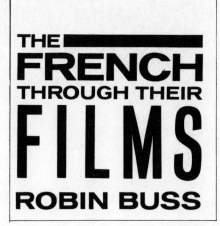

THE FRENCH THROUGH THEIR FILMS

ROBIN BUSS

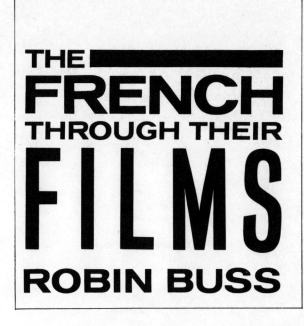

THE FRENCH THROUGH THEIR FILMS

ROBIN BUSS

B. T. Batsford Ltd · London

© Robin Buss 1988
First published 1988

ISBN 0 7134 5360 5

Printed in Great Britain by
Anchor Brendon Ltd
Tiptree, Essex
for the publishers
B. T. Batsford Ltd
4 Fitzhardinge Street
London W1H 0AH

Contents

Acknowledgements

I should like to thank the many people who have helped me in various ways during the writing of this book, in particular Michael Church, for his encouragement from the start of the project; Timothy Auger, my editor at Batsford; and Madeline Saunders for her help with compiling the reference material. I should also like to thank the staff at the British Film Institute Stills Library for supplying photographs.

Acknowledgement for permission to reproduce stills is given in the captions to the illustrations. Every effort has been made to trace copyright holders and to obtain permission from them to reproduce stills from the films.

Preface

'It is not with impunity' Marcel Carné writes in his memoirs, 'that young Frenchmen are taught, from the age of four or even earlier, to applaud the spectacle of Mr Punch giving the policeman a good hiding.' And he goes on to describe the hilarity that greeted Cécile Sorel's reply when she was summoned before one of the committees of enquiry set up after the Second World War to investigate collaboration with the German occupier: 'Gentlemen, if you did not want me to receive them in my home, you should not have let them into the country!'

Dislike of authority and a ready wit that appears (but, perhaps, only appears) to make light of serious matters, are characteristics that we think of as 'typically French'; the French themselves prize them just as the British prize their own peculiar sense of humour and fair play. But Carné is wrong if he implies that disrespect for authority should be attributed directly to the influence of spectacles, entertainments and literature. After all, Punch and Judy, *Guignol, Hanswurst und seine Frau* are also to be found in the Italian *teatrino di burattini* as *Pulcinèlla*, in the Spanish *títeres* as *Polichinela*, and no doubt elsewhere under names more various than the type of entertainment they provide. If *Le Guignol* were peculiarly French, one might have the basis for a piece of crude sociological theory. It would still have to contend with the fact that the forces of law and order are themselves staffed by Frenchmen and, as far as I know, the *Gendarmerie Nationale*, the *Garde Républicaine* and those other elements that make up the allegedly despised representatives of authority do not face any major problems of recruitment. French people who had applauded Punch and laughed at Cécile Sorel's reply to her accusers also made up that committee of enquiry. They were French, the men and women who in those postwar purges executed many thousands of their fellow-citizens (the precise number can never be fixed). The chuckles that acknowledged Sorel's witticism had the same accent as the jeers that greeted the shaven heads of those others accused of consorting with the occupier as they were paraded through the streets of Paris or Lyons.

It is not with impunity, as Carné might have remarked, that one sets out to define the 'Frenchness' of the 50 million or so individuals who can lay claim to that quality. A book that proposes to study, on the one hand, the French and, on the other, their films, suggests an equation to one element of which it is

7

impossible to assign any precise value. There are difficulties, too, with 'their films', given the substantial contribution of foreigners to the industry and the number of co-productions; but one can argue a way out of that dilemma. The temptation is to simplify the first part of the problem, either by recourse to sociological and statistical data which may give the appearance of scientific backing to a definition of the society at a particular moment, or by starting with what General de Gaulle called 'a particular idea of France' (when he wrote, with his usual grandiloquence, in a celebrated passage in his war memoirs: *'je me suis toujours fait une certaine idée de la France'*).

Statistics and other similar evidence can serve their purpose, and I shall use them from time to time, without wishing to suggest that they can describe more than some of the boundaries of what it means to be French. As for de Gaulle, even though the Constitution of the Fifth Republic which embodied some aspects of his 'particular idea of France' was accepted by 79 per cent of those who bothered to vote in September 1958, one is still left with one-fifth of this electorate who were opposed to it and, as later events were to show, a number who had apparently misunderstood precisely what he intended. Electoral approval declined, to 62 per cent in 1962 (of 77 per cent of the total electorate), to 55 per cent in 1965, to 46 per cent in 1969. It is no exaggeration to say that this decline represented in part the declining popularity of 'a particular idea of France'.

There has never, in any case, been *one* France; only, at various times, ideologies like de Gaulle's that would seek to impose unity on the diverse elements that make up the society and on the collection of individuals that is 'the French people'. Hearing Cécile Sorel's ironic reply to the commission of enquiry, a French man or woman might say that it was unlikely to come from a woman who had spent all her life in, say, Concarneau or Roscoff, while at the same time suggesting that there was an element of 'peasant slyness' in its false naivety. The women who have had to suffer the ravages of two wars between France and Germany in this century and the young peasants who have fought in them might have reason to question the 'gentlemen' in Paris who let 'them' into the country. Those living in a society and sharing its history, individual though they may be in their outlook, also necessarily share some attitudes towards the world and towards the society to which they belong.

This book is about those attitudes as they are expressed in the collection of works that make up French Cinema, each of them the product of the efforts of many individuals and designed to fulfil various needs of their producers and their audiences. I have not tried to write a history of French Cinema: there are already several of those. From time to time, especially in the first two chapters, I have found it convenient to adopt a broadly chronological approach, but I feel that such an approach can be, in many ways, misleading. We divide history into decades (the twenties, the thirties), implying fits and starts where there is, in fact, continuity. To speak of one generation and the next may make sense in a family, but not in a whole society where there is constant renewal and confrontation between the outlook and experiences of individuals born at different times. There are men and women still alive who have known the whole of cinema history, from the early silents to the latest Godard, and the society represented in films is a composite of ideas and attitudes belonging to individuals of many generations.

Film is the most powerful medium we have for investigating societies. Unlike literature or painting, which appeal to only one of our senses, a sound film conveys impressions on several levels at the same time. Moreover, because the camera is unselective, some of what it shows escapes the control of the person directing it and, because it is a mechanical means of representation, its images carry a minimum of interpretation. For this reason, a film made on location in Paris in 1908 has the value of an historical document: there is no better source for a knowledge of the physical appearance of the city and its inhabitants at that moment.

To understand how those people thought and felt, we turn to written sources. But as cinema developed as a narrative medium, and still more with the coming of sound, films were also able to bear witness to this, while retaining the ability to convey the actual appearance of things. Looking at a film, we have the nearest equivalent to real experience and a film about France may indeed tell us more about the country and its people than a visit, because it takes us inside the society in a way not available to tourists.

Still, we need to be cautious. The picture cinema gives of a society at a particular moment is necessarily incomplete. There is the hand of the censor, which has always fallen more heavily on cinema than on any other art form, precisely because cinema carries this conviction of realism, and because it is a popular entertainment. In virtually every country, at different times, censors and critics have worried about the image of their country that films might give to foreigners, and their fears are not entirely unjustified. The Italian woman who exclaimed despairingly: 'That's France!' after seeing *Quai des Brumes* at the Venice Biennale in 1938 confirmed such fears and should be a warning to us. There is more to the French than their films.

For one thing, each film exists in a particular cultural context and reflects preconceptions about art, characters, and so on. In addition, it is the product of an entertainment industry, made by people who belong to a particular social class or group whose work will reflect the outlook of that class, conditioning their answers to the questions 'what story shall we tell?' and 'how shall we tell it?' The preconceptions of film-makers and the expectations of audiences help to decide these things and to create stereotyped characters and situations. And, considering that the films themselves are part of the reality, that they help to condition the views of their audiences, nothing could be more problematical than to perceive the truth about that doubtful entity, the French, through the often deceptively clear mirror of their films.

What we can do is to study the actual image of France and French people in the French cinema and place it in some kind of social and cultural context. In trying to do so, in what follows, I have had to take into account chiefly what might be called 'quality' films. Many more 'popular' films have not survived from earlier periods (it is estimated, for example, that 70 per cent of the output of the French cinema industry between 1929 and 1939 is wholly or partially lost), and much of the 'popular' cinema is not available to an English-speaking audience, since it is never shown even in specialized film theatres. Since my purpose in looking at representations of French society in the cinema is to make film-going more enjoyable and films more 'readable', I see little point in discussing a mass of work that few people are likely to see. On the other hand, while I have stayed broadly within the canon of the 'quality' cinema and the product of France's better-known directors, I have tried to avoid aesthetic judgements on the films, leaving those to critics and historians; and I may, for example, devote some space to examining a film like *Ascenseur pour l'échafaud* [134]* which no one would count among Louis Malle's 'best' films. I hope that my reasons for analysing any particular film will be clear and I apologise for what may appear to be inexplicable omissions, eccentricities or partialities.

François Truffaut's celebrated article in *Cahiers du Cinéma* in 1954 ('Une Certaine tendance du cinéma français') was based on 'a particular idea' of French cinema: literary adaptations, giving priority to the scriptwriter and making the director merely 'the gentleman who adds the pictures'; so it is a surprise to find *The Times* writing in 1946, in a review of Maurice Cam's *Métropolitain* (made in 1938), that 'this film is *typically French* in that it tells its story in pictures. Sound, dialogue and, of course, sub-titles are there, but as embellishments . . .' – *typically French*: the emphasis is mine. The contradiction between these two 'particular ideas' of French cinema should serve as a reminder of the inconstant and changing nature of this cultural phenomenon.

Different interpretations of the character of French cinema itself are not irrelevant to the subject of this book, so its first chapter is an attempt to assess the place of film culture in France. Film has the peculiar ability to show and, simultaneously, to interpret what it shows, to represent a scene and to give an 'angle' on it. French cinemagoers, as well as foreigners, acquire some of their notions about the society in which they live through the cinema and French film-makers have learned to see it partly in films made by others, so that cinema representations of particular characters or locations take on a certain authority which influences subsequent perceptions of these same types or places. What Truffaut and the other writers in *Cahiers du cinéma* attacked in the 'quality cinema' of the postwar period was what they saw as that cinema's pursuit of certain themes because they were 'cinematic' and not because they corresponded to a continuing social reality, as if the art which a society produces were not itself part of its reality. No one doubts that the very fact of the nineteenth-century English novel's reticence about sexual relationships has something to tell us about Victorian society and Victorian attitudes, so

* Numbers in square brackets refer to the films listed in the reference section.

when French films of the 1950s depict gangsters or historical figures rather than dealing with social topics like abortion or political ones like the Algerian war, this too is not irrelevant to the understanding of attitudes at that time. And individual experience confirms that what may be 'untrue' in a sociological sense, can be 'true' in a personal one: that a film from the 1950s or 1960s, which might have seemed to its contemporaries deplorable, appearing scrupulously to avoid tackling some pressing social or political concern, is reviewed 20 years later and revealed as somehow containing the very 'essence' of its period. It is this fascinating and changing relationship of films to the society they represent and the society that produced them, that accounts for the popularity of old movies in the television age.

1 Film culture in France

Cinema was the product of science, industry and art, in that order. Auguste and Louis Lumière's invention, according to *Le Monde illustré* in 1896, could 'reproduce life and movement', transforming still portraits into a living record of loved ones: 'death will no longer be absolute', claimed a writer in *La Poste* after the demonstration on 28 December 1895 at the Grand Café in Paris – though for Louis Lumière the more prosaic aim was to sell cameras and the first films were probably designed not for exhibition as works of art, but for demonstration purposes to attract amateur purchasers of the machine. They soon became an attraction in their own right.

During the 20 years following the exhibition at the Grand Café, France dominated world production both of completed films and of film stock. Louis Lumière was the first to exploit the new medium as an industrial enterprise, sending out teams of operators to make and project films. His lead was followed by Georges Méliès and by Charles Pathé whose company, Pathé Frères, established itself as the giant of the industry up to the First World War. By 1907 it had offices in some 15 cities, including London, New York, Moscow, Berlin, Milan, Calcutta and Singapore; seven years later, the number had increased to 41 and Pathé enjoyed a virtual monopoly in many small countries. In a partially successful attempt to restrict their operations in the USA, Edison brought an action in 1904 against Pathé and Méliès, but it was the war in Europe, and the shortsightedness of the French government, that finally allowed the United States to establish its hegemony in the industry.

The hundreds of films made by the Lumières, Pathé and Méliès consisted of short documentaries, fantasies (showing the medium's ability to create visual illusions), melodramatic sketches and animated tableaux, like *L'Histoire d'un crime* (1901) which Ferdinand Zecca directed as head of production at Pathé. There was no inevitability about the application of the Lumières' invention to these genres: they were the use made of it in a particular society in which cinema was at first an extension of journalistic reportage and of the music hall. Despite early recognition of its potential as a scientific tool and as a method of 'living portraiture', cinema did not acquire the prestige of a science and, unlike still photography, was not immediately associated with painting. Instead, it took its place in the culture as a fairground attraction, on the level of the 'popular' culture of the music hall and the *fête foraine*.

The early Lumière 'documentaries' have acquired historical value as a record of contemporary events and scenes. They show children at play, washerwomen, Parisian street scenes, peasants ploughing with oxen. Camera-men travelled to bring back exotic films from Tunis, Cairo or Algiers and newsworthy events like the inauguration of President McKinley, the Universal Exhibition of 1900, the Carnival in Nice and Buffalo Bill's circus. Even these films, made by operators who simply cranked the camera in front of whatever they wished to record, are not neutral: the camera showed what the operator decided to film and its presence affected the subject. Passers-by in a New York street can be seen giggling at the contraption and a French peasant making hay is so distracted by it that he walks forward, staring fixedly towards the lens and waving his rake inches above the ground.

The invention also began to influence its operators' view of the world. One Lumière cameraman, Albert Promio, crossing the Grand Canal by boat, found himself visualizing the scene on film. A moving platform overcame the limitations of the early camera on its fixed tripod and, copying Promio's example, film-makers began to take travelling shots from boats, trains, trams, fire-engines, the New York El train and the lift in the Eiffel Tower, aware that the audience could be stirred by what happened behind the camera, as well as by what went on in front of it.

Méliès filmed the coronation of Edward VII in his Montreuil studio, before the event, using the form of service as a guide. On the day, the service in Westminster Abbey had to be shortened because the King was unwell and Edward, who was favourably impressed by Méliès's work, ragged him on the camera's startling ability to record even those parts of the ceremony that had not taken place! On the other hand, one should not be too quick to assume, because audiences would pay to see such reconstructions of events, that they believed in the actuality of what the camera portrayed. On the contrary, Méliès was a conjuror whose cinema was an extension of this form of magical entertainment and his audiences may have had a sophisticated awareness of different levels of cinema reality. Tricks with the camera were common, in Méliès's films and in comedies like *Onésime horloger* (1912), in which the central character speeds up time in order to obtain an inheritance. More important than the audience's ability to distinguish between direct represen-tation of reality, and trickery, is the fact that cinema, as a medium of information, was marginal: an audience would expect to be amused, not to have its perceptions of society and events formed by what it saw on the screen. Consequently, these early audiences' reliance on it as a representation of different levels of reality, was almost certainly less than our own.

Promio called his travelling shots 'panoramas', recalling a popular nineteenth-century vogue for panoramic displays mentioned in Balzac's *Père Goriot*. The attraction of this kind of display derives from three sources: the appeal of the unknown (Tunis, Venice, etc., to Parisians who had never visited these places); seeing the known from a new angle (when I lived in London near the Post Office Tower during the 1960s, when the observation platform was open to the public, I used to take visitors there and invariably we turned the telescope on my kitchen window); and the products of the imagination made real (bird's-eye views, tableaux of the Battle of Waterloo 'authenticated' by historical research, etc.).

Using the novelty of the camera, cinema exploited these three types of appeal to the taste for the exotic, the everyday and the imagined. There were 'genre' scenes (Lumière's 'feeding baby'), gags, mimes, Biblical tableaux and conjuring tricks. Comedy, using the slapstick forms of music hall, dates from *L'Arroseur arrosé* (in which the gardener is sprayed with his own hose) and the Lumières went on to do sketches involving a trick played on a concierge and a fight between two women (in which the 'actresses' are visibly laughing at their own antics) as well as brief historical scenes (Joan of Arc, the Duc de Guise, a battle). Méliès's plots included several on fantasy voyages or drunken nightmares, allowing him to evoke fantastic beasts and journeys to 'impossible' places (the Moon, the pole). Zecca, at Pathé, made moral fables and melodramas. The themes of the Pathé and Méliès comedies of 1905–6 have been analysed and leading subjects were absent-minded professors, Whites turned into Blacks, mishaps to photographers, the disastrous effects of alcohol (a large category) and accidents involving unpleasant smells and lavatories.

Like the views over the European quarters of Algiers or the 'picturesque' representations of the Casbah in the early Lumière documentaries, the comic themes of these films may give clues to attitudes in the early part of the century. But their interpretation demands caution, understanding and common sense. One should remember two things, above all: that, while the cinema was able to perform technical tricks (showing a man being automatically dressed up in a woman's clothes, for example), the themes and characters it used came directly from theatre and music hall; and secondly, that cinema was marginal as a form of entertainment, its audience was limited and its makers had little sense of social responsibility. What early comedy reveals, in its stock characters, are the stereotypes of popular imagination: the drunk, the concierge, the naughty boy, the cuckold, the bill-sticker, the maid, the cook, the baker, the beggar, the Auvergnat, the lovers, the virago, the cripple; surrounded by their props, from glue-pots and rolling pins to smelly shoes and lavatory brushes. Settings were 'downstairs' rather than 'upstairs', the apartment house rather than the *château*, the barracks of the *soldat de deuxième classe*, not the officers' mess.

* * * * *

However, within a decade the pioneers had realized the potential of cinema as an accessory to the 'superior' culture enshrined in literature, theatre and the schoolroom; and the economic advantage to be gained from extending its appeal to different classes at home and in an international market where France was dominant. They began to depict religious scenes as well as pornographic ones, historic events and a 'better class' of comedy. The comedies of Max Linder, André Deed ('Boireau' or 'Foolshead'), Charles Prince ('Rigadin', 'Whiffles', 'Moritz', according to whether the films were shown in France, Britain or Germany), Léonce Perret and others have begun to move into a lower-middle-class environment where, if the central comic character is not necessarily a bourgeois, his girl-friend's father probably is. 'Boireau' in particular was constantly committing social gaffes. By the early dramas of Louis Feuillade the environment of the country house is taken almost for granted as a 'neutral' setting, in *L'Oubliette* (1912), for example, or *L'Erreur tragique* (1913). *Le Coeur et l'argent* (1912) depicts the tragic consequences when an inn-keeper's daughter is persuaded to further her mother's ambitions by renouncing the man she loves and marrying an older man of superior class.

These Feuillade films starred René Navarre and Suzanne Grandais: the first was to make his name as Fantômas, while Grandais, who died in 1920 at the age of 27, had already by the time of her death established an image as a simple Parisian *midinette*, a lower-middle-class working girl around whom, in René Jeanne's words, 'hovered an atmosphere of a busy workshop . . . (and) peaceful apartment with a canary and a pot of geraniums'.

In Navarre and Grandais, French cinema had found two of its earliest non-comic 'stars'. The founding in 1908 of the Société Le Film d'Art, by André Calmettes and the Comédie Française actor Le Bargy, as well as creating the term 'art film', gave the medium a new aspiration. Partly controlled by Pathé, the company used well-known players from the theatre and its films mark the first serious attempts to depict character. Le Bargy himself appeared in *L'Assassinat du Duc de Guise* (1908), while Réjane (*Madame Sans-Gêne*) and Sarah Bernhardt (*La Reine Elisabeth*, *La Dame aux camélias*) gave prestige to later productions. The cinema was acquiring respectability, though some might say not necessarily to its advantage.

* * * * *

A respectful attitude to material and cast did not encourage experimentation with the camera or with narrative and reverence for literature and theatrical tradition were at times to weigh heavily on a medium which had to wait a long time before acquiring a status comparable with that of other arts. Many of the best actors and actresses in French cinema, if they did not belong exclusively to film, came to it from music hall, cabaret or the café-concert, rather than from the conventional stage. Max Linder, France's first international star, may have begun as an actor on the boulevards, but he was only 22 when he made his first film in 1905. Musidora, Noël-Noël, Maurice Chevalier, Jean Gabin, Arletty, Michel Simon, Fernandel, Paul Meurisse, Albert Préjean, Bourvil, Yves Montand, Simone Signoret and Jacques Tati started as singers or performers on the popular stage. Raimu's career began in the *caf'conc'* before Pagnol chose him to play Marius. Pierre Brasseur and Serge Reggiani had hardly made their stage débuts when they started work in films.

In contrast, the classical theatre has provided few stars: Madeleine Renaud, Jean-Louis Barrault, Françoise Rosay, Jules Berry, Charles Vanel, Charles Dullin, Fernand Ledoux, Marcel Levesque and, of course, Louis Jouvet whose celebrated clashes with Michel Simon (they once set out to get each other drunk during the filming of *Drôle de drame* – both succeeded and both played magnificently) seem like the collision of two worlds, Jouvet's quick wits, irony and distinction with Simon's coarse vitality: Voltaire and Rabelais, perhaps. As for Gérard Philipe, one of the few actors who, like Jouvet, could move easily between cinema and theatre, his stage and screen careers began almost simultaneously.

It was not so much that stage actors despised cinema (though, up to the Second World War, many did) as that film-makers, when they started to explore the potential of their medium, realized that it demanded a different style of acting from the stage. The great theatre director André Antoine, when he started to make films, chose to work chiefly with non-professionals, choosing an actor who had 'the right mug for the part'. Carl Theodor Dreyer used the same criterion, picking Eugène Silvain as Cauchon in *La Passion de Jeanne d'Arc* [13] not because he was a well-known actor, but because, as *doyen* of the Théâtre Français he had the 'authority' for the role; and casting as the English soldier Warwick a Russian café proprietor with the appropriate personality and physique. During the 1920s, several foreign actors, especially Russian émigrés, found work in France until their careers were cut short by the coming of sound.

But it was not only a question of that. Other directors (e.g. Bresson), like Antoine and Dreyer, have preferred to work with amateurs in accordance with a particular interpretation of cinema art and the distinction they see between its demands and those of the stage. Henri Troyat's novel *Grandeur nature* (1936), precisely because it is not written by a film-maker and because it attributes a relatively low cultural status to cinema, gives important clues to the way in which these questions might be perceived at a crucial moment in cinema history. The chief character in the novel is a middle-aged theatre actor who takes the opportunity to launch his 12-year-old son as a movie star: there are parallels with the career of a child star like Julien Duvivier's protégé, Robert Lynen. Manipulated by an unscrupulous director, the boy is an overnight success, then returns to obscurity.

Troyat makes a crucial distinction between the hard work and technique needed by stage actors, with the unforced, 'natural' technique of the screen, to show the screen actor as a fabrication of the director, cinema science and the cinema industry. Backstage, the theatre too may be sordid and the life of its employees precarious, but they find compensation in moments of contact with their audience and in work that calls for real artistry (Troyat makes his central character's father a mime artist, suggesting a decline from acting which gives total control over the material and a high level of artistic skill in a non-realist art, to the realism of the screen which demands no skills beyond those within the reach of an untrained 12-year-old). The implied conclusion is that the cinema is not concerned with art, but with hype and manipulation. Admittedly, its reputation had not been enhanced, at the time when he wrote the novel, by the collapses of Gaumont and of Pathé-Nathan, the latter a notorious fraud case which ended in Bernard Nathan's imprisonment.

On the other hand, as the industry became able to offer celebrity and money, an increasing number of actors and (especially, perhaps) actresses made their débuts in cinema and survived the fate of the matinée idol to establish solid reputations: Micheline Presle, Michèle Morgan, Danielle Darrieux, Gaston Modot, Martine Carol, Jean Marais, Daniel Gélin, Brigitte Bardot. By Bardot's time, even a fine actor most of whose work was done for the theatre (say, Georges Wilson) sacrificed much of his national and all international celebrity. As far as actors are concerned, La Poste could have been right in 1895 when it claimed that, thanks to cinema, death was no longer absolute.

* * * * *

Until some time around the 1950s, even in the country that pioneered cinema, dominated the industry in its early years, established the first film societies and specialist periodicals and invented the 'art film', the cultural status of cinema was not entirely resolved. Despite those early appearances by Sarah Bernhardt, silent cinema found its literary counterpart less in the 'high' art of classical theatre and 'serious' fiction, than in literature where events and action predominated: the roman-feuilleton (especially the serial novels of Eugène Süe whose Mystères de Paris were adapted in 1912 by Georges Denola) or the detective novel (Victorien Jasset's Nick Carter series of 1908–12). Thence developed of an original narrative form in Louis Feuillade's original screenplays for his series Fantômas [117], Les Vampires and Judex, in 1913–17.

By the 1920s, intellectuals like Louis Aragon were expressing admiration for the populist appeal of this cinema and for films 'with neither philosophy nor poetry' (a condescending recommendation that was not calculated to enhance the status of cinema in a culture where poetry and philosophy were considered the highest goals of art). What seems surprising now is that silent film was considered primarily a narrative medium, rather than being related from the start to the visual arts. Partly, this may have been because photography, as an art form, was associated with the academic or pompier realism most despised by the avant-garde, so it was not until the 1920s, thanks to the example of Russian, German and Swedish film-makers, that French artists began to experiment with film and to heed the Dadaist appeal for 'subjectless' cinema. It was not therefore until after the First World War, with what Sadoul calls the 'Impressionist school' (Louis Delluc, Marcel L'Herbier, Jean Epstein, Germaine Dulac, René Clair) that directors set out to explore the wider visual possibilities of the camera, and painters like Fernand Léger (Le Ballet mécanique, 1924) saw its potential as an extension of Dada, Cubism or Surrealism. Meanwhile, there was Abel Gance.

Gance was not an artist like Léger, Picabia or Man Ray. His ambition had been to make his name as a poet, writing verse plays and epics, and in spirit he was a product of the Romanticism of the 1820s. But he also turned to acting, on stage and on film, and to writing screenplays for Gaumont and Pathé. In 1912, he directed his first films for Le Film Français and in the same year wrote an article in *Ciné-Journal* (9 March 1912) proclaiming that cinema was 'a sixth art' and arguing that it was 'more than just a facile source of entertainment and, in fact, the synthesis of all previous art forms' (see Norman King's *Abel Gance*, BFI, 1984). Between 1915 and 1918, he was working for Le Film d'Art as a director and in 1920 formed his own company to produce *La Roue* (with support from Pathé who distributed the film in 1923).

Gance's relationship to the Romantics and the nature of his ambition are important for an understanding of his work. The Romantics had carried forward a process, already evident in the eighteenth century, through which the concept of poetry was extended beyond the realm of literature and the Poet elevated to the status of supreme creative artist. Gance shared with Cocteau this Romantic belief in his ability to find and make 'poetry' in everything he touched and both men believed in the 'poetic' quality of the cinematic image: much the same outlook is to be found in the theoretical writings of the Russian director Andrei Tarkovsky. With Gance (unlike Cocteau) this faith in poetry was combined with a populist approach that exalted the melodramatic genres of cinema, and Gance's combination of high artistic ambition and faith in these early narrative forms of cinema was revolutionary.

La Roue [84] is the story of a railway worker, Sisif, who becomes the rival of his own son and of another man for the love of an orphan girl. Exaggerated, over-acted, it ran for eight hours in its original version and for seven-and-a-half hours even in the version finally released by Pathé. But Gance's defects are also his qualities. His 'populist Romanticism' saw Sisif (Sisyphus) as a mythical hero, ennobled by work and by his love for the railway and its machines, standing at the head of a line of working-class heroes in French cinema; while Gance's belief in film as art encouraged him to experiment with techniques of montage to give the work extraordinary visual and rhythmic appeal. This technical experimentation, inspired perhaps by Gance's meeting with D. W. Griffith in 1921, was to be taken still further in his most famous work, *Napoléon* [12].

Though Gance was concerned with using such technical devices to tell a story, making form and content, as in an epic poem, indissoluble, his experiments with form led others to foresee the possibility of freeing film from its literary and narrative associations. René Clair dismissed the 'curious plot' of *La Roue* as irrelevant: 'If only this man ... was willing to create a pure documentary! If only he would renounce literature and have confidence in cinema!'; and he was joined by other 'Impressionist' directors: Dulac claimed that Gance was 'above all a poet', defining cinema as dramatic, 'but a drama conceived in a completely new way, completely divorced from the rules that govern theatre and literature', while Epstein stressed the view that 'poetry is not to be found only in verse'.

When Dulac wrote of 'the *rules* that govern theatre and literature', she was speaking as part of a cultural tradition that had been much concerned with debate on formal constraints and the definition of genres; and where the status of cinema as an art had to be decided partly by situating it in relation to other forms, and deciding whether it was essentially narrative (the novel), dramatic (the theatre) or visual (painting). The 'Impressionist' conclusion, that cinema was one of the visual arts – a form of 'visual poetry' – was theoretically consistent. But it overlooked the fact, recognized by Gance, that film had developed as a popular, narrative medium and that it was a narrative that it appealed to the public, who went to the cinema to be entertained. They enjoyed the narrative genres of Hollywood cinema, not the 'visual poetry' of the 'Impressionists'.

Simone Weil's journal of her experiences as a factory-worker in the mid-1930s records meeting a fitter who told her that the talkies had killed cinema which was, in essence, a perfect extension of photography. This nostalgia for the 'pure cinema' of the 'Impressionists' survived the coming of sound by many years: I remember being given it as an essay topic at school in the 1950s. But sound only confirmed what the industry had long appreciated: that the market was primarily for narrative films. The celebrated debate in the 1930s between René Clair and Marcel Pagnol was, in this sense, futile. Clair defended the thesis of cinema as primarily a visual medium; Pagnol argued that it was not truly an art in its own right, but a means to preserve great dramatic performances. In fact, both men were probably driven, in debate, to defend extreme positions and certainly ones which they did not hold to in practice. The films of Clair are narrative and those of Pagnol more than just records of his plays.

However, Pagnol's relegation of cinema to the subordinate role of preserved theatre was a threat to its claim as an independent art form and there was another more serious challenge to its status before the intellectual élite of the country could give it general acceptance as anything more than (in Marcel Duhamel's words) 'an entertainment for helots'. As an industrial product involving the work of writers, producers, technicians and actors, cinema failed to meet a major requirement of art in Western culture: that it should be the product of a single creator. This is the dilemma that had to be resolved in the 1950s by the writers who developed the theory of a *cinéma d'auteurs*: taking the most obviously commercial and industrial cinema of all, that of Hollywood, they argued that the central creative vision could be located in the director who thus became an artist in the same way as the author of a play or the composer of a symphony.

Gance had already come to the same conclusion: there was only one creator of *his* work. His shooting scripts (though not always strictly followed) prescribe every shot, angle, edit and even the reaction to be cajoled out of the spectator.

His directing style was frankly dictatorial (or, perhaps, 'Napoleonic'); in an appeal to the actors and technicians working with him on *Napoléon* in 1924, he proclaimed that the film would 'allow us to enter once and for all into the temple of the Arts through the great doorway of History. An inexpressible anguish grips me at the thought that my willpower, and even the sacrifice of my life, will be to no avail if you do not, each and every one of you, give me your undivided loyalty at every moment.' He demanded 'absolute dedication' from everyone involved in the production and the renunciation of 'all petty personal considerations'. No doubt about the *auteur* here.

The problem of the creator virtually disappeared, in any case, with Structuralism, which was more interested in the analysis of cinematic genres, and in the political climate after 1968 when collective work was seen as inevitable or preferable to the product of an isolated individual. When Marxist writers like Pierre Macherey were elaborating a theory of 'literary production' that treated the lonely writer as part of the productive chain of industrial society, the matter of whether film was the product of a single creator, or of many, came to seem meaningless. The generally accepted view was that expressed in a school textbook on contemporary French literature, published in 1970, which argued that 'cineasts' (a neutral word capable of referring to scriptwriters and directors) aimed not so much to 'rival literature as to express, by different means but with the same depth and perhaps greater intensity, what the writer expresses', adding that 'this has often been called *cinéma d'auteur*' (*La Littérature en France de 1945 à 1968*, published by Bordas).

* * * * *

The theoretical debates of the 1920s were academic in more than one sense. France had lost its hegemony in production and in sales of films and film stock during the First World War. The successful campaign of American producers to take over has been described by Kristin Thompson (1985). Where the output of new films in France stood at around 25,000–30,000 metres one year before the outbreak of war, it fell to less than 10,000 by 1916 and in December of that year only one-third of the films shown in France were home-produced, 27.8 per cent coming from the USA and 25.4 per cent from Italy.

American films filled the gap left by the decline in French production, due to the demands of the war effort, and they were more entertaining and better-made than the home product. The Americans had started to develop narrative techniques that were to become almost universally accepted conventions. Even when American imports fell during the 1920s, French producers were unable to respond and the result was an increase in imports from elsewhere, particularly Germany. The French and German film industries entered on a long period of collaboration that was to last through the 1930s, regardless of the difference in the political systems of the two countries.

To protect the industry against American competition, the French government, like others, adopted a quota system, adjusted in 1931 to take account of the introduction of sound. The rules restricted foreign films in original version to only 10 cinemas (raised to 20 after 1933) and demanded that dubbed versions should be made in Paris. Dubbing was only one solution to the language problem; another was the production of several versions of a film, shot from a script translated into perhaps 15 languages and using native actors.

During the 1930s, the press alternatively mourned the death of the French film industry and announced the birth of a 'national school' of cinema. There was justification for both views. The industry was not healthy, especially after the Gaumont and Pathé-Nathan disasters, but it maintained a steady flow of films: 1178 were distributed in the period 1930–39, as well as 156 French-language versions made abroad, which compares well with Sadoul's estimate (1962) of around 850 films in the decade before 1930 and 920 in the 10 years following the Liberation (including a large number of co-productions). The films of the 1930s were of high quality and most critics would argue that they made a distinctive contribution to world cinema (justifying the notion of a French 'school').

An industry with high capital costs requires a strong home market and French cinema attendance has always lagged behind that in Britain or the United States. Sound cinema increased audiences which stabilized in the 1930s at around 250 million admissions a year in around 4100 cinemas. The economic crisis brought a decline in box office receipts, but as the decade continued there was a rise in living standards and in leisure time. The deteriorating international situation may have brought an increased demand for distractions and the Second World War certainly did: admissions rose, reaching 402 million by 1945 and peaking in 1947 at 424 million. However, this should be compared with attendances in Britain where a slightly larger population achieved a peak in 1945 of 1585 million admissions, equivalent to around 30 visits per person per year, in contrast to the French average of around 10. Certainly there were reasons for this different use of leisure time in the two countries in social custom and habits (restaurants and cafés offered an alternative in France), climate, population distribution and availability.

Television did not make the same impact in France during the 1950s as in Britain or the USA, but cinema admissions fell despite this, to reach 355 million in 1960. From then on, as General de Gaulle realized, *la télé* had become a major source of information and entertainment: only a million sets in 1959, three times that number in 1963. Cinema admissions continued to decline, but less fast than in Britain and when, in 1969, they reached rough parity with Britain at 184 million, the decline was halted. In the 1980s, admissions were still running at between 180 and 190 million, equivalent to 3.5 visits per person per year. Broadly speaking, this was lower than the USA, considerably lower than the USSR, and higher than Britain (1.5 visits), Japan (1.3), Belgium, West Germany or Austria. This means that, in their cinema-going habits, the French were similar to the Italians, the Swiss and the Danes, but I doubt if it allows one to draw any far-reaching conclusions about the national character.

The industry was in fact healthier than the figures might suggest: some 230 feature-length films being produced every year (more than any country except India, Japan and the USA). This was partly because of government support, through direct grants and through a quota system imposed on television under which 50 per cent of televised films had to be French. The quality of French television, closely controlled by the government until the late 1970s, was generally admitted to be poor, while cinema, from the period of the New Wave onwards, had high intellectual prestige. Perhaps the battles over the cinema's status as art had not been entirely a matter of disinterested theory. On the other hand, the less elevating aspect of the high rate of admissions was that a good deal could be accounted for by the relaxation of censorship which allowed a flood of pornographic films in special cinemas. There was not one audience, but several, sometimes overlapping groups of cinema-goers: fans of porno movies, intellectuals looking for art films, children and adolescents attracted by the special effects of *Star Wars* and its successors or imitators.

* * * * *

The experience of cinema-going varied according to locality and so according to class. Bernard Barbey, critic of the *Revue hebdomadaire*, ventured outside the Parisian first-run theatres in 1935 to visit a country cinema and found conditions very different from what he was used to: the range of films was limited and programmes did not include the usual 'shorts' before the main feature. 'Is there a documentary? I like documentaries', says a character in Nelly Kaplan's *La Fiancée du pirate* [158], before the start of a show given by a travelling projectionist who has set up the projector on the bar of a village café (there isn't).

The industry soon discovered the profits to be made by giving a film an exclusive run at an expensive theatre before putting it on general release. This meant that, even in Paris, say during the 1950s and 1960s, there were four distinct outlets for films: on the one hand, the first-run cinemas around the Champs-Elysées and the Boulevard des Capucines showed French and foreign films (the latter sub-titled, not dubbed) *en exclusivité*, compensating for high prices with plush seats, carpets and, sometimes, an artificially scented atmosphere. There was no smoking and the usherette expected a reasonable tip to put in her little bag (after all, it was almost certainly her wage).

At the other end of the scale were the local *cinémas de quartier* where the seats felt more like public transport than the lounge of an expensive hotel. Here, foreign films were invariably dubbed, John Wayne and James Stewart having apparently had voice training from Charles Dullin, and standards of exhibition (for example, focusing) were less reliable. You might end up in the back row with a couple not concerned by the doing of John Wayne or James Stewart, or in the front rows with some rowdy *blousons noirs*. The commercials

23

were by Jean Mineur Publicité and in the interval the audience was encouraged to enjoy an *esquimau Gervais* or a packet of caramels.

These cinemas dealt in more or less the same modern films and were distinguished mainly by their standards of comfort. The *cinémas d'art et d'essai*, meanwhile, showed a mixture of old films, cinema classics, independents and some intellectually more demanding works. Their repertoire, even so, was broader than that of most London 'art houses' in the late 1950s: French critical opinion had been quicker to recognize the talent of Hollywood directors who tended to be dismissed by Anglo-Saxon critics as mere entertainers. *To Be or Not to Be*, *Hellzapoppin* and Westerns were perennial favourites, beside Ealing comedies like *Kind Hearts and Coronets* (*Noblesse Oblige* in France). These art cinemas were very small, centred on the Latin Quarter around the Rue Champollion or the Rue de la Huchette, catering for a student audience and one that took cinema seriously, without necessarily liking 'serious' films. Finally, there were cinema clubs, like the Ciné-Club at the Cité Universitaire which was open to residents and students and showed, twice a week for practically nothing, an astonishing range of films from everywhere in the world.

There was also the Cinémathèque, an unclassifiable institution, giving three shows a day of different films on its screens at the Rue d'Ulm and the Palais de Chaillot. It was open to everyone and very cheap: there were seasons of particular directors and other organized events, but the place was no model of efficiency and the best thing was often to take pot luck, pay a couple of francs and see whatever happened to be on offer. Once when I did this, a fat, flamboyant man, with his coat draped over his shoulders, walked to the front of the hall to introduce the film. I am sorry to say that I found him rather irritating. It was Henri Langlois.

Langlois had founded the Cinémathèque in 1936 with Georges Franju and two years later helped to set up an international body, the Fédération Internationale des Archives de Film. Eccentric, enthusiastic, he played a major role in French cinema history by encouraging preservation. But he was an individualist who resented interference. The archive grew well beyond his control and when he died it was found to be in an appalling state, with many films piled up unprotected or stored in the wrong boxes, and many wholly or partially damaged. It was said that Langlois's most publicized legacy was a huge task of restoration and cataloguing.

Despite this, the Cinémathèque was his monument and it played a crucial role in film education, especially for the young directors who were to make the so-called New Wave. In the brief period between 1958 and 1962, nearly 200 new film directors made first films, aided by the willingness of investors to give money to virtual unknowns and by the development of light, hand-held cameras. Technical polish was not, in any case, as important as the spontaneity and immediacy that their British counterparts were finding in work for television. Neither television nor the established procedures of the cinema studio were attractive to them: most never served the recognized apprenticeship as assistants. Against the background of a culture that tended towards academism, good taste and conformity, the cinema appeared as iconoclastic and far more open in access to both film-makers and audiences than most other means of artistic expression.

* * * * *

The director may be the 'author' of the film, and most directors would claim 'authorship' of their works, but no one is more acutely aware of the limits to their 'authority' than directors themselves. Carné, in the book of memoirs which he called *La Vie à belles dents*, devotes several pages to the problems he had dealing with his producer Grégor Rabinovitch during the making of *Quai des brumes* [2], pages which might sound racist if they did not reflect the usual grumpiness of directors at such constraints; he also speaks of actors 'I could work with', actors 'of whom I was sure' or who could 'be relied upon'. He tells us that the subject of *Les Portes de la nuit* [37] was one that he, personally, did not want to make and that he was 'unenthusiastic' about working with the two stars. He describes his problems with the censor (especially over a film that he tried to make about the juvenile detention centre on Belle-Île), his admiration for the set designer Alexandre Trauner, his break with the scriptwriter Jacques Prévert and, inevitably, the problem of raising financial support. Much the same can be read in the writings of any film director. Where other artists may speak of struggles to realize their vision against the constraints imposed by the material or by financial hardship, film 'authors' inevitably grumble about the restricting effects of having to work with producers and designers, scriptwriters and actors and against audience expectations, routine critical hostility and moronic censorship.

As well as these external constraints, the cinema 'artist' tailors his vision according to his own preconceptions about genre, setting, plot and so on, before finally coming up against the central requirement of translating it into the 'language' of film. The image on a cinema screen is not the 'real' world, but acts as a signifier of it. Within the context of the cultures and ideologies through which we ascribe meanings to the 'real' world, screen images have connotations which are expressed in the codes of 'cinema language'.

The cinema is especially privileged in its ability to exploit the connotative implications of its signifiers, because it combines the iconographic features of a visual medium with the narrative features of a literary one. Gabin's cloth cap and Jules Berry's hat, tie and checked overcoat in *Le Jour se lève* [90] mark one out as a workman, the other as a bourgeois, meanings which are reinforced by the fact that a contemporary audience would hardly expect Gabin to play a middle-class crook, or Berry an honest working-man. The connotations of such iconographic clues may vary according to audience and period.

As I mentioned earlier, Dreyer chose a Russian, Alexandre Mihalesco, to play Warwick in *La Passion de Jeanne d'Arc* [13] because he felt the man had the right 'look' for the part of an English captain. He dressed him in a peculiar uniform: flat helmet, dark jacket, Sam Browne belt, jodhpurs and boots, with a chain around his neck. The opening credits of the film, showing a hand turning the pages of the manuscript record of Joan's trial, emphasize Dreyer's wish to convince his audience of the authenticity of its representation of those distant events. In 1927, then, an English medieval army officer looked like that. Today, the flat helmet makes Warwick look like nothing so much as a Second World War fire warden.

La Passion de Jeanne d'Arc is not a still icon, but a continuous narrative and the final credits are preceded by a message recalling the enduring love of the French people for St Joan. Taking these credits in isolation from the film, we might assume that Dreyer had set out to give the conventional interpretation of Joan as a symbol of French resistance to foreign domination. This is the primary meaning of the story of Joan of Arc for a French audience and, less than 10 years after the end of a war in which France had driven off a foreign invader, that is how an audience would expect to interpret the film. What Dreyer does is to assert his own reading of the events, in spite of his final caption.

Having emphasized the veracity of its account by the first reference to the contemporary manuscript, Dreyer's film confines itself purely to the confrontation between Joan and her judges, leaving aside altogether the historical context of the Hundred Years' War. Warwick, the English officer, and Cauchon, the French bishop, stand side-by-side as allies against Joan, not as enemies. The concentration on Joan's persecution and suffering voids the film of any wider, nationalistic content and the contrast between Joan's simplicity and Cauchon's learning amounts to a class distinction that culminates in the final scenes of popular revolt, brutally suppressed, following Joan's execution. The cumulative effect is to shift the emphasis in the final caption from the *French* people's love of Joan as a nationalist symbol, to the French *people's* love of Joan, as a symbol of resistance to the oppression of the State (Warwick) and the Church (Cauchon).

Dreyer's film belongs to a particular genre: historical narrative based on reconstruction of real events (as opposed to period films that use a historical setting for fictional narratives), and it shows how a film conveys its meanings through visual and narrative means. But the representation of real events and the reading of history are not the only way in which a film can speak to its audience about questions of politics and religion, peasants and priests, nationalism and class. The writers of *Cahiers du cinéma* in the 1950s already perceived that a strength of cinema, especially of American cinema, was its ability to construct 'parables', using the conventions of genres like the thriller, the gangster movie, science fiction and so on, to translate into fictional narrative some profound concerns of society at a particular time. In general, the writers of *Cahiers* found French cinema lacking in such myths and parables, too little concerned with contemporary social issues and too much with 'quality' adaptations of literary works from the past. With the advantage of hindsight, however, we may disagree and in the next chapter, bearing in mind the many constraints that make cinema inevitably a distorting mirror of reality, I shall try to survey the myths and parables in which film-makers have encoded the underlying concerns of French society at different moments in the history of the twentieth century. *La Passion de Jeanne d'Arc* (a French film, though it was made by a Danish director), with its subversion of a nationalist story to convey a message of popular revolt and individual resistance to the oppression of the State, seems a good place to start.

I. DIRECTORS AT WORK

1. Méliès studio   (MUSEUM OF MODERN ART FILM LIBRARY)

2. René Clair filming   (NATIONAL FILM ARCHIVE)

3. Lelouch filming   (NATIONAL FILM ARCHIVE)

4. Renoir: *La Marseillaise*   (CONTEMPORARY FILMS)

5. *La Grande illusion*   (CONTEMPORARY FILMS)

6. *Les Enfants du paradis*   (NATIONAL FILM ARCHIVE)

7. *L'Espoir*   (NATIONAL FILM ARCHIVE)

8. *Fort Saganne*   (ALBINA/LES FILMS A2)

9. *Le Temps détruit*   (INA)

10. *La Passion de Jeanne d'Arc*   (CONTEMPORARY FILMS)

11. *Casque D'Or*

12. *Journal d'un curé de campagne*

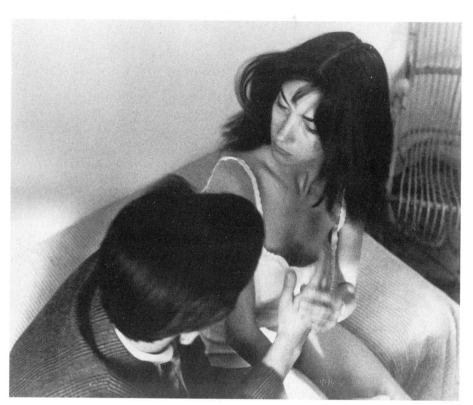

13. *Je vous salue, Marie*   (THE OTHER CINEMA)

14. *A nous la liberté*   (SECA/MARCEAU COCINOR)

15. *La Belle équipe* (NATIONAL FILM ARCHIVE)

16. *Le Crime de Monsieur Lange* (DOMINIQUE H. DES FONTAINES)

17. *La Bête humaine*   (NATIONAL FILM ARCHIVE)

18. *Le Salaire de la peur*   (MARCEAU COCINOR/CIC/VERA)

19. *La règle du jeu* (CONTEMPORARY FILMS)

20. *Le Jour se lève* (VAUBAN PRODUCTIONS)

21. *Les Vacances de Monsieur Hulot* (NATIONAL FILM ARCHIVE)

22. *Occupe-toi d'Amélie*   (NATIONAL FILM ARCHIVE)

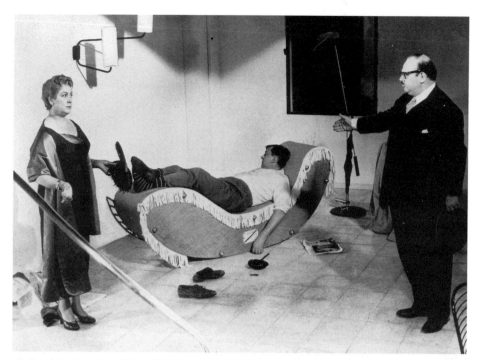

23. *Mon Oncle*   (NATIONAL FILM ARCHIVE)

24. *Hypothèse du tableau volé*   (BFI/INA)

2 The mood of the times

The struggle for individual rights against the normalizing pressures of institutions might be seen as one of the enduring themes of history, reaching a peculiarly acute stage in the twentieth century. At first glance, the French cinema has been consistently on the side of the individual, rather than the institutions, which is much to its credit. But this sweeping conclusion needs to be modified in several respects.

Firstly, it should not lead to any hasty assumptions about the French character or the national passion for individual freedom. A persistent struggle against normalizing institutions implies the persistence of these institutions. Secondly, while the leading characters in a film may be perceived as individuals and appeal for our sympathy in their struggles to achieve happiness and fulfilment, the cinema is a notorious creator of stereotypes and a host of secondary characters, some merely glimpsed in the background of the story, may combine to make cinema one of the most powerful media for reinforcing conservative values. Thirdly, film-makers belong to a particular social group; directors may have their origins in different classes, be they children of cabinet-makers (like Carné) or great artists (like Renoir), but their outlook will be conditioned to some extent by the industry for which they work. And, fourthly, their products will be conditioned by preconceptions about art, fidelity to literary sources and other constraints.

Love and sexual relationships have been the central theme of Western literature since the Middle Ages and remain the central theme of most films. To treat this theme in a mythical and universal manner, literature and cinema tend to seek a 'neutral' social setting which will vary from time to time. For medieval audiences, this was the castle of courtly romance, for Racine's plays it may be the Roman imperial court or Theseus's palace. The setting is a transparency through which the audience can identify with the actors. The emperors, kings and queens in Racine are not shown at work as rulers: like the oilmen in *Dallas*, they devote most of their time to private matters.

The bourgeois drawing-room in the Boireau comedies or the *château* in the early dramas of Feuillade, as I mentioned earlier, provides an equally 'transparent' setting. We take for granted the servants who hover in the background when they are required by the plot. And, though the cinema's contrary appetite for variations in background or local colour means that it is not possible to be dogmatic, one can none the less distinguish at different times the environments that came close to being 'transparent' or 'neutral' backgrounds for a particular period. The term 'drawing-room comedy', for example, is not insignificant and the French *comédie mondaine* which implies a particular social world, more or less corresponds. The films of Yves Mirande (*Baccara*, 1935; *A Nous deux, Madame la Vie*, 1937; *Le Chasseur de chez Maxim's*, 1939) evoke a wealthy class from the previous decade in their nightclubs and 'modern-style' salons, and only marginally to satirize it.

Another sub-genre of the 1920s and 1930s, with a similar 'transparent' location, was the Russian film, a love story of the Steppes involving beautiful aristocratic women and handsome officers in pre-revolutionary times. Between 1934 and 1938, Raymond Chirat has counted no less than 36 films on such Russian-imperial themes, inspired partly by the group of White Russian émigrés who were a significant feature of the cinema industry from the 1920s. Despite the military uniforms, there is little military action: ballrooms and drawing-rooms provide the settings; love, duels and occasionally espionage, the plots; and balalaikas and falling snow the mood. They have titles like *Nuits de feu, La Tragédie impériale, Les Nuits moscovites, Troika sur la piste blanche, Les Nuits blanches de Saint-Pétersbourg*, which promise extremes of passion and changing fortunes against the high contrast of black nights and white landscapes. When actors like Ivan Mosjoukine failed to make the transition to talking pictures because of their (genuine) Russian accents, directors turned to Gaby Morlay, Victor Francen or Harry Baur, removing the product still further from reality and deeper into myth.

Of course, there is in one sense nothing 'neutral' about this nostalgia for the Tsarist world, a mere 20 years after the Russian Revolution, at a time of violent confrontation between Communism and Fascism in Europe. But it would be ridiculous to think of these films as 'anti-Communist propaganda' in any real sense. They were not directed against Communism in France or towards the restoration of the Russian imperial régime. The attraction of the pre-revolutionary aristocracy, for the makers of such films, was precisely that it was a lost class and its romantic appeal, giving it such power as fantasy, lay in its unattainability, its separation from current concerns, its potential as myth. The same was true, to some extent, of the salons and night-clubs of the *comédie mondaine*, designed to appeal to the fantasies of the poor rather than to the actual experience of the rich.

In the period after World War II, especially, the underworld could supply a conventional setting for films that were less about crime and punishment, than about loyalty, solidarity and friendship. But the *milieu* is more conventional than 'transparent', and more overtly political because of the social nature of crime. The society that has defined a character as a criminal or a gangster is inevitably present in a film about him. Frequently such films can be seen as a form of political allegory: the emphasis on friendship and loyalty in the 1950s gangster movies, like *Touchez pas au grisbi* [131] or *Du rififi chez les hommes* [133], being a hang-over from the betrayals of the Occupation, and the 1960s and 1970s detective or gangster movie suggesting more or less openly that the 'alternative' society of criminals is much like the world of big business or politics (and, more importantly, vice versa), or that there is a 'police underworld' no more moral than the criminal one.

The very high proportion of literary adaptations in French cinema, especially up to the directors of the New Wave, was another way of achieving a kind of 'transparency', the contemporary or historical environment associated with a particular novelist serving as a screen through which the audience could become involved in the emotions of the main characters. This is by no means a necessary consequence of literary adaptation: Aurenche and Bost's adaptation of Emile Zola in René Clément's *Gervaise* [96] directs attention specifically to the problems of the working class and, before accusing directors of adopting the 'safe' solution of literary adaptation, one should remember that several chose to update the text, to make it more relevant, risking criticism for tampering with it. The most 'neutral' films are set in what Jeancolas (1979) calls '*le contemporain vague*', a period recognized by the audience as 'the present' but distinguished by no particular contemporary features. As Jeancolas also remarks, this 'vague contemporary' is found much less in films made after 1970 when period is often indicated by reference to precise events or by such hints as copies of newspapers or political posters, or intrusive clues (the intercutting of newsreel footage) which oblige the audience to locate the action precisely.

Increasingly, from the time of Vadim's *Et Dieu créa la femme* [153], made in 1956, the 'transparent' background is that of a particular class, leisured and comfortably well-off. The characters are not so rich that one asks where their money comes from, but rich enough to have the leisure to indulge in affairs with each other. Their possession of leisure may be emphasized by a holiday context, as in some of Eric Rohmer's Moral Tales or Comedies and Proverbs [e.g. 82]. If they have any profession, it is both glamorous and socially marginal, like the racing driver of *Un Homme et une femme* [78] or the 'big business' in which the characters of Losey's *La Truite* [81] are supposedly involved. These characters are seldom, if ever, seen at work, which is merely the means of play, or in relation to members of other classes who make brief appearances to service the needs of the central characters, as servants, shopkeepers and so on. The luxurious, modern-style furnishing of the thirties *comédie mondaine* gives way to a less obtrusive form of good taste in the sixties, and the motor car ceases to be a symbol of wealth and becomes an inevitable possession: driven in prewar films by a chauffeur and used to ferry its contents ostentatiously from apartment to night-club and back, it now takes to the open road, the means of their freedom and a testimony to it. Even films which set out to criticize this lifestyle often take it largely for granted and provide it with no real social context.

Paris or the countryside, when they are not particularized in some way, can

31

serve as 'transparent' urban or rural settings (which I discuss in Chapter 3); age, too, may be an element of 'transparency'. Jules Berry, as the impoverished and not entirely trustworthy bachelor André Leclerc in *Baccara* (1935), gives his age as 44 (Berry was in fact 46, so he is perhaps illustrating the character's untrustworthiness). Marcelle Chantal who plays opposite him as Elsa, must be in her thirties, even in the film's terms. There is nothing unusual, in thirties romantic comedy, in centring interest on members of these age-groups, especially when they have a sexual relationship that might be considered unacceptable in younger heroes and, especially, heroines (the relationships described in *Le Blé en herbe* [168] were shocking in 1954). The 'transparent' age was to be considerably reduced by the 1960s, its lowering being helped by the fact that, with changing economic and social circumstances, it was more plausible for adolescents and young adults, particularly as students at school or university, to have the leisure to enjoy romantic relationships without the need to define their social status. These 'transparent' contexts give the least interrupted view of love, sex and the emotions related to them, but the precise conditions which are most likely to allow audiences to forget work, money and other everyday concerns and indulge these more interesting fantasies, vary from time to time.

* * * * *

The Lumière and Méliès comedies of the first decade of the century, through a genre inherited from the music hall and popular theatre, enshrine a society of clear distinctions in class and status. They seem peculiarly appropriate, in retrospect, to *la belle époque*, in its supposed insouciance as well as its stability.

Despite the Belgian film *Maudite soit la guerre*, made by Alfred Machin in 1913 and released just before the outbreak of war, the image of military life in the cinema is predominantly that of the Pathé short of 1905 in which an unfortunate captain is mistakenly doused by his men with a bucket of water intended for a drunkard who is disturbing the barracks ... The Army, even outside comedy, is shown as a masculine world of disciplined high spirits and comradeship, and the occasional representation of military action, in Lumière sketches like *Défense d'un drapeau* (c. 1900), emphasizes heroism and triumph, completely outside any context of actual war.

The French authorities were slow to recognize the potential of cinema in wartime for information, encouragement and entertainment. A proposal to set up an official camera unit at the start was turned down by Marshal Joffre, so the first great engagement of the war (the Battle of the Marne in September 1914, when the French turned back the German advance on Paris) went unrecorded. A film unit was subsequently formed and newsreel footage produced. Not surprisingly, as a corollary to this, the war provided an excuse for creating a system of censorship, involving several levels, from the Ministry of the Interior and the Prefecture of Police, to the local authorities, who were able to prevent even the showing of films passed for exhibition elsewhere.

General censorship was applied to newsreels: when Marshal Pétain was shown wincing as he tasted the troops' wine, this evidence of fastidiousness, on the part of a war leader with a reputation for the 'popular touch', was banned.

As for encouragement, there was a succession of patriotic films, bearing the most eloquent titles in the history of cinema: *Alsace*, *Mère française*, *Coeur de française*, *Chantecoq* (the national cockerel being honoured), *Les Poilus de la revanche* ('poilus' was the civilian name for the soldiers, the revenge, presumably, was for the defeat of 1870), *La Voix de la patrie*, *Vendémiaire* (the victories of the revolutionary army against the Prussians could be recalled and isolated from the events of the Revolution itself). But it was as escapist entertainment that cinema came into its own, with an influx of American serials like *The Perils of Pauline* supplying the demand created by the drop in French production. Louis Feuillade, whose series *Fantômas* dates from 1913–14, was already working in the genre and, returning to Gaumont in 1915, began the 12 episodes of *Les Vampires*, followed by *Judex* (1916) and *La Nouvelle mission de Judex* (1917).

The plots developed like soap opera as they were being filmed and actors who arrived late on set or received their call-up papers were liable to be cut from the script at the last moment. This improvisation, and the occasional illogicality that resulted, thus reflected some of the insanity of the time. When the world goes mad, one must improvise. In the trenches another serial dragged on, apparently unending. The soldier on leave could be sure that a new villain would replace the Chief Vampire and that Musidora, as the evil Irma Vep (anag.), would be lurking in the shadows; returning to the front, he found the same mud, the same trenches and the same implacable enemy as before.

Apart from the Surrealists, who appreciated his imaginative improvisation, Feuillade did not appeal to postwar audiences and was only re-discovered, thanks partly to Henri Langlois, in the 1940s and 1950s. André Bazin remembered seeing his films at the Cinémathèque where characteristic uncertainties in projection enhanced the impromptu nature of Feuillade's method. During the war itself there were those who, with unintended irony, called for the banning of representations of violence and crime. As the conflict ended, attention was concentrated more on rationalization. Abel Gance, in the first version of *J'Accuse* (lost, except for a mutilated reconstruction), proclaimed that the war had been justified by the new society that would emerge from it. The final scene of the film showed the dead rising to demand this reparation for their sacrifice, and they did rise, haunting society for the next 20 years.

* * * * *

The statistics tell some of the story: 1,400,000 killed, one in 25 of the population, mainly young men; three million wounded; countless numbers bearing the psychological scars of fighting or bereavement. The landscape of northern France was devastated and the economy shattered by the war debt and the disruption of industry.

Industry, for its part, recovered rapidly and the surge of industrial growth drove a wedge between this 'modern' sector, and the 'traditional' sector of agriculture. Depression followed and films like *A Nous la liberté* [85] suggest conditions that made for the rapid rise or fall of industrial enterprises and suspicion of the new rich, as well as fears of the subjection of humans to machines in 'factory-prisons'; in contrast, there was to be growing nostalgia for the values of rural life. The peasant classes had made the greatest sacrifice of men in the war and their 'backwardness' was accentuated by the high average age of those who remained, pointing the contrast between 'country' (old men and women living a timeless existence on the land) and 'town' (dynamic, industrial and moving through *les années folles* – the Jazz Age).

The Russian Revolution, as well as supplying émigrés for the cinema industry, suggested one version of the future, the United States another. The Communist Party (PCF) was founded at the Congress of Tours in 1920, when the pro-Bolsheviks split away from the Socialist Party. The working class had come back from the front expecting conditions to improve (one part of the legacy of Gance's rising dead), but it was still relatively weak. Its new militancy, however, was threatening to the middle class which retreated into conservatism as a defence against Bolshevism, on one side, and the Bohemianism of Jazz Age Paris on the other.

Films dealt directly with these political preoccupations of the ruling class. In René Le Sompteur's *La Croisade* (1920), a war hero returns to find his region devastated and sets about rebuilding his father's factory on the basis of co-operation between management and workers: 'we must hope,' wrote the *Courrier cinématographique*, 'that all will end well as it does in the film, with a victory for common sense, and with a clear and beneficial union between Capital and Labour'. A similar message informed the 12 episodes of Le Prince's *L'Empereur des pauvres* (1921), a family saga adapted from the novels of Félicien Champsaur. There are corresponding appeals for a return to the land and to stable prewar values: Théo Bergerat's *La Terre commande*, Max de Rieux's *La Grande amie* and Jean Choux's *La Terre qui meurt*.

The theme of urban corruption, explicit or implicit in such films, became linked with that of financial corruption as the economic crisis worsened. Marcel L'Herbier's *L'Argent* [72], updating Zola's novel about the Stock Exchange, introduces a theme which was to take on sinister overtones as it became linked with the image of the 'cosmopolitan' financier: one critic accused L'Herbier's film of not being realistic because it failed to introduce these 'Armenians, Jews and Levantines'. *Baccara* (1935), to take just one example of a film that did, involves the disappearance of a foreign financier who has been speculating against the franc, and the trial of his mistress (also a foreigner) for complicity in his crime. In the event, she is acquitted, partly because she has entered a marriage of convenience with André Leclerc (Jules Berry), to keep her French nationality, and partly because André, despite his dissolute character, is a war hero.

The veterans were a continuing legacy of the war. The memorials and cemeteries that are a feature of every town and village in the country were constant reminders and the focus of local ceremonies. André Leclerc is modest about his medals, but most veterans wore them with aggressive pride. The Associations d'Anciens Combattants, and other related or 'patriotic' organizations, often saw themselves as guardians of the national conscience, liable to censor works which they considered insulting to the dead and to the country for which they had fought, through pressure on the mayors and *préfets* responsible for banning films at a local level. Buñuel's *L'Age d'or* was banned in 1930 after protests from the Ligue des Patriotes and an anti-semitic group, the Ligue Antijuive. A *conseiller municipal*, Le Provost de Launay, wrote an open letter to the *préfet de police* expressing disgust at the showing of the film 'a stone's throw from the monument to the Unknown Soldier' and *Le Figaro* (7 Dec 30) described the film as besmirching 'fatherland, family and religion' and, returning to the subject three days later, accused it of 'Bolshevism'.

Films using war veterans were liable to special difficulties. Raymond Bernard's *Le Croix de bois* (1932), filmed on the Great War battlefields, resorted to them, particularly when the Army refused its co-operation for certain scenes: 'you don't expect my regiment to march past a ham actor disguised as a general!', Bernard was told by one colonel, who also refused outright to let them be filmed covered in mud, instead of in their best dress uniforms. Eventually Bernard called on veterans who were happy to oblige. But the second version of Gance's *J'Accuse* [33] attracted criticism (see my note).

The veterans brought home two contradictory outlooks: a shared military experience, and a hatred of war. In peacetime, there were different ways in which these could be reconciled. One was in the comedies of military life so popular in the 1930s, stressing the positive aspects of service: comradeship and good-humour, while doing without the unpleasantness of fighting. The genre had in fact existed in theatre for many years before the war, often with musical accompaniment, and transferred easily to sound cinema, where music was an important element (during the first sound decade, film shows frequently included live performances by singers which preceded the film). Jeancolas (1983) has counted at least 20 of these military comedies or melodramas between 1932 and 1935 and they continued to be made, with actors like Bach and Fernandel specializing in them: *Le Champion du régiment*, *Le Coq du régiment*, *La Caserne en folie*, *La Mariée du régiment*, *La Garnaison amoureuse*, *La Margoton du bataillon*, *La Fille du régiment* and, the best-known, *Les Gaîtés de l'escadron*. They could be compared with the British military comedies of the 1950s, like *Private's Progress* and the first 'Carry On' film, *Carry on Sergeant*, though I can think of no French equivalents after the Second World War.

Another solution was to relocate the events in time or place by setting them in historical or colonial contexts. René Le Somptier's *Les Fils du soleil* (1924), Renoir's *Le Bled* (1929), Duvivier's *La Bandera* (1935) and Poirier's *L'Appel du silence* (1936) use stories of the Rif war, the conquest of Algiers, the Spanish Foreign Legion (with a dedication to Franco) and the life of Charles de Foucauld (officer and Catholic missionary killed in the Sahara in 1916). Fernandel met Robert le Vigan in *Un de la légion* (Christian-Jacque, 1936), to provide a mixture of colonialist epic and military vaudeville. The latter predominated. It was beyond the powers of Le Vigan to upstage Fernandel.

Both the musical comedies and the colonialist dramas exalted some, but not all, military virtues. In Maurice Gleize's *Légion d'honneur* (1938), a wounded lieutenant convalescing in the Camargue falls in love with the wife of his best friend, but decides to sacrifice happiness to return to the desert (a sort of secular Charles de Foucauld). Male comradeship is the value that unites the musical comedies to the romantic melodramas and behind both is an ethic of honour, patriotism and self-denial (accepting sacrifices with good humour or a sense of duty). The qualities of order and discipline and the efficient weaponry that make an effective fighting force are less prominently displayed.

Of course, the colonialist films have a disturbing lack of awareness of the less desirable side to France's 'civilizing mission' in Africa. After some 50 years, the genre has been revived, with clear critical intentions. The thesis of Bertrand Tavernier's *Coup de torchon* [51] is that, like the men around the pool table in the film, the colonialist either considers 'natives' as lower than animals, or goes crazy and, perhaps, like the police chief, becomes a mass-murderer. Alain Corneau's *Fort Saganne* [52] casts Gérard Depardieu as a legionary who is at the same time a typically individualist hero, becoming aware of the limitations of military values. With a feminist heroine and a climax that takes its hero to the horrors of the Great War, Corneau's film is an evident attempt to combine later perceptions with the excitement of the thirties epics. Its comparative failure perhaps shows, as Francis Veber remarked to me, that 'you can't make a left-wing colonialist film'.

Neither the political Right nor the Left wanted war, though their interpretations of the deteriorating international situation and the threats to peace were as divergent as their ideas of *la nation* and what constituted it. Newsreels took up where the military comedies and melodramas left off, showing the defensive preparations of the army and, more generally, exalting its achievements and traditions. Léon Poirier's *Verdun, vision d'histoire* (1928), remade in a sound version as *Verdun, souvenirs d'histoire* [29], advocated the government policy of rapprochement with Germany, while Marcel L'Herbier's *Entente cordiale*, which the director later described as 'something of a history lesson', giving 'not only an anecdotal, but also a diplomatic understanding', celebrated the alliance with Britain in 1939. In the same year, Jean de Loubignac made a documentary drama answering the question *Sommes-nous défendus?* (in the affirmative, naturally) and *Double crime sur la ligne Maginot* (1937), adapted by Félix Gandéra from a spy novel by Pierre Nord, was an opportunity to display France's famous eastern defensive system, as reconstructed in the studio.

Against these arguments (that the country was prepared, well-protected and secure in its alliances), there were more directly pacifist statements: Léo Joannon's *Alerte en Méditerranée* (1938) allegorized the spirit of Munich in a story about French, British and German captains co-operating against smugglers. The fact that Léonide Moguy's *Le Déserteur* (1939) had to be retitled *Je t'attendrai*, shows the sensitivity of the government at this moment and helps to appreciate the context of *Quai des brumes* [2], where Carné never explains the circumstances of Gabin's desertion from the army.

Of Renoir's film *La Grande illusion* [34], Prédal (1972) says that it 'faithfully reflects the state of public opinion in 1937' and, unjustly, dismisses the view that it shows class divisions as more important than national ones, also accusing it of 'disguised antisemitism' in its portrait of the Jew Rosenthal, because he is shown to be richer than the French prisoners and 'fighting only to protect his fortune'. Given the circumstances of the time when the film was made, and the film's argument (the need for solidarity between the representatives of modern French society, Maréchal and Rosenthal, as opposed to the outmoded aristocratic values of de Boeldieu and Rauffenstein), his reading is unfair to Renoir.

* * * * *

The films of the thirties offer warnings and reassurances, avenues of escape and the prospect of dead ends. They are less preoccupied with the personal concerns of happiness and misery, than with the public ones of cynicism and hope. Whether they depict human beings in an industrial environment as the prisoners of industry (*A nous la liberté*) or in a Utopian rural one (*Regain*), they show little faith in contemporary, organized society and even those films which accept it as an inescapable premise generally consider its institutions to be corrupt and propose as another inescapable premise that fulfilment can be achieved only through love, in the constitution of the ideal couple.

There was a moment, around the time of the Popular Front in 1936, when hope predominated over cynicism. The government of Léon Blum only survived a year (though, in name, the front lasted until 1938), during which it fulfilled some hopes with the Matignon agreements, ensuring trade union rights, paid holidays, security against unfair dismissal and the 40-hour week; and disappointed others, particularly in its failure to give military help to the Spanish Republicans. But the Popular Front mood extended beyond and went deeper than Blum's government. In May 1936, after the elections, there were strikes and factory occupations involving more than a million workers: Georges Monca's *Choc en retour* (1937) presages these in a right-wing comedy where the boss (played by Michel Simon) instigates the strike. Julien Duvivier's *La Belle équipe* [87] tells how a group of workers spend the money from a win on the lottery to start a restaurant outside Paris as a co-operative enterprise. Duvivier brings in several themes of the time: unemployment, foreign refugees, financial swindles, workers' co-operatives; and the film, which shows the original group of five friends reduced to two (Jean Gabin and Charles

Vanel), both in love with the same woman, was made with two contrasting endings. In one, the dispute ends in murder; in the other, they decide to bury their differences and give up the woman for the sake of their joint enterprise and their friendship.

La Belle équipe illustrates the attractions and the limitations of the 'populist' film, the sentimental theme and the melodramatic elements partly blunting the political message. But the very fact that so many of these films introduced working-class heroes and heroines was remarkable in European cinema at the time; and the mood of the Popular Front made it possible for film-makers to treat political themes in a new way, even when the context was romance. Some directors, like Jean Renoir and Jean-Paul Dreyfus (Le Chanois) were politically active, using their work to support the Front and the PCF.

Renoir's *La Marseillaise* [15] and *Le Crime de Monsieur Lange* [88] are probably the best distinctly 'popular front' films: the first tells the story of the Revolution through the ordinary people of Marseilles, flocking to Paris to support the revolutionaries; the second is about a writer of Westerns whose books are produced by a small printing works run by Batala (Jules Berry). When Batala disappears to avoid his creditors, and is presumed dead, his nephew agrees that the workers should run the firm as a co-operative. It is a huge success, but Batala returns (disguised as a priest!) and threatens to resume control, so the inoffensive Monsieur Lange (René Lefèvre) kills him. Lange flees with his girlfriend, is stopped at the Belgian frontier and tells his story to a group of workers in a café: the main action is shown in flashback. They discuss whether to hand him over to the police, and decide to let him escape.

Though there is an anticlerical joke in having Batala dress up as a priest, the PCF line was one of conciliation of different factions in the Front; the priest in Dreyfus' *Le Temps des cerises* (1937) says: 'one must also believe in a paradise on earth'. *Le Temps des cerises*, funded by the PCF, contrasts the fate of two Frenchmen born in 1895, one in a *château*, the other in a working-class family, and it ends with an impassioned plea for retirement pensions for old people – the kind of issue on which the Communists could expect wide popular support. This film, and *La Vie est à nous* (1936), directed by Renoir with the help of Dreyfus and Jacques Becker, show the PCF making intelligent use of the cinema in support of its election campaigns.

When André Malraux made *L'Espoir* (1939, finished in 1945), using men who were actually fighting in the Spanish Republican cause, hope had in fact gone. France was at the mercy of obscure forces and impulses beyond easy understanding. Ordinary people longed for happiness, peace, reasonable working conditions and the occasional breath of country air: Jean Boyer's *Prends la route* (1936) had used the excuse of the first paid holidays for industrial workers to show a couple of popular singers touring the country. But these reasonable expectations were to be denied. No wonder some believed that the world was at the mercy of pathological sadists and liars. No wonder it sometimes felt like being trapped in a room from which there was no escape. No wonder *Le Jour se lève* [90] has been seen as such a powerful metaphor for its time.

* * * * *

The period of the German occupation and the Vichy government has almost certainly received more attention from film historians than any other in French cinema history. Partly this is because of the almost prurient delight some take in reopening the sores. For left-wing writers, it is agreeable to remind the Right of past misdemeanours – the complicity of the French police, for example, in the deportation of Jews. Jeancolas (1983) and Prédal (1972) remind us that anti-semitism was already present in 1930s French society.

Others have felt an ambiguous attraction to the period: the novels of Patrick Modiano, for example, use for literary ends the themes of disloyalty and sexual and political corruption which carry over from the financial and social scandals of the 1930s; his script for Louis Malle's *Lacombe Lucien* [49] is bathed in this atmosphere and, if the period of the Occupation can be seen as a continuation of the struggles of the 1930s, so the various reinterpretations of the Occupation and the Resistance, from *La Bataille du rail* [35] onwards, are the extension of its political conflicts up to the present.

In 1939, a number of films, including *La Règle du jeu* [58] were banned as 'depressing, morbid [and] immoral' and, with the Occupation, censorship of films became exceptionally strict. From 1940 onwards, there were regulations demanding that cinema proprietors should exhibit notices on the screen, announcing measures against anyone demonstrating with laughter or catcalls during the newsreel and threatening cinemas with closure if such incidents took place. Lights were partly to be left on as a further discouragement.

Goebbels strongly believed in the power of cinema and especially fiction films (direct propaganda tending to become counter-productive), but he did not wish, either, to have French audiences attending high-quality films which might give an exalted idea of French culture; so he proposed that the French market be provided mainly with cheap entertainment. 'It is not our job to supply Frenchmen with good films,' he wrote. For this reason he described as an 'incredible lack of political sense' the decision of Alfred Greven, director of Continental Films in Paris, to allow Christian-Jacque to make *La Symphonie fantastique* (1942), which gave far too flattering a picture of Berlioz's achievement.

As far as the industry itself was concerned, the close prewar collaboration between France and Germany in this field meant that there was little difficulty for the Germans in taking it over.

Marcel Carné, for example, had already worked for the German firm UFA on *Quai des brumes* [2] when they obliged him to accept a producer, Grégor Rabinovitch, who was a Jewish refugee from the Nazis: 'business is business',

Carné remarks of this surprising choice which was to cause him numerous problems during the shooting of the film. Returning to Paris in 1940 ('the Parisians seemed to be completely unaware of the presence of the occupier'), he was called to see Greven, whom he found 'shifty, authoritarian and determined to take full advantage of a power acquired for him by others', and insisted on complete freedom in the choice of subjects and that any film he undertook should be shot in France. Eventually, according to Carné's account, this was reluctantly conceded and Greven invited him to his home, in the Rue Beaujon, where he kept open house to guests from the world of cinema and theatre every Thursday.

'I went there, just once . . .' If the Carné memoirs take on a defensive note at this time, and if he quotes with delight Cécile Sorel's reply to the postwar committee investigating her relations with the Germans, it is because, like many others, he was also investigated in the postwar purges. To work at all under German occupation meant compromises, so the tone is defensive. The many gradations of compromise involved can be measured by comparing Carné's fairly relaxed account of his wartime activities with the newsreel interview in which Maurice Chevalier tries to make light of his singing tour in Germany, his habitual *insouciance* sounding decidedly false. Sacha Guitry, in *Quatre ans d'occupation* (1947), writes of his association with the Germans in terms of 'the professional obligations of a man of my kind', 'the natural curiosity of the writer' and, incredibly, his publisher's insistent demands for a further instalment of his memoirs. Ernst Jünger, from the other side, describes Guitry welcoming him to his home and presenting him with autographed letters by Debussy and Octave Mirbeau. Deceptions and self deceptions were inevitable in the circumstances of the time.

One category of films made under the Occupation is easy to define: these are the films of overt, anti-semitic, anti-Communist or pro-Nazi propaganda, relatively small in number, including documentaries made by the Fascist militia, Marcel Déat's RNP or the Légion des Volontaires Français which were given a restricted showing at party meetings. There were also French versions or compilations from German films, like *Le Péril juif* and *Face au bolchevisme*, which got wider exhibition.

As well as these overtly Nazi films, there were others which in varying degrees may be interpreted as supporting the 'National Revolution', the official doctrine of Vichy France. Identification of these is to a great extent a matter of interpretation, since they were mainly feature films, not direct propaganda. The attribution of guilt by association is common among later writers on the period: films like Pagnol's *La Fille du puisetier* (1940) which contains a scene showing the family listening to Marshal Pétain's broadcast of June 17 and praised by *Le Film* in 1941 ('a great film . . . reconciliation in love for the country'), are obvious targets and have led to a revised assessment of Pagnol's pre-war work in the light of the 'National Revolution' appeal for a return to the land and the exaltation of traditional peasant values.

There is certainly a high level of continuity between the films made before the war and those made during the Occupation. Hollywood was out of bounds, but there was an increased demand for the kind of escapist entertainment it had provided, so the period was good for the industry. But an analysis by Jean-Pierre Bertin-Maghit of 140 films made between 1940 and 1944, seeking evidence of Vichy propaganda, yields rather dubious results. It is hardly convincing evidence of the population policies of the Vichy government, for example, that most films deal with young couples (70 per cent aged between 20 and 30) and have a happy ending which implies that they married and had lots of children: these are typical features of the kind of Hollywood films French audiences enjoyed. As for the observation that many of the films involve middle-class characters, often belonging to the liberal professions (especially artists and writers), it is one that could be made of most periods in French cinema: the middle classes and the liberal professions are 'transparent' elements, like the couple who live happily ever after.

The same is true of most other themes which Bertin-Maghit identifies: a contrast between sincere and insincere love related to the purity of women and the need for struggle to achieve happiness; appeals for social integration and an end to class conflicts; the city depicted as a place of perdition and the country as one of salvation. These themes are picked up from prewar literature or cinema, and offered for acceptance or reinterpretation in the light of circumstances.

Indeed, this continuity is the essence of Vichy. The 'National Revolution', despite its name, was not presented as a violent upheaval, but as return to the traditional values of *travail, famille, patrie*, a slogan that could be equally well adopted by Stalinist Russia, supporters of the American way of life and a host of others. *Premier de cordée* [107] was certainly not made as propaganda for Pétain, and others (*Le Mistral*, 1942; *Patricia*, 1942) may not have been either: to say they were, suggests looking for scapegoats. As for films made before the war, it is playing Vichy's game to attribute Pétainist meanings to them, demonstrating the very continuity that the collaborationist government set out to assert. In any case, the slogan *travail, famille, patrie* needs to be interpreted in a very loose way before one can apply it to *Regain* [103], a rural anarchist film, with a message of 'neither God nor master' which would have stuck hard in the throats of the authoritarian Vichy Catholics.

Most of all, the desire for national survival and recovery to which Pétain appealed, was a legitimate one in 1940 (though it became less so as resistance was organized and as Vichy began to demonstrate the extent of its subservience to the Nazis). There may have been a number of naive people who continued to work in the cinema industry, but there were few Fascists.

Interestingly, if one compares *Les Visiteurs du soir* [17] with the earlier Carné-Prévert collaborations, there is a change: the message of the final image of this medieval romance, with the lovers turned to stone, is one of hope. Their hearts continue to beat. Carné's story is precisely dated ('May, 1485'), but its

41

central theme of the triumph of love and faith, despite the pact with the devil, was capable of a particular interpretation in the light of circumstances. 'What is signed, is signed!' Gilles is told by Dominique, played by Arletty in a medieval version of the sophisticated and cynical women of her prewar films; and the devil (Jules Berry, again in a characteristic role) warns the lovers: 'you may forget your chains ... but I am still here'. These fatalistic pronouncements should, on the model of *Quai des brumes* or *Le Jour se lève*, prepare us for a tragic ending, but here faith triumphs over cynicism and the audience is left with a paradoxical message of optimism.

* * * * *

Around 1960, I was talking to a friend in his room at the Cité Universitaire, and he showed me a group photograph of himself and his classmates from the final year at his *lycée* in Limoges. He pointed to one of the faces: 'He's dead ... so is he.' Like Michel, about four of the young men on the photograph were students whose military service had been deferred; the rest, most of them, were in Algeria.

Writers on the history of French cinema tend to express surprise, and sometimes disgust or contempt, at the virtual absence from films of the colonial wars that divided the country and were directly responsible for the collapse of the Fourth Republic in 1958. While the country was experiencing these traumatic upheavals, the cinema could do nothing better than stare at some previously undiscovered fragment of Brigitte Bardot. To take such a view is to overlook two facts. The first, frequently cited by film directors themselves, is that the censor and producers simply blocked films proposing to deal with sensitive political issues, Indo-China and Algeria coming top of the list, or with those social topics like abortion which are sometimes also mentioned in the indictment against the cinema of the 1950s. Even books on the Algerian war were banned; literature has always enjoyed greater immunity from censorship than film because it appeals to a more select audience and because it is consequently less easily seen as 'an inspiration to crime, propagating immorality, dangerous even to the faith ... endangering the health of the soul', as Louis Salibert wrote in 1921. The case of *Les Nouveaux messieurs* [54] is exemplary: a play allowed for exhibition was banned on film; and the banning of Stanley Kubrick's *Paths of Glory* (1957), describing an execution of men from a battalion in the French Army during World War I that had refused to advance, demonstrates the extreme sensitivity of the censor to criticism of the military. Any film about Algeria that could have been made in these circumstances would have described the glorious achievement of the Legion or the *paras*, as the few films about Indo-China did; and that was not likely to please the critics any more than the cinema's battle to be allowed to reveal another inch of Bardot.

If anything, it was society that was at fault, not the cinema. And the second fact, sometimes overlooked by Anglo-Saxon critics, is society's need to recover from its wounds. The divisions caused by the political confrontations and economic disasters of the 1930s had been reconciled in Britain and the United States in the external alliances and national unities of World War II. British cinema of the war years is a potent expression of this theme: 'we was all one'. In France, the Occupation had greatly deepened the wound and there was a need to propose a myth around the fiction of a 'nation' united in resistance, through such films as *La Bataille du Rail* [35] (with only a few, excluded from this concept of the 'nation', collaborating with the enemy). It was not until the 1970s that the other side of the story could safely be examined. But, in the circumstances of the Cold War and the colonial wars, France was no easy country to govern, even without the added irritant of a politically engaged cinema.

The cinema that the French got, in fact, was the one most likely to heal their wounds and reconcile them to each other. The films of the late 1940s and the 1950s, described in *Cahiers du cinéma* under the disparaging label *cinéma de qualité*, were precisely that: a 'quality' product, of the sort that the French have always prided themselves on making well, like good clothes, good cooking or good wines. The directors, actors, scriptwriters and technicians were masters of their crafts, and, in relying largely on adaptations of novels, they emphasized the strength and continuity of the country's literary achievement.

Contemporary issues were certainly not absent from the films of this period, even outside the work of André Cayatte. Raymond Borde found plenty of relevance in such unlikely places as *Ali Baba et les 40 voleurs* [39] or *Papa, Maman, la bonne et moi* [152], where, apart from the comments quoted in my note on the film, he praises the non-racist portrait of a North African.

If critics were beginning to discover that a film could carry a hidden message about its politics behind the grotesque spectacle of Fernandel singing 'Je suis Ali, Ali Baba', so they were beginning to realize, too, that such meanings could be more powerfully conveyed when expressed in this kind of 'code'. By the end of the 1950s, some were detecting, beyond the conventions of a routine suspense thriller like Louis Malle's *Ascenseur pour l'échafaud* [134], a whole host of messages about France in 1958 (see my note to the film).

The thriller and the gangster film were treated at the time as mere bread-and-butter productions (hence Sadoul's regret that Malle, as a novice director, should be saddled with *Ascenseur pour l'échafaud* just to satisfy his producer's idea of a 'commercial' subject). In fact, such genre films are exceptionally instructive and revealing in relation to society at a given moment. The genre itself is like the framework of a traditional tale, which the storyteller can confidently adapt to fulfil or deny expectations and to suggest different levels of meaning. So a genre film is quite capable of dealing with the same basic material as any other type of narrative: the patient performance of a difficult task is much the same in *Du rififi chez les hommes* [133] as in *Un Condamné à mort s'est échappé* [42]. And, while thrillers, gangster movies and so on are made with a particular purpose (usually to do with pleasing audiences and making money), there is no harm in suggesting that some may owe their appeal to their aptness for their time. *Le Jour se lève* [90] and *Quai des brumes* [2] belong peculiarly to the late 1930s, as *Le Salaire de la peur* [95] belongs to the mid-1950s, with its despairing picture of men trying to escape from exile in a mythical South American town which has the atmosphere of a colonial backwater.

* * * * *

The cinema of the New Wave was the product of a society enjoying considerable material prosperity and at last emerging from its colonial entanglements. General de Gaulle, like Gabin in *Le Cave se rebiffe* [140], had been called out of retirement for 'one last job' and, in the shadow of his autocratic presidency and his 'particular idea of France', the middle classes began to enjoy the benefits of their prosperity, safe, after 1962, from the fear that their children would die on a hillside in the Aurès or a backstreet in Algiers.

The country's growing affluence and self-confidence were evident, and helped to disguise the poverty of some sections of the population. The cinema experienced an extraordinary burst of activity and some films (*Les 400 coups* [169], *Le Beau Serge* [111]) examined the realities and problems of life in Paris or the provinces in a fresh way: comparing *Les 400 coups* to other films of the period, I can think of nothing better than the old cliché that it 'spoke a new language'. Seeing it again recently, I was astonished at Truffaut's ability to capture the details of life in the Paris streets, the school, the small apartment, that were the everyday experience of the less well-off and their children at the time. It stands, for me, beside a quite different film, Chris Marker's documentary *Le Joli mai* [61], as a document for understanding the hidden face of France in the early years of the Fifth Republic.

However, the 'new language' was more often used to record the most visible faces of the country, if only because these happened also to be the most photogenic. The political ambiguities of the New Wave were summarized in the work of Jean-Luc Godard: the censor banned *Le Petit soldat* when it was made in 1960, and on its release three years later, left-wing critics were disappointed to find that the director had not made up his mind which side to support. Most of the new lightweight cameras, often in the hands of film-makers happy to admit that they were not sure how the things worked, were pointed at the new apartment blocks, the stylish interiors and, above all, the Citroëns DS and ID that symbolized the lifestyle of the new class. By the time of *Un Homme et une femme* [78], it seemed that the 'new language' might be contained in a pocket phrase book. Lelouch had something to say about fast cars, lovers on the beach, soft-focus lenses and windscreen wipers, and he said it over and over.

Despite attempts by rival gangs to persuade him to go back to retirement, the Boss clearly had no intention of doing so and there was a pervasive sense of frustration among my friends in the Union Nationale des Etudiants de France. In Strasbourg, the student union was taken over in 1967 by an anarchist group which promptly abolished it and published a pamphlet, *De la misère en milieu étudiant*, denouncing the 'opium of the intellectuals' and the misleading differentiation of equally inane products (Godard and Lelouch were given as examples). Advising students that if they had to read books, they should steal them, and unkindly describing the student class as 'the most faithful customer of theatres and cine-clubs and the most avid consumer of [art's] deep-frozen corpse, cellophane-wrapped in supermarkets for the housewives of over-production', it ended with a call for workers' councils and the outbreak of 'the revolutionary festival': '*play* is the ultimate rationality of this festival, and the only rules it can obey are life without boredom and enjoyment without let or hindrance'.

* * * * *

A year later, the authors nearly had their wish. 'Society is a carnivorous flower,' the walls of Paris announced in May 1968. 'Art is dead, don't consume its corpse.' Godard, described on the same walls as *le plus con des suisses prochinois*, began the process of self-criticism that was to occupy his films during the next 10 years.

The 'events' of 1968 themselves were television 'events' and, although Paris was certainly an exciting place to be in May and June of that year, the country was not slow to realize that revolution had passed it by. De Gaulle survived, to be succeeded in an orderly fashion by Georges Pompidou, then by Valéry Giscard d'Estaing. History, a character in a novel of the seventies remarked, seemed to be happening elsewhere.

The 'events' had not achieved what their instigators wanted, but they had not been entirely fruitless. Flanked by a powerful reactionary Right and a host of *groupuscules* on the Left, the Socialists and Communists concentrated their minds and united behind a joint manifesto, recalling the days of the Popular Front (a point made in Chris Marker's 1977 documentary *Le Fond de l'air est rouge*). There were benefits for education, the feminist movement, the ecologists. Most of all, there was a sense of *contestation*, a feeling of hostility to the establishment and anger at the awfulness of the world and the mess that had been made of it. Jeancolas (1974) underlines the conformity of the cinema under Pompidou, pointing out, for example, the 1930s archetypes which recur in films like Pierre Richard's *Je sais rien, mais je dirai tout* (1973) and the limits which the opposition appeared to accept; but noting that there was a much greater willingness to locate films in a real present, rather than the 'vague contemporary' of earlier times. But he observes, too, what is excluded from this: leftists and peasants, minorities and immigrants, and the *marginaux* of every description. By the end of the decade, there was a growing body of films dealing with the fringes of French society or offering a radical critique of society.

45

It would be wrong to exaggerate, however. There was also the matter of distribution and audience. The vast majority of people still went to the cinema for an entertaining night out, not for a hard look at social or political problems, and flocked to see Louis de Funès [183], rather than the latest Claude Faraldo [8]. By the mid-1980s, the cinema had certainly gained in scope. Film-makers dealt broadly with a range of social issues [163], attacked received ideas and dogmas [70], absorbed the lessons of contemporary sociology and historiography [27], examined the lives of the working-class, of women [161], of the family [162], of farmers [109] from a convincing and original point of view, and made works that defied classification in their effort to convey a variety of experiences [9].

In the main, the films of the 1980s, despite the economic depression, expressed the outlook of a prosperous, confident society. The *rétro* fashions of the early seventies had vanished and there was little of the dreamy nostalgia which seemed to afflict the British cinema revival of the same period (in *Chariots of Fire, A Private Function, The Weather in the Streets,* and a host of others, as if to be truly 'British' meant to live at some earlier time). But combining popular appeal, technical quality and social analysis usually meant working within a tested narrative genre; and, as it had been 30 years before, the most prominent genre in the 1980s was still the crime story or police thriller which could be adapted for formal experiments [10, 148], social analysis [116], political allegory [149], to show an alternative society [126] or to support the existing one (Maurice Pialat's *Police,* 1985). The cinema of the eighties certainly gave a rounded portrait of a country which might, or might not, be an accurate representation: it depended, as it always had, on which of its many social and geographical communities constituted your particular idea of France.

3 Geographies

'*J'ai deux amours: mon pays et Paris*', Joséphine Baker sang in what was to become her theme-tune, referring to her origins in the United States and to her adoptive home. But for a French man or woman, *mon pays* can have a variety of meanings, according to context. For François, in Claude Chabrol's film *Le Beau Serge* [111], *mon pays* could mean France, if he was speaking to a foreigner. In conversation with a Parisian, it might refer to the region of *le Limousin* or, less probably, to the *département* of Creuse, one of the three that make up that historical region. But for François (and still more for Serge, the provincial who has not taken the road to Paris), it is the little village of Sardent which would be most immediately and most intimately evoked by the word, and a French man or woman who sang of two loves, *mon pays et Paris*, would convey a quite different message from Joséphine Baker's: affection for Paris, as the capital city, a shared possession of all French people; and loyalty to some provincial homeland, *mon village, mon pays, mon petit bled*. There were many, and not only foreigners like Baker, who considered Paris as a second home.

There has always been movement from the countryside to the capital, but in France, where the proportion of the population employed in agriculture stood at over 40 per cent in 1910 and remained at over 35 per cent in 1945, the change from a largely rural to a decisively urban society came late in comparison with other industrialized European countries. It took place, in fact, within the period of cinema history and one would expect this fundamental social change to be reflected in cinema.

It is, but obliquely. The drift towards the town almost inevitably involves the younger, the more ambitious or the better-educated part of the population and it is these new urban-dwellers (François rather than Serge in Chabrol's film) whose lives find a reflection in cinema. Film, for reasons of production and of distribution, is an urban industry. The Provençal studios founded by Marcel Pagnol in the 1930s are an exception: the vast majority of French films have been produced in the Parisian suburbs from where they can call on the designers, technicians and actors who also, in the majority, make their base in the capital.

This does not entirely explain the use of Paris as a setting. In films made before the late 1950s, important exterior shots were not filmed on location, but on lavishly constructed sets. Marcel Carné got Alexandre Trauner to simulate the district around the Canal Saint-Martin outside the studios at Billancourt for *Hôtel du Nord* [120] and to build a replica of the Barbès métro station at Joinville for *Les Portes de la nuit* [37]: both were within a few miles of the actual sites. It was not convenience of location work that determined the choice of Paris as a setting for films in this period, but another form of 'transparency'. The décors for the two Carné films just mentioned are celebrated because they reproduce precise Parisian locations, but most 'Parisian' films cannot be identified with one particular quarter of the city. The action takes place mainly in 'typical' streets, with cafés, shops, perhaps a market, perhaps some street furniture like a news-stand or the *colonnes Morris* which carry advertisements for theatres and concerts; or in a 'typical' six- or seven-storey apartment block, around a central courtyard. This apartment block, in *Sous les toits de Paris* [118], provides a microcosm of society; its stairway, in *Les Portes de la nuit* [37], *La Belle équipe* [87] and *Le Jour se lève* [90], its courtyard in *Le Crime de Monsieur Lange* [88], serve as meeting-places for the characters or concentrate the drama; its age and eccentricities are exploited in *Mon oncle* [76] as a source of visual humour and a symbol of a traditional way of life. The Paris of these films is perceived less as a city different from other cities, than as a universal urban environment where workers, bourgeois, aristocrats, shop-keepers, writers, criminals and kind uncles live, but not peasants or provincials. This almost invisible version of Paris is the natural setting for the diverse characters that most interest French cinema.

* * * * *

Between this 'normal' human habitation and a place where human life is absent (for example, up a mountain in the Alps), there is a range of inhabited locations. These are the countryside and the provinces, where one or two cities (Marseilles, Lyon, Bordeaux) acquire a distinctive character. In the main, however, they exist primarily as generalized 'provincial' settings and the countryside is defined by the absence of features that characterize the town. In short, the norm (against which an increasing number of films made since the late 1950s appear, however, as deviations), defines Paris as the place where people live when they are not to be considered primarily as 'characters', 'provincials' or 'countryfolk'.

Not that Paris, and the ordinary life it represents, is necessarily depicted as an ideal. The theme of escape pervades French cinema. In *Le Crime de Monsieur Lange* [88], where the Parisian story is encapsulated in flashback between the scenes on the border, we understand that Lange and Valentine are fleeing not towards a better place, but towards a future time when social justice, not capitalist law, will govern France. But this optimism is rare. A host of films from the 1930s onwards centre on the idea of escape to an unattainable paradise: the remembered tropical islands which bring together the lovers in *Les Portes de la nuit* [37] or the 'elsewhere' towards which Gabin struggles in *Pépé-le-Moko* [32], *Quai des brumes* [2] or *Au-delà des grilles* (1949), only to die

48

within sight of the ship that will take him there. The image is reversed in *Le Salaire de la peur* [95] where the 'tropical paradise' turns out to be a kind of Devil's Island and the characters yearn for escape to Paris. But in all these cases, the hopes of 'ordinary' people for a better life are given a location in which they might, were it not for fate or the wickedness of others, be realized.

The tropical island or the unspecified place, outside the reach of the camera, where Gabin can restart his life, are by definition unattainable. The countryside of France, however, can give a tantalizing glimpse of what might be. The lovers in *Casque d'Or* [130], Becker's tale of the underworld and demi-monde at the turn of the century, have to leave Paris: in self-defence, Manda (Serge Reggiani) has committed murder and he is wanted by the police. After meeting Casque d'Or (Simone Signoret) by the river, he goes with her to a farm near Joinville where they can hide out in safety.

The next morning, Casque d'Or wakes alone; but she is reassured by the sight of Manda's bundle on the chair. In the courtyard, Madame Eugène is doing her washing. A change of scene reminds us that the police investigation continues, but the lovers meet, walk through the woods and, returning to the town square, hear music from the church. It could be a funeral, Manda suggests. But it is a wedding. 'Do you love me?' Casque d'Or asks him as they go inside.

They leave the church, its bell now tolling ominously, and meet Félix who tells them that Manda's friend Raymond has been arrested for the murder. That night, Manda ponders whether to return to Paris and give himself up. The next morning, Casque d'Or wakes to see that his bundle has disappeared. Their idyll is over.

The Joinville episode is all the more isolated by its parallels and contrasts with respect to the rest of Becker's film. The simple happiness and wisdom represented by Madame Eugène (an idealized figure of a countrywoman at peace with herself and the world) or the bride and groom in the church, are placed firmly beyond the reach of Manda and Casque d'Or, both in location and in time. Regardless of the period in which the film is set, they signify a past way of life and in this, as in many other films, the church, facing a village square, is made the focus of traditional values, but values which no longer apply to the 'ordinary' urban environment. Indeed, the church porch, with worshippers coming and going from mass, serves as a gateway to this now alien way of life. The lovers in *Casque d'Or*, aspiring to its promise of peace and respectability, hovered just inside; Mouchette [113], rejected by the village community, passes in front of it; François, in *Le Beau Serge* [111], sits on the church steps, talking to the priest who reminds him of his lost vocation; and in *Biquefarre* [109], a character remarks on the emptiness of the church square which, in the days of *Farrebique* [108], 36 years earlier, was a crowded meeting-place after mass. The camera, in these and other films, studies the coming and going of people through the church porch (usually old women in black) from the point of view, literally and metaphorically, of an 'outsider'. There is even an attenuated version of the same idea in *Sans toit ni loi* [163] when Mona is left sitting in the car while Madame Landier goes to attend a conference of agronomists.

'You said we'd go and pick lilacs at Easter,' Françoise (Jacqueline Laurent) tells François (Jean Gabin): the countryside as a paradise for urban workers can be evoked, in this case [90], by a greenhouse, but a car horn interrupts the conversation and brings them back to reality. In *La Grande illusion* [34], the German farm is a refuge not from city life, but from war and the class, national and racial distinctions that lead to it. '*Her* German, I can understand,' Gabin tells Dalio, as he starts to fall in love with the widow in whose house they are hiding. The unchanging work of the farm and the continuity of the natural environment across the artificial boundaries erected by men (the two prisoners cannot be sure precisely when they have reached the Swiss border), suggest an uncorrupted, prelapsarian world which in *La Faute de l'Abbé Mouret* [66] is a literal paradise, a walled garden untouched by guilt and sin.

This myth of the Fall of Man and of expulsion from paradise may be given very divergent meanings within the same formal structures: hence the confusion between the Vichy nationalist ideal of a return to the soil, expressed in some films made during World War II, which was an essentially reactionary yearning for a particular idea of 'peasant' France; and some prewar films, like those which Marcel Pagnol made from stories by Jean Giono, proposing a form of rural anarchism, *ni Dieu, ni maître*, with totally different implications. Both, admittedly, start from a premise of the corruption of city life inspired partly by the experience of France's industrial revolution and, more immediately, by the political and financial scandals of the interwar years. But they proceed to very different conclusions. In *Angèle* [100] and *Regain* [103], a girl is rescued from urban degradation to start life anew in the Provençal hills: the title of the second film means literally 'aftermath', the grass that grows in a meadow after the first mowing; but more commonly 'revival', 'renewal' or 'recovery'. As Gedemus, Fernandel is a comic figure, a knife-grinder who believes in 'progress', and he serves to bring together the couple of Panturle (Gabriel Gabrio) and Arsule (Orane Demazis) who will ultimately revive the life of the abandoned village of Aubignane.

In *Regain*, it is this couple, with their rejection of all social restraints, who are the 'real' characters: the closer the other participants get to the city and to society, the more 'unreal' they become and the uniformed characters (the station master, the gendarmes, the *garde champêtre*, the seed merchant) are mere puppets, alienated from the natural life of hard work and the open air. 'On the whole, dress for obedience is not dress for work,' Panturle remarks.

Rebuilding the church in Aubignane never enters Panturle's scheme of things: *Regain* belongs to a current in French provincial and peasant life largely neglected in literature and cinema, and only recently given its proper weight by historians. While in certain regions (e.g. Brittany) the peasantry has been Catholic and conservative, there are others which have a long tradition of revolt, ignored by the Right because it did not conform to an image of Catholic

France, and by the Left because it deviated from the Marxist assessment of the peasantry as a potentially unrevolutionary class, Marx himself being as dismissive of 'the idiocy of rural life' as he was of religion, 'the opium of the people'.

* * * * *

As Maréchale tends the 'German' cows in *La Grande illusion* [34], he is led inevitably to think of his grandfather's cows in France, and for Pagnol, too, the 'rural paradise' belongs as much to the past of childhood and grandparents as to the better world of the future. The reverse of the 'rural paradise' is the 'rural slum' depicted in such films as *Goupi-Mains-Rouges* [105] and *La Fiancée du pirate* [158], where country life is backward, repressive and hidebound by tradition. In short, the countryside is much like childhood, combining the contradictions of innocence and freedom from social constraints with the repressive control exercised by parents and grandparents. And, given the 20th-century migration from country to town, it is at least plausible that for many people the countryside should have some of these associations with childhood and the past.

Take the example of Pagnol whose father's weekend cottage in the hills (as he recounts in his fictionalized autobiographies) provided the family with a refuge from the confinement of Marseilles. Pagnol senior was a primary-school teacher, one of the *instituteurs* created in the 1880s by Jules Ferry with the introduction of universal primary education who went into rural communities as missionaries for republican and lay values. In the town, the conflict between State and Church over education could be ignored, but in a small country parish, the *curé* and the *instituteur* often confronted each other across the same market square.

Who gained the upper hand depended largely on location. In the West, the Catholic and Royalist counter-revolution of the Vendée in the 1790s remained a vital memory into the present century. In the southern *départements* of Hérault, Tarn, Vaucluse and Bouches-du-Rhône, the Restoration 'White Terror' left a strong republican tradition which survived and is still reflected in electoral terms. Further distinctions can be made between small peasant proprietors, who would vote according to conscience, and tenants of large landowners, who often voted with their landlords. The rural ideal in the films of Pagnol is not so much one of a simple return to nature, as of the liberation of rural society from town, Church and large landowners, viewed in the light of the strict republican morality of Pagnol's father and the happy memories of hunting and wandering across the Provençal hills.

Pagnol was in touch with one strand in the complex ideological geography of rural France, and was able to express it because of his love of the countryside, his family background and his acquaintance with the work of Giono who turned to a rural, anarchist ideal as a result of his experiences in World War I. But, like Pagnol's Marseilles film studio, this identification of and with a particular region is a rarity and the increasing urbanization of the country meant that fewer and fewer film-makers (with the exception of Chabrol and Rouquier, discussed below) would have such direct associations with regional and country life.

The introduction of paid holidays by the Popular Front government of 1936, as well as offering the urban worker the means to realize his dream of lilac-picking, gradually brought the countryside back into the cinema in a new role. In the postwar period, *Les Vacances de Monsieur Hulot* [110] and *Le Blé en herbe* [168] virtually abolish the specific features of Brittany; the location becomes an anonymous middle-class seaside resort. Much the same had happened to the Mediterranean coast some 20 years earlier in such films as *Pension Mimosas* [102], though the clientele is naturally richer; and it was to happen 20 years later, again to Brittany, in *Pauline à la plage* [82], except that here the characters live in second homes: they are no more part of the region, or more interested in it than Monsieur Hulot; they just own more of it. Already, by the 1950s, Antoine Doinel's longing to see the sea [169] marks him out as an underprivileged child. The privileged majority saw provincial France in August and as tourists.

* * * * *

You do not have the feeling that the prewar Pagnol-Giono films are addressed primarily to an audience of town-dwellers and this is something else that differentiates them from most of the films of Vichy. *La Terre qui renaît, Jardin sans fleurs* and *Croisade de l'air* (all made in 1942) define themselves by their subject-matter as films reacting against rural depopulation and small families, or in favour of Pétain's policy of giving city children a country holiday. The restriction of wartime cinemas to one feature film per programme encouraged the making of documentary 'shorts', and these, too, tend to depict rural craftsmen, implying an audience not familiar with their techniques and products. A company called 'Artisans d'Art du Cinéma' made 24 documentaries, mainly on such topics, between 1940 and 1942: the title of one, *Petits artisans, grands artistes* (1942), sums up their message. But the best-known of this type are the documentaries of Georges Rouquier, *Le Tonnelier* (1942) on the work of the cooper, *Le Charron* (1943) on the cartwright. Like other 'artisanal' documentaries and like his full-length works *Farrebique* [108] and *Biquefarre* [109], they celebrate the continuity of peasant life, but, paradoxically, assume an audience which needs the film-maker's mediation to understand it.

In fact, *Biquefarre*, filmed in 1982 as a return to the family depicted in *Farrebique*, no longer makes any assumptions. Its thesis is that, faced with competition inside the EEC, peasants have no alternative but to become *agriculteurs*, or proletarians of the land, and it suggests that they are unable or unwilling to renounce the traditions of individualism that prevent this transformation. Only after a bitter struggle does the central character manage to buy the plot of land that will keep his farm as a viable unit and the film deals convincingly with this perennial problem of *remembrement*, placing the audience in a position where it can understand and sympathize with the farmer's attachment to the soil and his alleged 'greed' and 'acquisitiveness'.

Though the film ends on a note of guarded optimism, the impression it leaves is painfully depressing. Rouquier, whose work seemed reactionary in the context of 1940s Vichy, turns out to have a progressive concern for the environment, in the light of the ecological movement of the 1970s. The fertilizer that we see destroying the wildlife at the edge of the field, poisons the farmer himself when a sack of it breaks open. Piglets drop dead and cows have become machines for the production of milk.

Farrebique and *Biquefarre* were precisely located in the villages of Goutrens and Rignac in the Aveyron, and between the two films Chabrol's *Le Beau Serge* [111] went to the director's own village of Sardent to write an ambiguous morality about the young man who has escaped and the one who stayed behind. With more than a hint of Hitchcockian guilt, it reverses its original thesis of François, the success, and Serge, the alcoholic failure; and, more than for this contrivance, the film is memorable as one of the first to reverse also the established formula, making Sardent the tangible location in which 'real people' live, and Paris the illusion.

Ultimately, however, in this as well as in his later films, Chabrol turns out to have a town-dweller's view of provincial society, exploiting the secrets behind the surface of village or small-town life in his thrillers just as, say, Agatha Christie used English village settings for the same purpose. However precisely they are located (*Poulet au vinaigre* [116], for example, acknowledges the participation of the inhabitants of a particular village in south-east France), most audiences perceive such films as taking place in a generalized 'provincial' environment. And the increased use from the 1960s onwards of colour film-stock has introduced a new variant on the idealized rural setting. Jeancolas (1979) praises *La Veuve Couderc* [115] for its attention to the Burgundian landscape, but it is doubtful whether the film brings its audience any closer to the reality of the place. A church, with sunlight and shadow revealing the different tones of the surface, suggests beauty unchanged since the Middle Ages, only to recall the images in medieval illuminated manuscripts, the paintings of Courbet or the Impressionists. Human figures become passers-by, hardly distinguished by accidents of dress from their ancestors 500 years earlier and the traditional women in black make their way to church or to market. As with Chabrol's references to Hitchcock, art intervenes even in these later perceptions of rural life.

* * * * *

Two films may sum up aspects of the representation of the countryside in French cinema: Louis Malle's *Lacombe Lucien* [49] and Bertrand Tavernier's *Un*

Dimanche à la campagne (1984). The first of these subverts the proposition that rural life is either paradise or slum, by depicting it in terms of both stereotypes.

The film is set in and around Toulouse during World War II. When we first see Lucien he is in his parents' farmyard, killing a chicken, and the archetype of the brutal, ignorant peasant boy. This image seems to be confirmed when, after the local *instituteur* has rejected his overtures to the Resistance, he joins the Fascist *milices*. In the tawdry society of these collaborators, he discovers a sense of power and self-importance, apparently as indifferent to the interrogations going on in the basement as he was to the spectacle of the headless chicken running about the yard.

His 'work' brings Lucien into contact with M. Horn, a cultured Jew who lives with his mother and his daughter in an apartment that expresses the refinement of the *haute bourgeoisie*: Lucien fingers the art objects that symbolize this culture as if they had arrived from an alien civilization.

The transformation starts when Lucien falls in love with M. Horn's daughter. Her race means nothing to him, his Fascism going no deeper than his commitment to the Resistance. His ignorance becomes simplicity, his simplicity innocence, and as the war ends the two lovers escape to the mountains to enjoy one of those brief rural idylls which are a cinema cliché. The story of the Fall is thus reversed and Lucien absolved ('innocented', in Franglais) before a brief title on the screen tells us that he was arrested, tried and executed as a collaborator. Faced with this compound of two modes, reversing the usual story, audiences and critics found the film ambiguous and were unsure about its political message.

As for *Un Dimanche à la campagne*, one can just imagine a particular type of spectator emerging from the cinema: 'the colour! A painting by Monet!' 'The interiors: pure Vermeer!' Tavernier's film makes continuous reference to painting through its use of colour and photography, and concerns in fact a painter, now an old man, entertaining his son, daughter and grandchildren at his country home. It is the period before World War I, the son is a conventional family man, the daughter a modern young woman preoccupied with a tormented love affair. The old man just wants to preserve harmony for what he realizes may be one of their last Sundays together.

Tavernier gives us all the elements a Parisian audience would associate with the countryside: interpreted primarily through the perceptions of painters, it means peace, childhood, nostalgia, family and the past. Above all, perhaps, it means food. After all, France is a major agricultural producer and all those market vegetables, meats, wines and cheeses start way beyond Les Halles ('how can you govern a country which has over 300 cheeses?' De Gaulle is supposed to have asked). Appropriately, the characters in Tavernier's film never seem to stop eating. The housekeeper, Mercedes, usually appears up to her elbows in flour or at the chopping board. The old man's appetite may be flagging, but he does not forget to invite the others for lunch, dinner or a snack. Indeed, the only crisis in an understated film comes when the daughter threatens to drive back to Paris early, to see her lover, which might spoil the dinner *en famille*. The table around which they eventually eat symbolizes their re-found unity.

A tarragon omelette, in Renoir's *Une Partie de campagne* (1936) is a work of art. An ability to appreciate a potato salad, properly made, in *La Règle du jeu* [58], is more important than the right family background. For Renoir, both as a director and as a character in his films, attitudes to food can indicate anything or everything. Early in *La Règle du jeu*, when Octave (Renoir) refuses breakfast, it is a sign of distress. Bit by bit, the misunderstandings that have disturbed him are resolved and he begins to accept what eventually grows into a substantial breakfast, decidedly more English than continental in menu terms.

Though food continues to occupy a central place in social life, Renoir's gargantuan enjoyment came, with time, to look like over-indulgence. Ferreri's *La Grande bouffe* (1973) took criticism of Western appetites to sickening extremes, but reaction had set in some time earlier. Office workers used to have a two-hour lunch break, this being the minimum necessary to progress through hors-d'oeuvre, main course, salad, cheese, fruit and wine that, until the arrival of *le fast-food*, was considered essential to sustain life between a light breakfast and a heavy dinner. Women would traditionally devote much of the day to family meals, planning, shopping and cooking. The further one got from the fast-moving and 'artificial' centre of urban life, the older one was (young people were able to manage with the tin plates of student restaurants, though they still got five courses on them), the greater the part food would play in one's life, both as a preoccupation and a time-consumer. To the Parisian, the provinces have always offered the supreme attraction of regional cuisine, from the Provençal magnificence of the Oustaù de Baumanière in Les Baux to the solid Alsatian *chou croute* or the Breton pancake, peasant food elevated to a regional delicacy. Exotic cuisines may be sampled in Paris, as can regional specialities, but they are better enjoyed *sur place*.

Clearly, the pressures of modern life conflicted with the total gastronomy of Renoir (food as the measure of all things), and by the 1960s reaction had started to set in. The 'modernity' of the characters in Lelouch's *Un Homme et une femme* [78] lies partly in their preference for fast cars over slow dinners. When Jean-Louis, Anne and her two children meet in a restaurant, the table carries nothing more enticing than a vase of flowers, some hors-d'oeuvres and a salad: a presage of *la nouvelle cuisine*, perhaps, but hardly a feast. They toy with some shrimps, which the children refuse, and there is a discussion about tomatoes. Before we know where we are, Jean-Louis has lit a cigarette and the waiter is clearing the table. As Tati observed in *Mon Oncle* [76], the postwar bourgeoisie was starting to show an American concern with health and hygiene, and is more likely to be seen picking at appetizers or mixing drinks, than sitting down to enjoy a sumptuous dinner.

Sharing food still remains important, however. Sleeping together may be just another episode in the sex war, but eating together signifies harmony. Father and son trying to get by in the kitchen of *Les 400 coups* [169], in the absence of the mother, the 'natural' provider, who is gallivanting around; father and daughter dining in a restaurant in Alain Cavalier's *Un Etrange voyage* (1981), to denote their reconciliation; the 'children' in *Les Enfants terribles* [167] teasing the guests in the restaurant at the seaside hotel or discovering the erotic possibilities of crayfish; the marriage feast in *Gervaise* [96]; the members of the co-operative around the table in *Le Crime de Monsieur Lange* [88]; the bourgeois dinner in *Subway* [126]; these, and innumerable other examples, indicate some of the many meanings food can acquire, its obtrusive presence in the films of Renoir and its virtual absence from those of, say, Bresson and Godard, suggesting polarities of sensuality and austerity, physicality and intellectuality.

* * * * *

The countryside of *Un Dimanche à la campagne* might be pleasant to look at, a provider of good things and somewhere to pass the weekend, but only an old man, too tired to paint, would want to live there. The life of a provincial town did not even have those advantages in Henri Decoin's *Les Inconnus dans la maison* (1942), in Clouzot's *Le Corbeau* [106] and *Les Diaboliques* [132], in Chabrol's *Le Boucher* [114] and *Poulet au vinaigre* [116] and in a host of other thrillers with provincial town settings, down to the Franco-British co-production *Les Louves* (1985), directed by Peter Duffell and set in wartime Lyons. Inquisitive and sometimes murderous old women seem to be the principal inhabitants of these places. Though it is true that with time they have become more specific as to location, Tavernier's *L'Horloger de Saint Paul* (1974) or Chabrol's *Les Fantômes du chapelier* (1982) not only recall those Vichy films about rural crafts with the watchmaker and hatter in their titles, they also find provincial town life interesting chiefly because it seems a good setting for murder. Some Frenchmen may have objected to the implications of the German title given to *Le Corbeau* [106] – 'A Small French Town' – as if what the film showed was true of all such, but French directors have not shown themselves particularly averse to perpetuating the myth.

This is why a few films, including Pagnol's Marseilles trilogy [99] and Jacques Demy's musical *Les Parapluies de Cherbourg* [112], that celebrate the lives of 'real people' in the provinces, are so refreshing. Pagnol loved the Provençal hills as he loved the free, generous and affectionate peasant boy who was his companion (in his autobiographical *Le Château de ma mère*, published in 1957), but they were separated by background and education: Lili, he tells us, left his village for the first and last time to die in Flanders. But Pagnol understands Marseilles society from the inside and while César and the others in his bar in the old port belong to a convention of picturesque regional 'characters', Fanny, with her illegitimate baby, Marius, with his yearning to escape to that 'elsewhere' the dream of which he shares with so many other figures in French cinema, and, ultimately, César, too, as an affectionate grandfather and loyal friend, are universal characters exhibiting universal emotions.

Les Parapluies de Cherbourg may be very different in idiom (all the dialogues are sung on a kind of recitative), but it is remarkably similar in plot. Again, the young girl, pregnant, abandoned by her lover, has to choose single parenthood or a safe marriage to a man she does not love. The film celebrates Cherbourg, as Pagnol celebrated Marseilles, as a real place and since, in Demy's film, the young man goes off to do his national service in Algeria, we are reminded all the more forcefully that these events are not happening in the closed environment of some province, comprehensible only to those who live there, but in a part of France that has shared the country's recent history.

* * * * *

The quaintness of the provinces was precisely what attracted Jacques Tati and, after the country postman of *Jour de fête* (1948), he discovered in Monsieur Hulot [110] the ideal vehicle for his comedy: ungainly, oddly acrobatic, contending with an environment not built for someone of his size or shape, he provides a walking observation post on the foibles of mankind.

The counterpart of the 'rural slum' is the progressive, modern city; that of the 'rural paradise' is an urban environment which is dangerous, dirty and industrialized. When Hulot returned from his holidays, he found Paris threatened and in *Mon Oncle* [76], *Playtime* [125] and *Trafic* (1970), he denounced the threat with increasing bitterness. The films are beautifully made and very funny, full of visual gags that are as out-of-tune with the tradition of French comedy since the arrival of sound, as Hulot is out-of-tune with 'progress'. In *Mon Oncle*, made in 1958, photography and soundtrack point the contrasts between Hulot's old quarter of Paris, housing a perfectly integrated society (almost a fragment of provincial city tucked away in a corner of Paris), and the modern suburb inhabited by his brother-in-law Arpel, an industrialist whose mechanized contemporary home is a monument to pretentiousness, discomfort and soulless lack of taste. Between them, father and uncle struggle for the soul of Hulot's young nephew. They are also struggling for the soul of France.

What Tati stood for in *Mon Oncle* was not the antique in itself. Like any city that has been inhabited continuously since medieval times, Paris retains vestiges of different periods, from the Roman Arènes de Lutèce, through its medieval cathedral, Tour Saint-Jacques, Musée de Cluny and so on, up to the Centre Beaubourg and beyond. What is special about Paris, however, is the city that emerged from the massive restructuring by Haussmann in the 1850s. This Paris was a space which its inhabitants felt was created to their size. It was large enough to contain everything necessary for human happiness (even, if your delusions should get the better of your common sense, the railway stations and later air terminal through which you could escape to some 'elsewhere'); yet it was possible to walk the length of it from the Place de la Nation to the Place de l'Etoile and the breadth of it, after a day or two of rest, from the Sacré-Coeur to the Parc Montsouris. Its 20 *arrondissements*, spiralling out from the centre, were bounded by the exterior boulevards, more or less following the line of the old fortifications. You would not be able to walk these, because of distance and boredom, the dullness of the scenery prefiguring what Parisians supposed was the dullness of the suburbs beyond.

Within these easily-defined spaces, was a public city remarkable for its variety. A tourist coach would take you to the outstanding monuments, recorded in early films by the Lumière cameramen and others or featured in René Clair's fantasy *Paris qui dort* [175] and numerous other films: Notre-Dame, the Louvre, the Conciergerie, the Panthéon, etc., and those post-Haussmann monuments like the Eiffel Tower and the Sacré-Coeur. Each had its accumulation of history. Then there were the different quarters, associated with different pursuits or occupations: les Halles, the Latin Quarter, Montmartre, Montparnasse, the elegant districts, the great shopping streets, the popular areas. Sacha Guitry even made a film recounting the history of France, in a highly romanticized form, through the story of one avenue, the Champs-Elysées [16].

This public city, then, seemed as varied as its inhabitants; but, to those inhabitants, the most striking feature of Paris was its homogeneity. Hunting for somewhere to live, perhaps a cheap maid's room on the top floor of an apartment building, you would emerge from an unknown métro station into streets that were immediately familiar, with the same cafés, little local restaurants and shops, and 19th-century apartment blocks from the top floor of which you would look out through your window onto a familiar pattern of leaded roof-tops. Only as you began to explore this new quarter more thoroughly would you discover its individual charms, the *passages*, the courtyards, steps, squares and parks that made it different from any other.

It is this homogeneity, which allows it to be at once unfamiliar and yet undeniably Paris, that makes it such an attractive location for cinema. It combines the particular and the universal, and never more clearly than in the typical Parisian apartment block. The first French talking picture of real quality, Clair's *Sous les toits de Paris* [118] discovered a city of lovers, *apaches*, workers, concierges, clerks, bourgeois and eccentrics, brought together in these buildings, with their gradations of wealth and status from lower to upper floors, their courtyards and their stairways. The courtyard in *Le Crime de Monsieur Lange* [88], the stairway in *Le Jour se lève* [90], the two together in *La Belle équipe* [87], natural theatres in which a small community can react to a win on the lottery and a blind man stumble across a corpse, provided writers and directors with the opportunity for marvellous inventions. The stairway sees its inhabitants resolving their conflicts as they adjust to the postwar world [37], but can also observe the loneliness of a boy going down to empty the rubbish [169].

These intermediate locations, linking the private space of the apartment to the public ones of cafés, shops, *bistrots*, markets, bars, *brasseries*, workshops and cabarets, may do something to explain the popular bias of French cinema in contrast to that of Britain or the USA. In Britain, for example, the rows of back-to-back cottages provided no overlap between private interior and public meeting-place. Henry Cornelius's *Passport to Pimlico* (1949) and Charles Crichton's *Hue and Cry* (1947) make use of the bomb-sites created by Adolf Hitler's plans for redesigning London, but the playgrounds offered to London children by the Luftwaffe had no history and a brief future. The British pub was, until recently, a largely male preserve and the weather is usually no encouragement to lounge around on the street (*Passport to Pimlico* adopted the pretext of an exceptionally hot summer). A film like Maurice Cam's *Métropolitain* (1938), in which a worker travelling to a building-site by the overground métro thinks he witnesses a murder, could transfer easily to a London setting, using the overground sections of the tube, to be re-made as Herbert Mason's *A Window in London* (1939); but there were no British equivalents to most of the popular or working-class locations around which the majority of French films of this type revolved.

* * * * *

When Jacques Becker made *Casque d'Or* [130] in 1952, though the story was set in the 1890s, he was able to show a Paris that had changed little in the intervening years. He takes pleasure, in fact, in superficial differences: costumes, the riverside *bal musette*, the workman's *bistrot*, Serge Reggiani stepping off the back of a horse-drawn omnibus (in 1952, it would have been the rear platform of a motor bus). Behind these, the fabric of the city is unchanged. Two years later, he used similar themes of underworld loyalties and betrayals in a contemporary context, in *Touchez pas au grisbi* [131], and the two films, thanks to the continuity of the setting, come together as part of a timeless Parisian myth, instead of being divided by half a century of history.

Because of the survival of this fabric from the mid-19th to the mid-20th century, history tends to be perceived as a continuity, rather than as a fracture between past and present. Paris could be 'seen by' Emile Zola either updated, as in Marcel L'Herbier's 1928 version of *L'Argent* [72], or left in the original period, as in René Clément's *Gervaise* [96], without losing authenticity or relevance. The urban environment of Zola's Paris was easy for film-makers to recapture and for audiences to accept. Zola's novels were, in fact, popular with film-makers from the early years of the century: *L'Assomoir*, as well as Clément's adaptation, was made in 1909, *Nana* by Jean Renoir in 1926, *Thérèse Raquin* by Jacques Feyder in 1928 and by Carné in 1953, *La Bête humaine* by Renoir in 1938, and so on. The depiction of the seamier side of Parisian life was also part of his appeal. An adaptation from Eugène Süe's *Mystères de Paris* in the first years of the century and the use of urban locations in the Feuillade serials [117] also imply that just beyond the broad boulevards and elegant residential quarters, within the same space bounded by the exterior boulevards, lies a dangerous underworld where criminals, prostitutes, police and masked avengers lead a parallel existence. This marginal Paris, dramatized to thrill respectable cinema-goers, has remained part of the Parisian myth, from Georges Denola's *Mystères de Paris* of 1912 to Luc Besson's *Subway* [126], a box-office success of 1985.

Subway, like *Métropolitain*, is a celebration of the métro, but of a system that bears little resemblance to the art nouveau railway that endured, virtually unchanged, into the 1960s. In that decade, pressures of transport and population profoundly altered the face of the city. It bowed to the motor car and motorways were constructed around and through the centre of the city. De Gaulle's arts minister, André Malraux, initiated a programme for washing clean the façades of the great monuments. Touching-up was accompanied by rebuilding, first in the huge complex at La Défense, then the Tour Montparnasse and a host of other glass and concrete erections. The market at Les Halles was removed to Rungis, outside the city, and replaced by the Forum, an underground complex of shops and cafés, and by the most blatant legacy of the Pompidou era, the Centre Beaubourg, all paint and pipes, precisely evoking the former President's taste for contemporary abstract art in the sixties international style. The building and the performance area in front of it have proved a success, but the street theatre outside and exhibition areas, libraries and other preserves of high culture inside marked a break with the traditional high and low cultures of Paris. Outside and in, the performers were younger and more international, like the Hollywood-influenced young directors who had made the New Wave in cinema 15 years earlier.

Standing on the Montagne Sainte-Geneviève in 1835, Balzac's hero Rastignac looked out over the rooftops of the city towards the Place Vendôme and the Invalides, to launch his challenge to Parisian society: '*A nous deux maintenant!*' From the same spot, 125 years later, he would have seen much the same prospect, with the addition of the Eiffel Tower to the left and, away in Montmartre, the Sacré-Coeur. Another two decades, and he would hardly have recognized the view as Paris. In the vast housing estates of the new suburbs like Sarcelles, he might have doubted he was still on planet Earth. But if the old Paris had appealed to film-makers because of its continuities with the past, so the new one appealed to a new generation because of its ruptures and its international associations. The New Wave directors who wrote for *Cahiers du cinéma* preferred the modernity of American films to the 'quality cinema' of France and their own country was beginning to offer them comparable locations.

Louis Malle's *Ascenseur pour l'échafaud* [134] had already made use of them. Its central character is an ex-paratrooper whose plans for murder involve climbing up the outside of an office block with a rope. This cool modern character is contrasted to the young crook who tries to emulate him but only manages to commit the incompetent murder of a German tourist: unlike

25. *A nous la liberté*   (SECA/MARCEAU COCINOR)

26. *Touchez pas au grisbi*   (NATIONAL FILM ARCHIVE)

27. *Ascenseur pour l'échafaud*
(NOUVELLES EDITIONS DE FILMS)

28. *La Chinoise*   (GLENBUCK FILMS)

29. *Themroc*   (THE OTHER CINEMA)

30. *Police*   (ARTIFICIAL EYE)

VIII. THE COUNTRY

31. *Regain* (ARTIFICIAL EYE)

32. *Casque D'Or* (NATIONAL FILM ARCHIVE)

33. *Lacombe Lucien*
(NOUVELLES EDITIONS DE FILMS)

34. *Sans toit ni loi*   (ELECTRIC PICTURES)

38. *Subway* (ARTIFICIAL EYE)

39. *Poulet au Vinaigre* (MK2)

40. *Les 400 coups* (NATIONAL FILM ARCHIVE)

41. *Mon Oncle*   (NATIONAL FILM ARCHIVE)

42. *Les Tricheurs*   (SILVA)

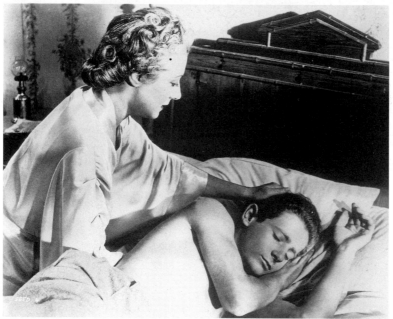

43. *Le Salaire de la peur*   (MARCEAU COCINOR/CIC/VERA)

44. *Le Blé en herbe*   (NATIONAL FILM ARCHIVE)

45. *Le Blé en herbe*   (NATIONAL FILM ARCHIVE)

46. *Du rififi chez les hommes*
(NATIONAL FILM ARCHIVE)

47. *Poulet au vinaigre*   (MK2)

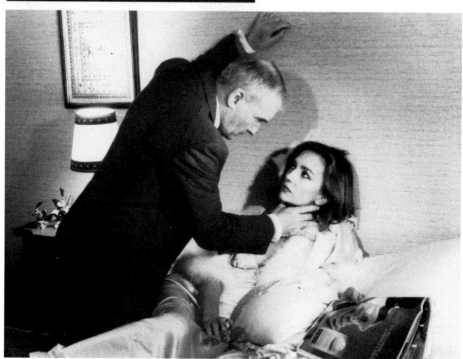

48. *Jules et Jim*   (GALA)

49. *Fort Saganne*   (ALBINA/LES FILMS A2)

50. *Subway*   (ARTIFICIAL EYE)

51. *Je vous salue, Marie*   (THE OTHER CINEMA)

Ronet, he still belongs to the backstreet world of the *chambre de bonne* and the corner florists'. He cannot handle the pressures of fast living. But the old world gets its revenge: Ronet is trapped in a lift when the night-watchman (a former NCO who, to Ronet's annoyance, still calls him '*mon capitaine*') cuts off the electricity. Colonial entanglements and unreliable lifts (to find one in Paris you only had to look for the words *en panne* or *en dérangement*) were among the frustrations encountered by the smart young technocrats trying to steer France into the fast lane.

Technocracy won out in the end. Gaullist hostility to US economic, social and linguistic influence, in an age of mass communications, was impossible to combine with a drive towards modernization. The take-over by General Electric of the French computer firm, Les Machines Bull, in 1964 had a symbolic as well as economic significance. Even before that, the battle was lost: just as the rediscovery of Hollywood led the New Wave in cinema, so American literary influences led the New Novel: in the 1950s, university students who opted for a degree course in English found that one-quarter was devoted to American literature, so they emerged knowing more about Faulkner and Dos Passos than most of their counterparts in British universities. The chief character in *Subway* is called Fred, the police, nicknamed Batman and Robin, swear in English and the inspector drinks J & B whisky. The Brahms concert at the end of the film is interrupted by reggae.

The thriller moves out of the reassuring comradeship of the Parisian backstreets and into the anonymous, international locations of the contract killer [145], or the confusing styles, multiple references and breathless pursuits of Godard [138, 142, 143]. When it returns to Paris, the old sense of homogeneity has gone. Instead, it discovers disturbing parallel police forces [144] and in quarters like Belleville, exploits the 'foreignness' of the immigrant population [149], for stories of prostitution and drug-dealing, that, in films like Maurice Pialat's *Police* (1985), veer towards racism. The thrill of the Becker and Dassin films of the 1950s was the thrill of being told that the man beside you in a corner bar might be a gangster, even though the bar and the man looked just like a hundred others in Paris. The North African drug-pushers and pimps in *Police* are defined by their difference from the Frenchman beside you at the bar, as well as by their criminality, and they inhabit what the film also defines as a 'foreign' enclave within the city. Wherever you chose to stand, in the Paris of the 1980s, in front of the Centre Beaubourg, in Belleville, in Montparnasse, on the Place de l'Etoile/Général de Gaulle, or watching the traffic on the Quai d'Orsay, you would be struck by the discontinuities with the largely 19th-century city so often celebrated during the first six decades of French cinema.

4 Histories

During the Cultural Revolution in China, a visiting French journalist is supposed to have asked an official what he considered to be the significance of the French Revolution for China. The Chinese Communist thought for a while, then gave his opinion: 'It is too early to say.' Perhaps it is also too late: great historical events tend to become progressively devoid of meaning as time goes on. If you go to Orléans in May and listen to the revolutionary anthem played at the celebrations to honour Joan of Arc, you witness the meeting of two universally recognized symbols from French history. What they mean depends very much on your point of view.

The cross of Lorraine, Joan's province, was adopted by General de Gaulle in 1940, but Saint Joan was also brandished by Vichy as a symbol of a contrary version of national survival. Rouget de Lisle's 'Chant de guerre pour l'armée du Rhin', the 'Marseillaise' as the Parisians called it, has been mouthed by right- and left-wing presidents, each imbuing it with whatever meaning he chose. A country that in the past 200 years has experienced several changes of political régime (five republics, two royal houses, two empires, one commune and Vichy) has an acute need for some national symbols so devoid of meaning that different factions can salute them with a clear conscience.

The first film devoted to Joan of Arc was made by Georges Hatot as early as 1898. The story was well-known from the account in Michelet's *Histoire de France* and from popularization in numerous nineteenth-century schoolbooks, so it made excellent material for silent film. The publication of the records of Joan's trial, and her canonization in 1920, emphasized a rather different figure from the military leader. It is not surprising that Bresson [19] should make a sound film concentrated solely on the trial, but that Dreyer should do so [13], despite the limitations imposed by silent cinema, shows a strong commitment to Saint Joan, rather than Joan the warrior. In the court, the military and their values are all on the other side. There are no battles in the film, and no royal pageantry. The angry crowd scenes at the end make Joan's defiance of authority potentially a call to revolution.

While Dreyer was asserting the rights of this individual against the state, Abel Gance followed a very different course in his version of Bonaparte [12]. In the most celebrated French film of the silent era, the aspirations of the Revolution find progressive expression in the personal ambitions of Napoleon.

The mob is assembled, realized and eventually controlled through its representative, the visionary genius of history. It all reads like the opening of Lucan's *Pharsalia* where the poet, addressing the emperor, proclaims that the disasters and suffering of the Roman Civil War have been worthwhile since they culminated in Nero's glorious reign. The difference is that Lucan was writing in a spirit of irony; Gance is serious.

People of different political persuasions can celebrate Bastille Day and salute the figure of Joan of Arc, without worrying that these national symbols cover divergent meanings: Catholic Joan is incompatible with 'protestant' Joan, the bourgeois revolution with the proletarian one. Wajda's *Danton* [26] analysed the confrontation between the last two through the personalities of Danton and Robespierre, but was perhaps more concerned with answering the question: 'what is the significance of the French Revolution for Poland?' In this respect, historical films are not at all 'safe', though they were one of the few genres encouraged under the Occupation. They speak about the past, but they speak *for* the present, because they speak in the present, though on three different modes of present time. There is the present of the period depicted on the screen, which may be any moment in the past; there is the present of the time when the film was made, which alters perceptions of the past; and there are the successive present moments at which the film is seen by its audiences. An audience in 1986 will be more aware, perhaps, of Gance's Romanticism, but less of the way in which his Napoleon can be 'read' as a type of Mussolini. And if they did see him as Mussolini, it would be Mussolini as the ally of Hitler, a very different plate of pasta from the dictator of 1927.

Nonetheless, the distance of historical events from immediate social and political concerns gives a perspective which allows one to contemplate both with detachment. A shared national past, even one involving civil war, revolution and a struggle between rival concepts of the nation, remains above all a *shared* past; and this perhaps explains why an opinion poll taken in the decade following World War II put historical films top of the list with French audiences.

The further away it is, the more the past can serve to unite. The Middle Ages have been especially popular as a setting for films, in different modes from fantasy [17, 24] to assertive realism [21]. The significance of the Revolution itself may still be a matter of debate, but a national history divided by it into old and new régimes offers an additional bonus: the French royal court can be enjoyed with none of the nationalistic overtones of Herbert Wilcox's *Victoria the Great* (1937). So Bertrand Tavernier's *Que la fête commence . . .* (1975), set in the Regency of Philippe d'Orléans between 1715 and 1723, indulges in the court tittle-tattle that makes Saint-Simon's memoirs of this period so delightful to read and gives a sympathetic picture of the Regent as a man of relatively advanced views, but does not in any way subscribe to the ideology of his régime. In fact, the conclusion is that the political order he represents is doomed.

The nearer one gets to the present, however, the more dangerous certain historical subjects become. There are several major films about the revolution-ary period and the Napoleonic epic, and literary sources from the nineteenth-century novel have provided the basis for numerous historical adaptations, as well as the detailed social background for original plots. There is one large gap. The 1970s saw the centenary of the Paris Commune of 1871, three years after it had been specifically evoked by the student movements of 1968. But there have been no major features made in France on the period, only a total of some 10 films, for cinema and television, mainly documentaries and shorts of less than 30 minutes running time (though Jean Grémillon did make plans for a feature-length film that was never produced). In Soviet cinema, on the other hand, there are several films on the Commune, including the massive silent epic *The New Babylon* (1929). The reason why this episode has been virtually ignored in France, despite a good literary source in the novels of Jules Vallès, could be that the Commune has acquired a fairly unambiguous political meaning for both Right and Left. It is an historical subject, but by no means a 'safe' one.

The 1970s saw instead some historical films, for television as well as cinema, which gave a sensitive analysis of politics under the Ancien Régime. Superficially, *Que la fête commence* ..., the television drama series about Mazarin, and others, may have resembled the bedroom history of *Caroline chérie* or *Remontons les Champs-Elysées* [16], but in fact they were concerned with a relationship between personalities and politics which, under the régime of President Giscard d'Estaing, remote and yet personalized by initiatives such as the President's breakfasts with 'ordinary' French families, suggested a degree of cynicism with the process of decision-making. They also demonstrate the continuing strength of the *cinéma de qualité*: excellent scripts, lavish sets, a strong cast. The genre does not usually inspire great originality in technique or interpretation, but it is often a framework for thoughtful and entertaining cinema.

Tavernier demonstrates another feature of cinema history: unlike historical writing, both fact and fiction, film cannot be limited to purely political events, however much it may seem to confine itself to the court. The tragedies of Racine unfolded in a court setting that belonged to classical mythology or biblical story, but found an immediate response in the court of Louis XIV for which they were performed. The cinema is required to be specific, in a way that Racine was not, about details of appearance, costume and furnishings. If it ventures outdoors, it must illustrate features of the landscape and buildings, show crowds and their occupations and, in general, pay attention to the surface texture of everyday life. The realization of historical scenes and dramas was one of the first concerns of cinema and it is perhaps no accident that the medium has developed in parallel with a shift of emphasis in historical writing from high politics to low life. It is hardly possible for a film totally to ignore the lives of ordinary people, and director, scriptwriter and art director will need

65

answers to a host of questions that even the historical novelist can overlook. An historian can write that the treaty was signed, the film-maker must show that the signatories did not use ball-point pens.

Historiography has been one of the major achievements in French writing over the past two decades, involving historical studies that combine meticulous study of contemporary documents with sweeping revisions of the matter of history. These historians, who have grown up in an age of sociology, structuralism and also of the cinema, include writers like Jean Delay, a doctor and psychologist, who has set out in *Avant Mémoire* to study his maternal ancestors from the sixteenth century to illustrate, among other things, the extent of class mobility in a Parisian family from that time. The project which these historians have undertaken finds a direct reflection in cinema. It includes: disinterring local histories to reverse the centralizing tendency of orthodox political history [23], reinterpreting conventional views of the past through structuralist, Marxist or other insights [21, 24], and giving a historical dimension to aspects of human behaviour, such as sexuality and sexual attitudes, previously considered outside the domain of history, through the application of sociological and anthropological methods of investigation to historical periods [27]. Over the past 80 years, film has provided a growing archive of increasing value for both political and social history, and is making a direct contribution to the study of the past; but it may also have played a less obvious part in the way that we interpret historical events.

* * * * *

In a sense, every film is a piece of history. The same reasons (mainly commerce, censorship and convention) that have discouraged film-makers from tackling certain historical subjects, have discouraged them still more from looking at the contemporary political process and documentaries about this are rarer than features, the relaxation of censorship coinciding with television's affirmation of its supremacy in the field (though see [67]). But a fragment of the history of class relationships, for example, can be seen in every film set in the present, however closely it approximates to Jeancolas's idea of the 'vague contemporary'. And, in particular, the way of life and the behaviour of the bourgeoisie have been subjects, often for attack, sometimes taken for granted as 'transparent'.

The majority of French people appear bourgeois to an outsider, but do not consider themselves as such. They prefer to say that they belong to the working-class, or to the *classes moyennes*, the terms 'bourgeois' and 'bourgeoisie' having acquired derogatory connotations, largely because of their use in literature. Usually, the bourgeois is the other, of superior or inferior class depending on the status of the speaker, and especially the representative of conventional society for the artist: 'I call anyone who thinks in a vulgar way *bourgeois*,' Flaubert wrote. The exception is *la cuisine bourgeoise*, good plain cooking which may even be preferable to any other, including *la haute cuisine*;

but feminists would probably consider that when a Frenchman calls his wife *la bourgeoise*, the derogatory implication is still intended.

In film, at least, the outward signs of dress and behaviour that indicate a member of the *bourgeoisie* are seldom meant to flatter. The rural petty bourgeoisie is contrasted with the hard-working peasantry in *Regain* [103] and represented by the seed merchant Monsieur Astruc with his three-piece suit, watch and panama hat. We learn the guilty secrets of the provincial bourgeoisie in *Le Corbeau* [106], *Thérèse Desqueyroux* [77] and *Poulet au vinaigre* [116] – the last being perhaps a sample of *cuisine bourgeoise*. And the Parisian new and upper bourgeoisie has been treated with every degree of contempt from the gentle humour of *Mon Oncle* [76] to the savage ironies of Buñuel [79].

This conventional middle class is often seen as so close to its nineteenth-century ancestor that literary sources depicting the bourgeoisie of the last century are frequently updated, suggesting this continuity (see [71], [72]); the same technique to emphasize class continuity was later used on literature depicting the working class (see [89], [96]). In both cases, this implies a society in which the forces of social control have been consistently monopolized by one group against the other. The link is not one that the ruling class itself likes to underline. When it represents itself, it depicts its behaviour as normal or 'transparent', and its films prefer to show the army through the conventions of the military comedies of the 1930s and the police as Maigret, providing the solution to a mystery for the benefit of the audience, or Louis de Funès, the comic gendarme [183], no more credible than the officer of military farce. The real face of the conservative 'silent majority', and its strength, could be seen at the rallies in support of De Gaulle in 1968, and it was quite unlike its cinema image.

The dominant conservative class is by no means wholly Catholic: there is a strong tradition of scepticism in conservative France which is both regional and historical in origin. But the Catholic Church is, with the army, the police and the ubiquitous state bureaucracy, a force of social control. Léon Poirier's biography of the Catholic soldier Charles de Foucauld, *L'Appel du silence* (1936), illustrated the alliance, but the majority of film directors, Amédée Ayfre remarked in his book *Dieu au cinéma* (1953), seemed to lack any religious conviction. This was partly to do with the Church's narrow view at that time of what constituted a 'religious film'. Film-makers like Delannoy were clearly concerned with social and spiritual themes (see his adaptations of *La Symphonie pastorale* [59] or Henri Queffélec's *Dieu a besoin des hommes* (1950)). But the Church, especially after the experience of the worker-priest movement (see [61]) which had tried to perpetuate the rapprochement between Catholics and Communists or Socialists from the years of the resistance, was wary of any association of religious and social themes. 'In [Dassin's] *Celui qui doit mourir*, all rich people are uniformly bad and all poor people uniformly good,' *La Croix* wrote in 1957, criticizing what, on a literal reading of the New Testament, might be considered an essentially Christian stereotype.

Church and State may sometimes be at odds (as they were over the issue of Catholic schools in 1984 when the Socialist government was forced to abandon plans to merge the two systems). But governments come and go, while the establishment, to which the Catholic establishment belongs, endures.

The Catholic bourgeois is probably more bourgeois than Catholic, and the Catholic intellectual closer to the intelligentsia than to the Church. The intellectual tradition is free-thinking and anti-clerical to an extraordinary degree, in comparison with Britain or the USA. The Church is sensitive to direct attacks on its institutions or its doctrines, as it showed in reactions to *Suzanne Simonin* [63] and *Je vous salue, Marie* [70]. In face of more general anti-clericalism, it is learning the virtue of dignified silence. When you consider the stereotypes of churchmen in British cinema and compare it with the ferocity of Franju ([66], [77]), or the jolly feminist send-up of Catholic and bourgeois conformism in *La Fiancée du pirate* [158], you sense the power of an institution that inspires such hostility.

Catholic intellectuals, sandwiched between their beliefs and the free-thinking tradition of their class, tend towards Jansenism and the austere, individualistic spirituality of Bresson [60], finding nothing more distasteful than the association of religious orthodoxy and political conservatism. For real hatred of the bourgeoisie, you have to read the novels of Georges Bernanos (see [113]) and François Mauriac (see [77]), two Catholic writers who considered hypocritical, devout, right-thinking bourgeois as criminal; atheists were merely unenlightened. After all, Mauriac's preferred adaptation of *Thérèse Desqueyroux* [77] was made by a notorious non-believer. Mauriac collaborated on the script, knowing that his name would help Franju with the censor and the Catholic Office.

* * * * *

The ordinary people of the middle and working classes, among whom the majority of the French would put themselves, were faced during the 1920s and 1930s with three major crises over which they felt they had little or no control. The first was a steadily deteriorating international situation, threatening a repetition of the Great War which had devastated the country. The second was rapid industrialization which appeared to regiment workers, subjecting them to the power of machines and explicitly, in René Clair's *A nous la liberté* [85] compared to imprisonment. The third was the economic crisis, attributed to financial corruption and speculation and, as contemporary reviews of Marcel L'Herbier's *L'Argent* [72] illustrate, considered to be different in type as well as in scale from previous crises.

One line of escape from all these problems is simply to drop out of conventional society, after taking a close look at what it has to offer, like René Clair's heroes or Boudu in Renoir's film *Boudu sauvé des eaux* [73]. The central character in Agnès Varda's *Sans toit ni loi* [163] tries to follow the same route some 50 years later, but the director implies that it is now closed. The figure of the tramp has always been a utopian one and, in fact, the picture that Renoir gives of the real lives of migrant Italian workers in *Toni* [101] is no more rosy than the one Varda gives of North African migrants in her film. Those who really exist on the fringes of society and whose national origin or poverty exclude them from full participation in it, are not to be envied.

The society that Emile and Louis reject at the end of *A nous la liberté* is not only one which reduces ordinary workers to the status of machines, but one where the political system actually encourages corruption. In *Avec le sourire* (1936), Maurice Chevalier plays an unprincipled 'hero' in a world where venality, not honesty, is rewarded, while Feyder's *Les Nouveaux messieurs* [54] and Pagnol's *Topaze* [57] suggest that the worker or lower-middle-class schoolteacher who tries to participate through the system is bound eventually to be corrupted by it. 'There is nothing dishonourable about wanting to be a member of parliament,' a character remarks in *Eusèbe député* (1938), while André Berthomieu's film tends to imply precisely the opposite: Michel Simon plays a simple-minded clerk, elected because of a mistake on the ballot paper and too innocent to realize that Jules Berry is using him to obtain government money for developing the spa waters in 'Sanzeau-les-Bains' as cover for a profitable speculation. Eventually, Simon is happy to be allowed to resign his post and return to his desk, leaving politics to the politicians.

The politicians are a class on their own. At election time, naturally, 'all candidates are for the people, it's more convenient', as one of them remarks in *Eusèbe député*, so, for the time being, they pretend also to be of the working class: 'take off your monocle ... we're sons of the people!' This cynicism about the political process suggests both disillusionment with society as it is, and disbelief in the ability of ordinary people to change it. The strength of the class system in the 1930s is underlined by Albert Valentin's film *L'Entraîneuse*, in which a night club hostess falls in love with the son of a bourgeois. Recognized by the young man's father, who tells her 'you don't mix towels and dishcloths', she returns to her job. The father, a customer of the club, suggests that in compensation for breaking off her engagement to his son, he will set her up as his own mistress.

Even the films of the Popular Front era which may appear to propose a radical critique of the system, often end in only partial solutions. *La Belle équipe* [87] and *Le Crime de Monsieur Lange* [88] find that narrative conventions oblige them to personalize the issues to the point where their message becomes ambiguous: Duvivier's film certainly touches on most of the issues of the time, from co-operative enterprise to political refugees, but ends with a dispute over a woman. Renoir also pleads strongly in favour of co-operatives and worker management, but makes Batala cynical in his personal as well as his business dealings, thus weakening the film's attack on a class that makes a distinction between personal and business morals.

Similarly, the Communist Party's *Le Temps des cerises* (1937), made to support the PCF campaign in the 1937 local elections, starts by contrasting the fate of two children from different backgrounds and contains some memorable scenes, notably the one where an old peasant confronts the local *châtelain* responsible for his wife's dismissal from her job. But it resolves itself into a relatively uncontentious plea for old-age pensions, a reform behind which people of different political ideologies could unite, at a time when the generation most depleted by the Great War was having to support an earlier one, now forming a very visible class of elderly people. In Julien Duvivier's *La Fin du jour* (1939), the inmates of a private home for retired actors, inspired by a trouble-maker (Michel Simon), start to demand their right to participation in running the home (an evident reference to the demands made by workers during the Popular Front period). The director, however, has to tell them that the management has run out of money and, unless a donation is made, the home will close and their 'little family' be dispersed to state-run asylums. 'You don't like private charity,' he announces. 'See how you like public charity, then.' In the end, of course, the 'family' is saved at the last moment and Simon humiliated, the implication being that people of the same 'social layer' (a term which the politician Léon Gambetta preferred to 'class') are happiest together: towels and dishcloths don't mix.

What is remarkable about French cinema of the 1930s is its willingness to study the 'dishcloths' and the sympathetic picture it gives of them. Few British or American films of the time, if one excludes gangsters from the ranks of the working class, treat workers as real people, 'heroes', capable of emotions and aspirations with which the audience is expected to identify. Still fewer see them against the background of their work. The factory in *A nous la liberté* [85], like the one in its successor, Chaplin's *Modern Times* (1936), is a caricature. But the railway of *La Roue* [84] is real enough, if romanticized, and the entire working environment depicted in *La Bête humaine* [89] is a carefully-observed portrayal of the conditions in which railmen worked at the time when the film was made. Gabin, in *Le Jour se lève* [90], is a paint-sprayer who knows something about health and safety at work, and in *Remorques* [91], a tug-boat captain whose personal and working life are seen as activities involving a single character, not as completely distinct. Surprising, too, in comparison with British cinema of the period, is the fact that he has both a wife and a mistress, a luxury seldom allowed in Britain to any outside the upper-middle classes.

When, at the turn of the century, Jules Renard asked Lucien Guitry what work by Victor Hugo he should read to the ordinary people of Chaumont, he was told *Ruy Blas*, because 'peasants are more interested in duchesses than in themselves'. Sacha Guitry, in his films, seems to have followed his father's advice and directors who wanted to make films about the lives of working people were liable to encounter the prejudices of producers who felt that they were 'bad box-office'. Films like *Le Jour se lève* and *Remorques* were made in the face of a prejudice that said audiences wanted to see either the doings of duchesses or those of prostitutes. The censorship that forbade the use of 'bad language' in films, also inhibited realistic portrayal of working-class life. The salon remains the conventional setting for a majority of films, but this may not be entirely the fault of film-makers and if the picture given of French society by its cinema during the 1930s appears incomplete, one should perhaps consider the films being made in other countries and be grateful that the image we are given, despite some stereotypes, often has the power to evoke a credible picture of contemporary life.

* * * * *

Even while asserting this presence of working people in French films during the 1930s, one has to recognize that it gives only a glimpse of working-class culture, and that a romanticized one. An analysis by Véronique and Pierre Sefani (*Cahiers de la cinémathèque*, 23–24, 1977) gave the professions of leading and secondary characters in 47 films made between 1930 and 1939. The Sefanis set out primarily to study female characters, but included males for purposes of comparison. Scientists (13 per cent) and criminals (12 per cent) came top among male leads, followed by artists and industrialists or financiers, then the army/police, politicians, lawyers and journalists. Workers (8 per cent) and tradespeople (6 per cent) came bottom of the list of those with jobs.

Work is the most obvious link between the individual and society, one point above all where the personal history of each among us joins the schoolbook history of Saint Joan, the rulers of the Ancien Régime, the revolutionaries of 1789 and the class struggles of the last century. How we identify with these depends largely on our social position, which decides how we perceive the society and how it perceives us. The postwar films of misbehaviour among young people (e.g. [170]) featured students and the children of the rich bourgeoisie who, because they had no work, could be considered part of a social problem, not a political one. The films of factory occupations after 1968 (e.g. [68]) were something quite different. As Claude Faraldo illustrates in *Bof!* (1971) and *Themroc* [8], the most fundamental rejection of society is to walk out of your job.

It is not an option open to most women in the films of the 1930s. The Sefanis discovered that, in their sample, nearly half (43 per cent) of the female leads had no profession (and a further 14 per cent were students or intellectuals). The remaining categories were represented, in this order, by: artists, tradespeople, prostitutes, spies/thieves, domestic servants (the largest group among secondary characters, after those with no job), workers or shop assistants and charitable workers.

Of course, neither of these sets of figures for male and female workers has any obvious relationship to the real distribution of employment at the time. The jobs given to men (and still more, as I suggest later, those given to women) perform a narrative function, putting the characters somewhere between the people next door and the princes and princesses of fairy stories: a 'typology of employment' among the characters in Hans Andersen and the brothers

71

Grimm would produce far more surprising results. Those in scientific, intellectual and artistic professions are freer to become universal characters, like the ones Eric Rohmer uses in his Moral Tales, and Comedies and Proverbs [82], and to criticize film-makers for wanting to achieve this universality ignores the need for the industry to maximize its audience and denies the right to artistic freedom, which seems a trifle unjust. Taking the official statistics in one hand and your 'typology' of cinema characters in the other, is entertaining rather than informative, because film has more subtle ways of depicting society and social attitudes.

Whole areas of popular culture are certainly omitted from prewar cinema partly because, as 'entertainment' in their own right, sport, music, etc., did not need to be transferred to another medium, any more than later films have felt obliged to depict characters spending much of their leisure time watching television (though Jean Boyer's Prends la route in 1936 showed two popular singers cycling around the country, combining popular music with a major sporting and leisure activity). More important than the gaps left by the non-representation of such and such a job or activity, is the impression that, once defined in a particular social role, few characters show any signs of mobility. Those from any section of society may want to get away, they may yearn for the country, or for another country, but it is not often that they succeed in moving upwards or sideways. Dishcloths or towels at the start of the film, they are still hanging on the same peg at the end. Fifty years later, much greater mobility, both social and geographical, is not only possible but often taken for granted. The worker's son in Claude Sautet's Un Mauvais fils (1980) comes home after serving a jail sentence in America for pushing drugs. He learns that the economic crisis has made it far more difficult for young people to find jobs than when he left France, but manages to get work loading lorries with some North Africans. One of them tells him that the work is so hard that few Frenchmen can stick it, the implication being that these immigrant workers alone are trapped at the bottom of the pile. Bruno moves on to an antiquarian bookshop and finally gets the job he has always wanted, working with his hands, as a cabinet-maker. On the way, he has acquired a middle-class girlfriend and almost a substitute father in the scholarly, homosexual bookseller who is determined to help him and Catherine to kick their heroin habit.

Bruno's job-hunting is incidental to the main narrative of the film, which concerns his relationship with his father, and so all the more persuasive as an indication of mobility. Even more striking when one compares recent films with those made before 1960, is the obliteration of distinctions between the material culture of the different classes. Of course, there are still great differences between the homes of peasants and those of aristocrats: the peasant boy in Louis Malle's Lacombe Lucien [49], as I mentioned in the last chapter, is fascinated by the elegant furnishings in Monsieur Horn's apartment, and the young criminal in the same director's Ascenseur pour l'échafaud [134] covets the sports car that he steals, knowing he will never be able to afford one like it. Leaving aside certain extreme cases, however, one is struck by the convergence of taste and means among people of different classes. In the 1930s, it was easy to show social distinctions: art directors put Gabin in a single room with a wardrobe, a cupboard and a bed, pinned some photographs of men with bicycles on the walls, and arrived at the 'typical' unmarried worker's room; the upper middle class lived in 'contemporary' surroundings, with much more space, carpets, glass, objets d'art, cocktail cabinets and so on. Distinctions of taste, style and housing, dress and leisure activities which persist in reality, despite levelling influences, have become less obtrusive on the screen.

* * * * *

In Jean Vigo's *A propos de Nice* [55] and Eli Lothar's *Aubervilliers* [92], there is documentary evidence of the contrast between rich and poor in the 1920s and the 1940s. From time to time we are reminded that the Italian immigrant workers in *Toni* [101] are the predecessors of the inhabitants of the shanty-towns in Nanterre whose living conditions shocked the students living on the nearby university campus in 1968. Some films, like Mehdi Charef's *Le Thé au harem d'Archimède* (1985), make serious attempts to investigate the culture of minorities, but the mainstream cinema is content to exploit its picturesque qualities. When, in Bob Swaim's *La Balance* [149] or Maurice Pialat's *Police* (1985), this means equating it with the drug-dealing, pimping sub-culture of the 'dangerous quarters' of Paris, the result is disturbing. The image of the Arab is no longer that of the noble desert prince who rides again in the final scenes of *Fort Saganne* [52], still less that of the pleasant neighbour who is an incidental character in *Papa, Maman, la bonne et moi* [152], but more alien and considerably more sinister.

Cultured and civilized though it may be, France has not always shown itself especially enlightened in its treatment of social problems. The racism of the 1980s, directed mainly against North Africans, is only superficially different from the anti-semitism of the 1930s. The public execution at the end of *Casque d'Or* [130] reminds us of a practice that continued into the 1930s (and beyond, if you include the executions of collaborators in the postwar purges). The death penalty itself was not finally abolished until the early 1980s, making France one of the last European countries to take this step, though there had been a long campaign in which films by André Cayatte [see 129] and Claude Lelouch [146] played a part with gruesome accounts of the way in which 'the widow' carried out her task.

Criminals, according to the cinema, are not much unlike the rest of us and their society a part of ours. During the war, resistance was a 'criminal' activity and the gangsters of *Touchez pas au grisbi* [131] possess the same qualities of loyalty and courage as *résistants*. What they want, ultimately, is for the war to end so that they can retire to enjoy a peaceful old age. When their counterparts in *Du Rififi chez les hommes* [133] pause to reflect on their ambitions, they turn out to be no more greedy or violent than the rest of us. The Italian Cesare wants the money for his sisters' dowry, Tony le Stépanois hopes to regain his health and his girlfriend Mado and the third member of the gang is concerned chiefly with ensuring a reasonable life for his family. Though they live in an enclosed world of night-clubs, cafés, apartments, empty houses and deserted banks, mixing only with those of their own 'social layer', this lack of contact with ordinary society only serves to emphasize that, far from being dangerous to us, they are eager to break out of the trap and join the audience on the other side of the screen.

The postwar economic recovery brought obvious benefits, but the need to bring together the elements of a society divided by the occupation may have helped to discourage reform of its institutions. The offices of 1930s bureaucrats, and the petty officials themselves, have hardly changed 20 years later. The school yard and the classroom in *Remontons les Champs-Elysées* [16] could be the same that Truffaut uses for *Les 400 coups* [169], with the difference that Guitry is complacent and Truffaut is angry. Women obtained the vote in 1944 and equal pay two years later, but they are still often treated as little more than bargaining counters between the men in the gangster films of the 1950s. This may or may not be true of the behaviour of criminals, but it is bad news if you consider these films as metaphors for politics or business.

As well as employment, the Sefanis also examined the relationships of female to male characters in their analysis of some films from the 1930s. The largest categories were young girls or fiancées, and wives or mothers. About 15 per cent were prostitutes or demi-mondaines, followed by mistresses. There was one Lesbian relationship and a small number of servants or governesses among leading characters, but these, like mothers-in-law and other female relatives apart from mothers or wives, were much more common in secondary roles. Only as actresses or singers could women in these films really hope to escape from dependence on the male characters. Indeed, the relative frequency of prostitutes as central characters suggests that they become more than just a portrait of a single social group, merging with wives and girlfriends to suggest the dependency of most women in a society where men control political and economic power. Older women, in the roles habitually played by Arletty and Françoise Rosay, often have considerable independence of mind and means, but even they seldom take an active part in the development of the plot. The passivity of the younger women is still more striking. When not actually bought and sold, like Orane Demazis in *Regain* [103], they wait, like Jacqueline Laurent [90] and Michèle Morgan [2], for Jean Gabin to liberate them from the dominance of repulsive, but apparently irresistible lovers; what happens to them at the end of these films, after Gabin has met his inevitable fate, seems irrelevant. The only way out of an intolerable marriage is probably murder, the solution adopted by the wives in *Le Dernier tournant* [128], *La Vérité sur Bébé Donge* [151] and several others. If Gabin himself turns out to be a sadistic sex-fiend [89], the outlook is bleak indeed.

Naturally, these films betray some male anxieties about the 'unreliability' of women, who may easily be seduced by the charms of that evident rogue, Jules Berry, or harbour secret thoughts of doing away with the master who, though he looks like a harmless imbecile with a bald patch and a pot belly, enjoyed considerable powers over his wife even after the changes to the Code Civil in 1938. The Women's Liberation Movement of the 1970s has accomplished a great deal, including a change in attitudes, but there is still evidence of masculine insecurity about women's behaviour. In the thrillers of the 1980s, the women pass from lover to lover, as often as not from the criminals to the police. The difference between them and the girlfriends of 30 years earlier, is that they are no longer the subject of bargaining. Charlotte Rampling in *On ne meurt que deux fois* (1985) and Sophie Marceau in *Police* (1985), hop into bed with their respective policemen for just one reason: they happen to feel like it. The genre, and the film-makers, are faintly disturbed by them.

Earlier independent women were often, for the sake of credibility, given professions in show-business or acting, as the analysis of 1930s films by the Sefanis demonstrates. This served, too, as a convenient excuse for bringing music-hall stars into film roles: Edmond Gréville built *Princesse Tam-Tam* (1935) around Joséphine Baker; Christian-Jacque put Baker's rival, Mistinguette, into *Rigolboche* (1936), neither being remarkable films, except perhaps for the implausibility of their plots. In the second, Mistinguette makes her way in life despite a fatherless child and a charge of manslaughter pursuing her from the colonies. What is worth noting is that the fictional show-business career that provides the vehicle for these stars had in real life given them fame and independence. Demazis, Morgan and others might be asked to play passive characters, but Baker and Mistinguette were not actresses – their films prove that, if nothing else – and it is harder to imagine them taking subordinate roles. Older film stars were not only given strong characters because of a stereotype of the forceful experienced woman, but also because they had established reputations. The screen image of an actress or actor is carried over from one film to the next, accumulating meanings and, while films create stars, stars in their turn create films.

In prewar cinema, this took time. But when the young starlets of Marc Allégret's *Futures vedettes* (1955) put on their dancing shoes, they heralded the arrival of a new version of screen woman, young, yet not innocent, independent without either social position or prostitution, who seems to owe her relative freedom from men to a pervasive curiosity about male society that invites her to explore it and to exploit its weaknesses. The year before Allégret's film, Françoise Sagan had published *Bonjour tristesse*: at 19, she could write authoritatively about adolescent girls. And the year after appearing as one of those *Futures vedettes*, Brigitte Bardot achieved the promised stardom in *Et Dieu créa la femme* [153]. The old dichotomies were resolved: young women did not have to be either innocent or prostitutes, and independent women did not have to be middle-aged. There was a possibility that some of these women might, as they grew up, refuse to swallow the story that they did not need political power, since they already exercised power in the home.

* * * * *

The public face of Catholic conservatism worn by the régime instituted by De Gaulle in 1958 and typified in Madame de Gaulle ('Tante Yvonne'), applied one set of values to private morals and another to politics. De Gaulle may have been right to give independence to Algeria, but the army brought him to power on the understanding that he was a supporter of *l'Algérie française*; Max and Tony le Stéphanois would have known how to respond to this apparent betrayal of trust and the gangsters of the OAS saw themselves less as terrorists, more as characters in the movies. De Gaulle responded by setting up the undercover, parallel police whose ends justified adopting the same means as the people they were fighting: the identity of police and criminals in many thrillers since the 1960s comes directly from the reputation acquired by these *barbouzes*. The OAS was certainly evil, like any organization prepared to use indiscriminate violence for political ends, but the purpose of their opponents was more the maintenance of state power than a moral or democratic crusade. In fact, De Gaulle's determination to weaken the parties of Right and Left, and to create and hold a strong, 'non-ideological' Centre established its own morality of power and efficiency, with an undoubted appeal for the technocrats of the new France. They were happy to operate under the umbrella of a well-oiled government machine, not a creaking parliament, welcoming the Franco-German rapprochement (see Raymond Borde's comment on the German businessman in [134]), putting prosperity and energetic action before ideology. Their values are reflected, more than criticized, in Godard's *Le Petit soldat* [45], and show as much in the lack of motivation of the characters in his early thrillers [138, 142, 143] as in the sugary romances of Lelouch [78] or that director's hymn to the brotherhood of man [25].

However, as Godard demonstrated, the technological revolution contained the seeds of its own destruction, not only in its environmental effects [64], but in the bewildering growth of communications which meant that French society was bombarded with simultaneous messages from outside and in. In *Lumière d'été* [75] or *Le Point du jour* [94], Grémillon and Daquin found conventional forms adequate to contain their stories of working-class life and industrial conflict. Godard, for *Tout va bien* [68], starts with a kind of Brechtian political drama about a strike in a textile factory, but by the end we are listening to a lengthy (and, frankly, boring) debate about sexual politics between Jane Fonda and Yves Montand. Self-criticism and criticism of the culture that the middle-class prized as its most valued possession, was not something to be indulged in from time to time, but a permanent state of mind. The events of 1968 could not be confined more than momentarily to the educational system: they involved everything, from the *bidonvilles* at Nanterre, to the Third World, the Vietnam war and the Thoughts of Mao Zedong [6].

Since 1968, it has been impossible to consider French society without at the same time taking into account the international patchwork of *Sans soleil* [9]. It is not so much a feeling that history may be happening elsewhere, as the realization that it is happening everywhere. They were right after all, those films of the 1930s: it is an illusion to think that we can escape from our history if we cannot get to the gang-plank of the ship that is waiting to take us away.

This is the place, as Wordsworth remarked in the context of the French Revolution, in which we find our happiness, or not at all. The word hangs on that episode of French and universal history (often seen from this side of the Channel as merely a bloody episode) like a charm. Happiness is a new idea in Europe, announced Saint-Just before Dr Guillotin's 'widow' claimed him, while the Marquis de Sade, whose concept of happiness was rather special, invited his compatriots to 'one more effort' if they wished to become true republicans. His recipe was as personal as Saint-Just's was political, insisting that republican liberties start, not with a reform of political institutions, but with incest, inviting the children of the Revolution to add a literal interpretation of fraternity to the liberty and equality they had acquired. The policy is still usually considered extreme. In the dull days of the 1970s, however, when political action seemed condemned to disappointment and economic recovery was giving way to recession, it was not only feminists who decided that it was time to look again at the most basic of social institutions, and to suggest that structural reform might start inside the family.

5 Families

'I perspire with anxiety,' Eugène-Marie's mother says in Roger Vailland's *Un Jeune homme seul*, 'whenever his father forces me to let him go to the cinema, because I know full well that bad thoughts are born in crowds and in darkness.' And in 1954, three years after Vailland's novel was published, the *Revue international du cinéma* noted that one-quarter of films on 'love or sentimental themes' had been given unfavourable moral ratings by the Catholic Office du Cinéma.

The films of the 1950s look harmless today, but at the time the anxieties of Eugène-Marie's mother and the Catholic Office were ordinary enough. The cinema frequently encourages 'bad thoughts'. Going there is like going to school: the child is taken outside the family and discovers fantasies beyond parental control.

It is no accident that a large proportion of French films have as their central characters a couple without family ties. Orphans and widows are not unknown in a country which has experienced both world wars and, still more recently, colonial ones. But the orphans and widows, prostitutes, mistresses enslaved by sadistic animal-trainers, or unhappy wives married to war profiteers, with whom the heroes of French cinema up to the 1950s fall in love, have a social status which serves another function: that of freeing them from the imprisonment of family and class. 'There's one person who bothers me . . . If I had known he was your father . . .', Gabin tells Jacqueline Laurent in *Le Jour se lève* [90]; but Jules Berry isn't her father and, that misunderstanding sorted out, the director is not interested in supplying the missing relative. *Déclassées* by their liberation from the family, these women are free to fall in love with men who, as often as not, enjoy a similar lack of immediate relatives. Past attachments may haunt the widow of *Un Homme et une femme* [78], but only, we suspect, for the length of the film.

It is not easy to make love with mother looking over one's shoulder, unless she is the mother in *Le Souffle au coeur* [172]: in that case, it is hard to know what she might do. The absence of relatives for these heroines (and often for the heroes as well), helps to universalize their situation, or their predicament, but at the same time illustrates the strength of the institution from which they have been released. The bourgeois parents of *Le Blé en herbe* [168] may not be too concerned if their son stays out all night, but bourgeois audiences in 1954 were shocked by his seduction of the girl next door. On the other hand, the desire to escape may imply the search for a happy ending which will unite the lovers in a new family to replace the one they have lost (or, apparently in some cases, never had in the first place), so there is some ambiguity in the desire for freedom. The institution is by no means ideal, but we are led to believe that the ideal couple might reform it. The alternatives tried in the more liberal climate of the 1960s and 1970s do not get to the heart of a problem that lies, as Maurice Pialat understands [162], in parents and children being able to redefine their relationship as time goes on.

For young children, the problems are minimal within the traditional family, and only occur when the normal pattern is disturbed: young orphans [164] are entirely to be pitied. Childhood, outside school, is a state of poetry and fantasy: the grown-up 'children' of *Les Enfants terribles* [167], encumbered only by Gérard's benevolent uncle, possess the genius that allows the child of Albert Lamorisse's *Le Ballon rouge* (1956) to transform a drab urban environment. Not that Montmartre was ever that drab, and dozens of French children have played across the screen through its squares and up its stairways, innocently observing its more seedy inhabitants. This child-like vision accuses us, in *Les Jeux interdits* [38], but consoles us, in *Les 400 coups* [169], for present and remembered miseries.

In the teasing games of children we can envy the first rebellion against the prison house that has now firmly closed around us: they play, without malice, in *Mon Oncle* [76] as in *L'Argent de poche* [173], and assert their independence from the class-ridden historical world of their parents. But already in *Un Dimanche à la campagne*, the boys tossing their caps in front of the church and the little girl obediently tending her doll, remind us that there is no avoiding its stereotypes.

Most of all, there is no escape from the inevitability of school. The entrance to the Maison des Examens in Paris, featured in numerous films, symbolizes the fear of failure as well as the promise of success in a meritocratic society. 'Passe ton bac d'abord': the title of Maurice Pialat's film (1979) sums up that long interval between the unknowing freedom of infancy and the enjoyment of adult privileges. French schools built during the past 20 or 30 years are open prisons which disguise their function behind pleasant modern exteriors, sometimes made still more attractive by a government policy which allocated subsidies to modern artists for work on public buildings. Their inmates, wearing no uniform, discovering the compensations of mixing with fellow-sufferers of their own age, seem to make the best of a bad job. Older school buildings are more honest: those rain-swept courtyards, with the corrugated roof of the *préau* offering little shelter and a row of unhygienic lavatories making their special contribution to the atmosphere, lack only the figure of the *surveillant*, the officer responsible for school discipline, to complete the image of a nineteenth-century jail. In the classroom and outside it, they certainly expressed respect for intellectual discipline.

Even Jean-Louis Trintignant, playing a would-be drug-smuggler invented in the course of the film *Trans-Europ-Express* [5], is obliged by the gang for which he works to pass a series of exams and, like a schoolboy, hides his bondage magazine inside a copy of *L'Express*. The train may liberate him from the narrative conventions of the traditional novel and permit him, like Alain Delon and Nathalie Baye who meet on the train in *Notre histoire* [83], to be invented as he goes along, but it is not that easy to get away from one's early schooling.

* * * * *

In extreme cases, Franju says [136], the middle-class family will see delinquency as madness and have the offender put away. In France, as in other countries, the older generation after the war was obsessed with the behaviour and misbehaviour of young people, whether from a working-class background [171] or from the wealthy middle class [170]. The second of these, Carné's *Les Tricheurs*, was an attempt to get inside the skins of the students and *fils de papa* who migrated in the evening from their homes in the 16th *arrondissement* to the cellar clubs of Saint-Germain-des-Prés. They were a new version of Jazz Age youth, lower down the social scale, higher on the scale of car ownership and allegedly more cynical about life and more likely to sleep around. Critics of the film, which was not the success Carné had hoped, found it less daring than it pretended to be, but this relative respectability was shared by the young people it depicted. The family provided a safety net for most of these rebels, as it would continue to do. One of them, no doubt, became the mother in Francis Veber's *Les Compères* (1983) who, when her own son drops out and joins a gang of hippies to be with the girl he loves, and her conventional husband will make little effort to find him, enlists the help of two former lovers (Pierre Richard and Gérard Depardieu) by convincing each of them that the boy is really his son. By the 1980s, the events and characters from the tragedies of 25 years earlier were repeating themselves as farce.

That a respectable middle-class mother, in Veber's film, should have had two lovers at the very moment when she was supposed to be conceiving a child with her husband, is good comic material, like the Rabelaisian infidelities of the baker's wife [104]. The figure of the cuckold has been a farcical one since the Middle Ages and a society long tolerant of men's sexual irregularities, has gradually extended this tolerance more generally, with the vote and equal pay, to women. The behaviour of the girls in *Les Tricheurs* is 'punished'; but fate in Carné's films was never on the side of the deserters and outsiders. And Mic and Clo, daringly modern in 1958, did nothing exceptional by the standards of Cholé in the last of Eric Rohmer's Moral Tales, *L'Amour l'après-midi* (1972) or his later Comedies and Proverbs [82]. The title of this second series refers back to the plays of Musset: their bitter-sweet treatment of the entanglements of love, in which the satisfaction of sexual desire is a necessary episode, but not a central obsession, also reflect the priorities of nineteenth-century Romantic literature.

A more liberal moral climate meant a more ready acceptance that young women might give up their virginity before marriage, but there was no lack of warnings of the emotional risks to these Paulines [82], and occasionally, as in Claude Goretta's *La Dentellière* [98], of the danger of crossing social boundaries to mix dishcloths and towels. Dissatisfaction with the restrictions of conventional marriage also led to the proposal of radical alternatives in films like Coline Serreau's comedy *Pourquoi pas?* (1977) where the three central characters live together in harmony and their example starts to become infectious. Why not? There was nothing very new about this: *La Règle du jeu* [58] had been about the failure of an 'open' marriage. Truffaut's *Jules et Jim* [44] and *La Peau douce* [157] examined the pains and possibilities of the eternal triangle. The anarchic central character in Claude Faraldo's *Bof!* (1971), a close relative of Themroc [8], begins by rejecting his boring job delivering wine and is soon sharing his wife with his widowed father. Having accepted this, the revelation that the father was responsible for his own widowhood (the mother was an invalid, obviously bored with life) is dismissed after a few moments' reflection. In Faraldo's radical revision of social conventions, the baby is first drowned in the bath-water to make sure that everything goes.

In the more austere 1980s, most of the alternatives enthusiastically welcomed ten years earlier were starting to look tarnished. Mona [163] does not find happiness even among the hippies and drop-outs she encounters in her wanderings around southern France: the North African worker rejects her because of pressure from his peers, the hippie farmers demand even harder work from her than she would have to give in a conventional job and the others she meets belong to a violent sub-group of drug-takers and thieves. None of them can offer her the absolute freedom that she seeks. During her brief life, she is envied by those caught in the trap of orthodox society, but ultimately she is to be pitied. Agnès Varda's film joins a long line asserting that the dream of escape is an illusion, to be indulged only in the cinema.

* * * * *

Between this life *Sans toit ni loi* [163] and *Le Destin de Juliette* [161], trapped in a forced marriage with an alcoholic husband, there must be some middle term offering hope for the free couples who outwit fate and settle down after the happy ending. Surely Godard's married woman [156, and 124] is not *all* married women? Does the bourgeois couple need the stimulus of jealousy and murder [80] to survive? Can true love only exist in the criminal underworld of *La Balance* [149]?

There are, of course, alternative kinds of love, though in *Pension Mimosas* [102] and *Les Enfants terribles* [167] these too are a recipe for tragedy. Comradeship can supply support and fulfil some emotional needs. In the cinema, with its bias towards action and violence, this usually means friendship between men; and the preference for romantic themes also often leads to women being presented as rivals for the love of the central male character. But if you read the secondary plots, you can find the occasional recognition of the support that women give to each other, in contrast to this (masculine) image of women struggling for a mate.

As for friendship among men, it is probably prized above any other form of relationship. Its essential quality is tenderness, one that distinguishes the really seductive heroes, from Gabin to Depardieu, from the mere seducers (Jules Berry is the prewar archetype) whose charm is more superficial, based on a way with words, power, money or ambiguous sexual appeal. The solidarity of *La Belle équipe* [87] is more important than any woman. The songs of Georges Brassens (whose only screen appearance was in *Porte des Lilas* [123]) celebrate 'Les Copains d'abord', and it is significant that René Clair's much earlier film, *A nous la liberté* [85], ends on the truly happy image of Emile and Louis free and reunited, dancing away from the divisive influence of money and respectability, singing that the earth is round and you can find women anywhere.

This fundamental tenderness in relationships with others, which one finds in the great screen heroes, is valuable socially and personally. It makes them protective towards women and loyal to the friends with whom they may be asked to face the dangers of war and resistance. They are often in conflict with the state authorities which are too impersonal to command affection: what matters is the solidarity of a sub-group (gang, cell, 'family'), its superiority proved precisely by this quality in its members. We side with Max [131] and Tony [133] because they are prepared to risk their lives for their friends.

Tenderness also creates a set of altruistic values which may be personally liberating: these men are not slaves to sex, money or similar imperatives and, once more, Emile and Louis, rediscovering this affection that is *the* important thing in life, also attain Nirvana. Freedom is for us, not for me: *à nous la liberté*, not *à moi*. The most important lesson you learn in school is not the classical literature or maths that enable you to advance in the meritocracy, but the comradeship that unites Antoine and his friend despite differences of background [169]. In Truffaut's film, the oppressive nature of the system to which Antoine is subjected is proved by its separation of the two friends, and one of the most poignant images in the film is Antoine standing behind the glass door at the reformatory, able to see René, but not allowed to talk to him.

Maréchale and Rosenthal [34], Max and Riton [131]: brought together by war or crime, these masculine couples (with Gabin as the dominant figure in each case), show a nostalgia for the simple values of the playground, at times exploited to conservative ends in military comedy or farce. More often, though, the friends belong to, or form, a sub-group against the authorities, like the schoolboy groups where 'Them' means teachers and *surveillants*. Freed, like pre-adolescent children from sexual desire, or simply experimenting with it like adolescents (*A nous les p'tites anglaises*, Michel Lang, 1975), they reconstitute their own version of the ideal family. Members of an adolescent gang; they recognize that serious commitment to a woman (*La Belle équipe, Les Enfants terribles, Jules et Jim,* and many, many others) threatens to undermine their solidarity. It is because of a woman that the best-laid plans of gangsters are undermined.

As contemporary critics of *Le Salaire de la peur* [9'5] observed, there is an element of sublimated homosexuality in this, as well as more general sublimation of sexuality or a desire to return to the 'pre-sexuality' of childhood. Max [131], as Colette Audry observed at the time, prefers to sleep alone at his age. The old man of *Un Dimanche à la campagne* (Bertrand Tavernier, 1984) holds the family together because he is an old man, released from urgent desires, while his daughter's affair with her unseen lover in Paris threatens to divide the group.

Homosexuality is acceptable when sublimated, as it is in the thrillers, and, like other expressions of sexuality, it leads to the constitution of a new family. Cocteau realized this in *Les Enfants terribles* [167]: unable to write directly about his own homosexuality, he obliterates it by elevating the brother-sister relationship to the status of myth, while at the same time showing that this 'unnatural' couple form a solid unit against threats from outside. The homosexual couple in *La Cage aux folles* [160] are a genuine family (there is even a child whose mother, a successful businesswoman, further reverses the male-female stereotype by setting out to seduce her man with typically 'male' aggression). In contrast to the bourgeois couple in the same film, the two gays possess the tenderness, affection, sympathy and solidarity of the heroes of French cinema and, while we laugh against the bourgeois family, our laughter at Ugo Tognazzi and Michel Serrault is complacent of their eccentricities and thus acknowledges their tenderness for each other.

* * * * *

'For a few days, I felt I was a young girl like other young girls,' says Suzanne, the night-club hostess of *L'Entraîneuse* (1938). Excluded by circumstances or sexuality (see, as well as homosexuals and others, the hermaphrodite in *Mystère Alexina* [27]), the majority of outsiders want only to return to the group. They can do it by constituting an ideal family outside the norm, by changing the repressive attitudes that have excluded them and (a theme of several recent films) returning to the nuclear, bourgeois family to establish healthier relationships within it. The trouble with the family is precisely that it serves as a transmission belt for repressive patterns from parents to children. Juliette's fate [161] is determined not only by the SNCF regulations which mean that her family loses its tied railwayman's cottage, or the accident of marrying an unsuitable husband who becomes an alcoholic, but by attitudes towards wives and children which are carried from one generation to the next. Setting out to look for their son, the two 'fathers' of *Les Compères* (Francis Veber, 1983) find out about him and about themselves, to arrive at a more balanced view of paternity and of the needs of children. The son (Pierre Beuchot), who made the documentary *Le Temps détruit* [53] to resurrect his own father and two others killed in the 'phoney war' (the writer Paul Nizan and the composer Maurice Jaubert) was impelled by a desire to abolish the fateful cycle of generations and to encounter a young man like himself: time destroyed.

In Alain Cavalier's *Un étrange voyage* (1981) a man's mother disappears during a routine journey; convinced that she has fallen off the train before arriving in Paris, he enlists the help of his daughter and in the course of their search they come to know one another as people for the first time. Maurice Pialat's *A nos amours* (1983) has a similar father and daughter coming to terms with each other (the father played by Pialat himself) and Claude Sautet's *Un Mauvais fils* (1980) examines the same process of re-education between father and drug-addict son. There is nothing facile about these films: their conclusion is arrived at without underestimating the generation gap and they show that crossing it requires as much revision of the child's stereotypes and preconceptions about his or her parent(s), as vice versa. Where the 'teenage-delinquency' films of the 1950s and 1960s assumed an older generation immobile in its attitudes, these suggest that there can be movement from both directions.

All very encouraging, the more so since these films suggest a genuine escape from the old stereotypes. From *Marius* [99] in 1931 to *Les Parapluies de Cherbourg* [112] in 1964, young men yearned for somewhere else, leaving their pregnant women to choose between becoming social outcasts or the wives of men they did not love in a 'safe' marriage that could as easily fail as succeed (*Le Miroir à deux faces* [154]) and leave them thinking of murder, like Bébé Donge [151] or Thérèse Desqueyroux [77]. 'Do you think one can be happy for more than an hour, or a night?' asks Suzanne, the night-club hostess. Perhaps the question itself is wrong. Perhaps the issue is not happiness and misery, inside the old categories of comedy, melodrama and tragedy, but wisdom. Perhaps we can escape from the fatalities of history and geography, learn a mature tolerance of others and infiltrate the structures of the repressive family with those qualities of tenderness and solidarity that gangsters and *résistants* find against their common enemies. Perhaps we can make here the 'elsewhere' to which we have always longed to escape. I doubt it. But the cinema's mission, beside that of reflecting the societies in which we live, is also Utopian. Its ideal couples and reconstituted families, its stereotypes of social categories, its parables of political struggles, its geographies of idyllic provinces to which we can escape from the archetypal urban environment of the Paris of René Clair and Marcel Carné, its mythical revivals of the past and its recollections of childhood games and the dreary courtyards of school, are a transformation of the chaos and disorder of everyday experience. The French cinema may have little to say on the subject of the future: science fiction is not one of its favourite genres; but it is still somewhere to dream.

Conclusion

Having reached the heart of French society, the family and the relationships that hold it together, I have still not come to any conclusion about the French character or any definite 'idea of France'. I hope to have shown, at least, that the films French men and women have made over the past 90 years may contribute to our understanding of the society in which they lived. The early efforts of Lumière did not preserve reality entire, as some people naively expected they would. They remain valuable historical documents which, like all films, incidentally contain a mass of information about the physical appearance of people and things at the time when they were made. And, as the cinema develops its own strategies of story-telling and its own genres, it allows us a less literal, but more profound insight into the world beyond the camera.

However, there are many dangers in trying to 'read' such messages. The Italian woman who came out of the cinema at the Venice Biennale in 1938 after seeing *Quai des Brumes* [2] and exclaimed: 'that's France!', made the same mistake as Vittorio Mussolini, the dictator's son, who walked out of a screening of Luchino Visconti's *Ossessione* four years later angrily insisting: 'that's not Italy!' In retrospect, we may feel that Visconti's film did, indeed, have a great deal to say about the state of Italy in 1942, even if it was not something that Vittorio Mussolini wished to hear.

As for Carné's sombre story about yet another 1930s hero caught up in corruption and denied his simple dream of happiness by the workings of evil men and blind fate, it reflects the state of mind of its director and his scriptwriter, Jacques Prévert, not the state of their country. They made films on this theme before, during and after the war, and the Venetian spectator who interpreted this particular example as an accurate image of French prewar society, was suffering a delusion which belonged to her own society, that of Fascist Italy, with its beliefs about the weakness and corruption of the European democracies. Certainly, these repeated stories of frustration and the desire for escape may guide us towards asking reasonable questions about the social or political mood of the time; and, with hindsight, the false hopes of the heroes and heroines in the Carné-Prévert stories of the 1930s do appear quite apt as a metaphor for the false hopes of the period; but the coincidence is just that and the meanings that we read into these films about the state of society are not to be taken too literally.

On the other hand, the cinema does give evidence about the way people lived, thought and felt; sometimes negative evidence, for example in the failure of almost all films during the 1950s to deal with the colonial wars that dominated the political scene. But even in that period, films of social comment, literary adaptations, crime thrillers and comedies add to our understanding of how audiences wished to see the world. We can learn a great deal, too, from the Popular Front cinema of the 1930s and the 'anarchist' films which reflect the events of 1968. Where, except in the cinema, is it possible to know so fully the aspirations of these times or to share their vision of a better, freer and more equitable society?

Perhaps, to see the French through their films, we should not try to look through the screen, but instead examine the audience. The French, like other people, go to the cinema because it gives them pleasure. They enjoy the visual spectacle, the architecture of Paris in films from René Clair to *Subway*, the landscape of Burgundy in *La Veuve Couderc* or that of Provence in the films of Pagnol or in *Jean de Florette* (1986), a recent adaptation of a novel by Pagnol which was a splendid and highly successful tribute to his work. Sometimes, they enjoy these landscapes because they remind them of paintings. Part of the pleasure of the cinema is that it also gives intellectual stimulation and can refer to other forms of art. Many French people, it is true, are proud of their country's cultural heritage and the popularity of literary adaptations and historical films may be the reassurance they give of continuity with the past.

The 'well-made film' of the 1950s had its strengths, even though it was despised by the young directors of the New Wave. One was the talent of the actors, and especially the mature actors of French cinema. Scriptwriters, like Aurenche and Bost, set designers like the great Alexandre Trauner, photographers like Eugen Schufftan and musicians who might include Georges Auric or Joseph Kosma contributed to making films which deserved the label 'cinema of quality', but without the sneer that was given to the phrase.

What the audience enjoys, too, is laughter. It is said that French comedy tends to be verbal, rather than visual. Tati is certainly the exception, but there are others. There is a tradition of comedy, right down to Francis Veber (*Les Compères/Father's Day*, 1983) and beyond, in which situation, script and slapstick combine to make hilariously funny films. What one can say, perhaps, is that these comedies are on the whole reassuring rather than disturbing. Just as the audience likes to see people on the screen enjoying a meal, because eating symbolizes friendship and a warm family environment, so the most popular comedies derive from sympathy with the victims of disaster and an affectionate look at the foibles of mankind. Comedies end with a slightly sentimental return to a norm of affection and simple pleasure in the good things of life. Here, as elsewhere in French cinema, friendship and companionship are among the most valued qualities, often triumphing over passionate love, despite the belief among foreigners that *l'amour* is what most interests the French.

There are certain things that the cinema takes for granted, because film-makers or audiences take them for granted, but which, at a distance, appear less self-evident. At times when a large percentage of the French population lived on the land and belonged to the peasantry or the working-class, the norm represented in the cinema was overwhelmingly Parisian and bourgeois. The exceptions, films in which rural or provincial or working-class life was salvaged from this neglect, take on a particular significance. Rural society often appears to offer an illusion of escape from 'reality' or an ideal, anarchistic society. In the Pétainist films of the 1940s, there is a reaction: life in the country is officially promoted as spiritually and physically healthier than life in the city, so that the depiction of peasant life as brutish and retarded takes on a subversive meaning. And, in reaction to all these interpretations, there were attempts in the postwar period to unload all this ideological baggage, and to return to rural or provincial France for locations that were specific and characters whose hopes and feelings were shown to be little different from those of anyone else.

In this way, in dealing with the various geographies or histories of French society, the cinema sets up a kind of 'dialogue of myths'. For a time, one image becomes established: an image of the peasant, of life in a provincial town, of the behaviour of medieval knights and ladies, of the Revolution, of the honest worker or the good wife or the femme fatale or the seductive male. Then, because the cinema is a medium which has always had a peculiar pretention to 'realism', the image is challenged. *Remontons les Champs-Elysées* [16] offers us one version of history, *La Marseillaise* [15] or *Danton* [26] another. Gérard Depardieu is not the same kind of seducer as Jules Berry, and the films in which he appears suggest an entirely different attitude to seduction. And, while none of these films says everything about the time when they were made, together they suggest some of the many, often contradictory frameworks in which French people have constructed their images of reality.

It is this diversity and these contradictions that I want to expose. Like all societies, that of France is built on the conflicting interests and aspirations of individuals, belonging to a bewildering mixture of groups and classes, with their own priorities, their own interpretations of the society and its aims. If I have given no single idea of France in my chapters on the mood of the times, the histories and geographies of the country, and the various concepts of the family and other social institutions, I am glad. Any single notion of these would certainly be false. What I have tried to do is precisely what is indicated in the title of this book: to show, not the French, but the French as they appear in their films. I hope that cinemagoers will be encouraged by it to look again at these films and to consider them in the context of the times when they were made. Most of all, I hope that the book will give its readers some clues towards a better understanding of French cinema today and its place in the continuing dialogue through which film-makers tell us something – but not all – about the world beyond the screen.

References

ARMES, Roy, *French Cinema*, Secker and Warburg, 1985.

JEANCOLAS, Jean-Pierre, *Le Cinéma des Français*, Stock, 1979.

JEANCOLAS, Jean-Pierre, *Quinze ans d'années trente*, Stock, 1983.

PREDAL, René, *La Société française 1914–45 à travers le cinéma*, Armand Colin, 1972.

SADOUL, Georges, *Le Cinéma français*, Flammarion, 1962.

Readers should refer to Armes for an extensive bibliography of books in English and French.

The Filmographies

A NOTE ON THE FILMOGRAPHIES

The reference material that follows consists of entries on 183 films arranged under 12 headings:

   I. CULTURE
  II. HISTORY
 III. WAR AND EMPIRE
 IV. POLITICS AND RELIGION
   V. THE MIDDLE CLASS
 VI. WORKING CLASS AND INDUSTRY
 VII. PROVINCIAL AND RURAL LIFE
VIII. PARIS
 IX. CRIME AND THE LAW
   X. WOMEN AND THE FAMILY
 XI. CHILDHOOD AND YOUTH
 XII. FANTASIES

The attribution of any given film to one of these categories is necessarily arbitrary: most films could have qualified for more than one category, some for almost all; so I do not intend to suggest in any case that the meaning of a film can be reduced to what it has to say about a particular topic. Within each category I have tried to include a wide range of films, and I hope that within the categories and between them there are some suggestive comparisons and stories of changing attitudes or consistent themes.

The first category, 'Culture', lists ten films which I have put under that head partly because they did not fit neatly into any other list, but also because they illustrate particular moments in French intellectual life. The other headings should be self-explanatory, with the possible exception of 'Fantasies' (science fiction, horror and a couple of popular spy films). As for 'Women and the Family', I would not like this title to be taken as indicating that I consider women's role to be confined to the family circle. The films I list there and my comments on them should tell quite a different story.

The films are numbered consecutively from [1] to [183] and, in each section, listed chronologically, with the exception of Franju's documentary on Méliès [174]. After the title and date of each film, the credits are given, using the following abbreviations:

  d   director
  p   producer

pc	production company
ph	photography
m	music
sc	screenplay/script
ad	art direction
with	leading actors

It is usual to attribute a film to its director. I accept this convention, while recognizing that it ignores the co-operative nature of film production. The star system means that some actors (Gabin is an obvious example) determined a good deal of the meaning of any film in which they appeared: that is what makes them 'stars', not 'character actors'. When a director does not write his own script, the scriptwriter also makes an undeniable contribution to the work: the names of Charles Spaak, Jean Aurenche, Pierre Bost and others recur in many of the films listed here. The team of Aurenche and Bost was unfairly criticized for its part in what the New Wave disliked about *le cinéma de qualité* – too much literature, too little spontaneity. But the Aurenche-Bost credits include *Les Jeux interdits*, *Gervaise*, and several other films that would not be on the supporting programme of anyone's history of French cinema.

A study of the filmographies reveals the important contribution of cameramen like Eugen Schüfftan, Claude Renoir, Henri Decae, Léonce-Henri Burel and Raoul Coutard; of musicians like Maurice Jaubert, Joseph Kosma, Georges Auric and Michel Legrand; of designers like Alexandre Trauner, Max Douy, Georges Wakhévitch and Léon Barsacq. A piece of music may achieve recognition because it can take on an independent existence, but it is very rare for photographers or art directors to get the acknowledgement they deserve beyond a credit on the film. When the National Film Theatre in London devoted a season to Alexandre Trauner in October 1984, it was almost a unique occasion and a tribute to the versatility and longevity of the designer, who was born in 1906 and has worked in European and American cinema for some 50 years.

The filmographies are followed by passages of commentary on each film. These contain a summary of the plot or an indication of the main themes and suggest why a particular film has been included and why it has been put under that heading rather than any other. There are also in some cases translations, of varying length, from critical articles.

These critical extracts have been chosen almost exclusively from contemporary reviews. Because this is a book about film and society, I have also avoided quoting comments on the aesthetic qualities of the film – 'beautifully edited', 'excellent performances', 'fine photography', and so on. Readers who want this kind of evaluation can find it in the many histories of French cinema and in the collected articles of critics. What interests me here is comment that situates a film in the context of the time and society at the moment when it was made, or first shown. For the same reason I have turned principally to newspapers and reviews with a marked bias, either moral or political, which will encourage their critics to judge films in those terms; and I have deliberately sought out evidence of bias in the review.

This has not proved as simple as it might appear. The Catholic Office du Cinéma and other related organizations have graded films according to the age groups for which they were deemed suitable and, ultimately, according to whether they were appropriate for showing to people of any age; and their judgements, at least until the period following the Second Vatican Council, were gratifyingly free of the usual aesthetic considerations. Films which were blasphemous, sexually suggestive or which failed to give the necessary moral uplift to the audience were condemned more or less regardless of artistic worth. I have quoted some of these grades and the comments that accompanied them. However, from the mid-1960s onwards the Church became much more liberal in its attitudes at the same time, paradoxically, as films became more sexually explicit and less morally uplifting. Nowadays, only pornography which has clearly been made with the sole purpose of exploiting the market is condemned. When a poor sequel to a comedy about homosexuals [160] can be graded 'suitable for adult audiences', with only a regret that the topic was not given more serious treatment, at a time when (as far as I know) the Church still deplores homosexual relationships, it makes one wonder whether the Catholic Office is taking its task seriously.

Something similar applies to the political press. Reading Maurice Bardèche and Robert Brasillach's history of the cinema, published in 1935, it is possible to find quotes illustrating their right-wing views and their dislike of the 'internationalism' of French cinema; but it is not that easy. The critics of the Communist daily *L'Humanité*, whom one might expect to carry on a ferocious campaign against the product of a capitalist industry in a bourgeois society, prove, in the main, to offer judgements very little different from those to be found in the pages of *Le Figaro*, with only the occasional denunciation of 'a Fascist work', etc. Films, being an art object, are usually treated as being outside the range of the moral, social or political judgements that would be applied to, say, historical studies or political speeches, unless they have been produced with a clear message. Brasillach, whom it is surely not unfair to describe as a Fascist, shot in 1945 for collaboration with the German occupier, once wept with frustration when he was unable to get into a ciné-club showing of Eisenstein's *Battleship Potemkin* (which is like a Communist begging to be allowed to see *The Triumph of the Will*).

Despite this, I have managed to dig out some comments which illustrate how contemporary critics saw the films in relation to the society of their time. This search has not only been motivated by the fact that extreme comments are more entertaining than trite appreciations of artistic worth. Like the measurement of the water level of the Seine against the Zouave on the Pont de l'Alma, looking at extremes can be instructive, especially in a country where moderation has seldom been the most prized quality in political and social life. Not all French Catholics thought or felt like the Office Catholique du Cinéma, but when it was shocked by a film, one can be sure that many other French people also found that film shocking. The judgements of right- and left-wing newspapers reflected the opinions of at least a fraction of those on the political Right or Left, as well as the opinions of the author who signed them.

The periodicals or newspapers from which I have drawn most of this material, then, are those with a marked tendency: for the Left, *L'Humanité*, *Les Lettres françaises* and *Les Temps modernes*; for the Right, during the war years, *Je suis partout*, and in the prewar period the conservative *Revue hebdomadaire* and occasionally *L'Action française*; for Catholic opinion, *Télé-Ciné*, *La Croix* and the ratings of the Office Catholique. I doubt if any of them fully represents my own views, and, in some cases, I should be very sorry if they were thought to do so. Only in one (François Vinneuil's attack on Cocteau in [3]) have I let myself be carried away to the extent of commenting on an opinion.

The translations, except in a few instances where an English source is indicated, are my own. I regret that space has not allowed me to give the French originals, even when this would demonstrate the inadequacy of my attempt to translate a particularly well-turned phrase or apt comment. Out of it all, I hope, will come some interesting stories of changing attitudes and past polemics, providing further evidence of the part that cinema has played in French life and culture.

I CULTURE

[1]   *Un Chien andalou* (1929)
   d Luis Buñuel, Salvador Dali *p* Buñuel *pc* Studio-Film *ph* Albert Dubergen
   sc Buñuel, Dali *with* Simone Mareuil, Pierre Batcheff, Jaime Miravilles, Dali,
   Buñuel.

'A commitment to violence, sadism and morbidity,' was how Lucie Derain described Buñuel's 17-min. short in *Cinématographie française* (23 Nov 29), concentrating 'all the harm that Freud could do with his psychoanalysis'. *Pour Vous* saw it appealing to the artistic circles of Montparnasse where 'scandal is theoretically accepted as a necessity'. *La Revue du Cinéma* (15 Oct 29), describing it as 'astoundingly logical', took a similar view: it would enjoy 'un succès de snobisme' in art houses; and later, in its 'review of reviews' for 1 Feb 30 cited Henri Ghéon's remark in *Latinité* that the film was stupid, but that 'stupidity is forgiveable', adding: 'Henri Ghéon is wrong: let him re-read his articles and he will see that, beyond a certain point, stupidity is unforgiveable'.

   Un Chien andalou, the best-known Surrealist venture into cinema, remains a powerful assault on bourgeois and cinema conventions.

[2]   *Quai des brumes*/US: *Port of shadows* (1938)
   d Marcel Carné *pc* Rabinovich *ph* Eugen Schufftan *m* Maurice Jaubert
   sc Jacques Prévert, from the novel by Pierre MacOrlan *ad* Alexandre Trauner
   with Jean Gabin, Michèle Morgan, Michel Simon, Aimos, Pierre Brasseur.

The insane violence of the Great War, the subjection of human beings to the implacable operation of fate and the inhumanity of the machine age found expression in the 1920s in Surrealism (*Un Chien andalou*, Léger's *Ballet mécanique*). The 1930s brought a sense of impending disaster: Gabin, the ordinary man aspiring only to individual happiness, is hounded to death within sight of the ship that offers escape to a new life. As the deserter in Carné's film, 'disgusted by people and things ... he is not a "miserable wretch" because, despite doubt, stupidity and fear, he retains some character and self-respect', Bernard Barbey wrote in *La Revue hebdomadaire* (June 1938). 'From all this horror, these haggard or debased faces, emerges ... an impression of purity, which is essentially the purity of art.' Earlier (*RH*, Apr 1938) Barbey quoted an Italian woman who, after seeing the film at the Venice Biennale, exclaimed 'with pity or reproach': 'That's France!' The remark 'shows what may be considered abroad as the dominant or obsessive theme in the inspiration of French artists: sordid milieux, criminals, the lower depths, pimps and whores'.

   The Carné-Prévert films fell out of favour with critics after the war, perhaps because they no longer reflected the postwar mood. Jean Cau, writing in *Les Temps modernes* (Feb 1952), saw the film with an appreciative student audience but said that, for him, 'time has not been kind to the work'.

[3] *Orphée/Orpheus* (1950)

d Jean Cocteau *p* André Paulvé *pc* Films du Palais Royal *ph* Nicholas Hayer
m Georges Auric *sc* Cocteau *with* Jean Marais, Maria Casarès, François Périer, Marie Déa.

Partly in response to a dislike of Surrealism, Cocteau attempted to revive and modernize themes from Classical mythology and the legend of Orpheus, with its images of art, death and love, particularly appealed to him. The messengers of the underworld are sinister motorcyclists who suggest the uniformed agents of the Nazi occupation, but Cocteau's ambition is to create a timeless myth, as free as poetry.

In 1943, Cocteau scripted a version of the legend of Tristan and Isolde, *L'Eternel retour*, in which some English critics saw Fascist overtones. Admittedly, the film did appeal to François Vinneuil, critic of the Fascist *Je suis partout* (15 Oct 43): 'a rejuvenation of old myths has nourished literature and the arts in all ages ... [Delannoy's film] has reopened a window on the domain of the supernatural ... Our cinema is re-learning that pre-eminently French language, poetry, at the moment when it is cut off from Hollywood ...' But his approval did not extend to Cocteau: 'it is not that [your critic] has discovered any sudden liking for that morbid and now bedraggled clown called Jean Cocteau, for the grimaces of that perpetually inverted intelligence, for that aged weathercock of the third sex who turns in his female capriciousness from Surrealism to the most hackneyed imitation of Henri Bataille, for this mountebank ... like a frenzied coquette ...', etc. The attack, especially that on Cocteau's homosexuality, is worthy of the writer and of *Je suis partout*.

[4] *L'Année dernière à Marienbad/Last year at Marienbad* (1961)

d Alain Resnais *pc* Terra *ph* Sacha Vierny *sc* Alain Robbe-Grillet *with* Delphine Seyrig, Giorgio Albertazzi, Sacha Pitoeff, Françoise Bertin.

The New Novel of the 1950s challenged the conventions of chronological storytelling and of character in the 19th-century naturalist novel, so it is not surprising that writers like Robbe-Grillet and Marguerite Duras (*Hiroshima mon amour*) were interested in the opportunities provided by cinema. Their films may hint at some of the disquiets of postwar France (political turmoil, colonial wars), but they reflect mainly the tastes of an increasingly prosperous cultured middle-class, able to enjoy such intellectual enigmas. In *Marienbad*, the characters meet, couple and part in a timeless environment, to give a feeling of musical abstraction.

'The anti-novel ... now the anti-film', wrote Gérard Bonnot in *Les Temps modernes* (Dec 1961); *Madame Express* says 'everyone' is playing the *Marienbad* game, 'meaning ... that bourgeois fringe ... no less proud of its secondary culture than of its bank account ... As I write, men whose only crime was to have the wrong kind of face, and show it, are being thrown into the Seine [a reference to murders of Algerians in Paris during the Algerian war, for which the French police were held responsible] ... In the most austere, the most abstract work by Beckett, for example, there is a hidden awareness of our daily struggles and pains ... while in a long analysis of *Marienbad*, I have the feeling that I am betraying, not a particular cause, but the very possibility for mankind still to defend any cause whatever.'

[5] *Trans-Europ-Express* (1966)
       d Alain Robbe-Grillet *pc* Como *ph* Willy Kurant *sc* Robbe-Grillet *with* Jean-Louis Trintignant, Marie-France Pisier, Nadine Verdier, Christian Barbier, Robbe-Grillet.

A further advance in the undermining of traditional narrative: a film about a man making a film about the railway train. 'The New Novel version of the Christian myth of original sin,' Didier Anzieu wrote in *Les Temps modernes* (March 1967); or perhaps 'a denial of the Christian myth: despite the myth, that is to say, despite the feelings of guilt evoked in us by any enterprise in love or artistic creation, happiness is possible on this earth; you can accomplish many things, like a happy love affair or even a film ...' Decidedly, *Les Temps modernes* has taken to playing the *Marienbad* game: 'the success of *Trans-Europ-Express* derives from the fact that the film actualizes at the same time the fantasy of the obsessed man and the defence mechanisms of the conscience against the human subject's complacency towards his fantasies and against the resulting agony of guilt.'

On a more prosaic level, it may be said that the film exhibits some of the sadism evident in Robbe-Grillet's later novels, as well as the cinema's perennial love of trains. But, while films like *La Roue* and *La Bête humaine* longed to be train-drivers, *TEE* is with the passengers.

[6] *La Chinoise* (1967)
       d Jean-Luc Godard *pc* Annouchka/Prod. de la Guéville/Athos/Parc *ph* Raoul Coutard *with* Jean-Pierre Léaud, Anne Mazemsky, Juliet Berto, Michel Semeniako.

The Vietnam war, the Chinese Cultural Revolution, the Third World were beginning to penetrate the French national consciousness by the late 1960s. Godard was among the directors who contributed a sequence to *Loin du Vietnam* (1967), though the film also included Claude Lelouch's notorious hymn to the beauty of American bombers. *La Chinoise* is quintessential Godard: splendid colour photography and wordy conversations among a group of students who set up a Maoist cell in a Parisian apartment.

Its precise political orientation is hard to pin down and *Les Temps modernes* had still not decided to like Godard. An article by Jean Pouillon (Sept 1967) said 'this film is in reality perfectly conservative, not to say reactionary, but its originality of form makes the traditionalism of content acceptable'. It gives 'a stereotyped picture of youth' and an unthreatening one of revolution: 'Godard has for him those who do not hate to be worried and those, often the same, who want to be reassured.'

[7] *Jeu de massacre*/US: *The Killing Game* (1967)
d Alain Jessua *pc* AJ/Coficitel/Films Modernes/Francinor *ph* Jacques Robin
m Jacques Loussier *sc* Jessua *with* Jean-Pierre Cassel, Claudine Auger, Michel
Duchaussoy.

This story of a strip cartoon artist who becomes absorbed by the fantasy world of his
creations (drawn for the film by Guy Pellaert), acknowledges an important sub-culture.
Especially before 1968, French schoolchildren were subjected to an academic regime
that demanded rigorous application and left little room for creativity or imagination.
Not surprisingly, they would escape into comics like *Spirou* or *Tintin*. *Astérix* made the
genre more respectable and by the 1970s there was a rich literature of *dessins animés*
from the traditional children's stories to pornographic comics. I have put Jessua's film
here, rather than under Childhood and Youth, because the year after it was made the
country was shaken by the repressed products of that school system who turned the
walls of Paris into a comic strip with slogans like: 'Creativity, Spontaneity, Life!',
'Society is a carnivorous plant' and 'I believe in the reality of my desires'.

[8] *Themroc* (1973)
d Claude Faraldo *pc* Filmanthrope/FDL *ph* Jean-Marc Ripert *sc* Faraldo
with Michel Piccoli, Béatrice Romand, Marilu Tolo.

In *Themroc*, a production-line worker, disgusted with his mindless existence, reverts to
the stone age, taking his neighbours with him. Eventually, they turn to cannibalism
and (since this is France) eat a policeman. Jean-Louis Bory in the *Nouvel observateur* (6
March 73) saw Themroc's anarchism as 'a gut rejection, provoked by disgust with actual
experience ...', and a loss of faith in progress: 'persuaded that progress is not
civilization, instead of a step forward, he suggests taking a thousand steps back.'

[9] *Sans soleil/Sunless* (1983)
d Chris Marker *p* Anatole Dauman *pc* Argos *ph* Sana Na N'Hada, Danièle
Tessier, Jean-Michel Humeau *sc* Marker

A testament by one of France's most original film-makers, *Sans soleil* is a personal
documentary that travels from a road in Iceland to Cape Verde and Japan, and ranges
across themes of individual happiness, the variety of human cultures, the struggle for
political liberation, information technology and the cinematic vision of reality. Marker
is concerned, too, with time, as experienced by people and by peoples. He has something
important to say about what it means to be a human being and so a Frenchman, in the
last quarter of the century.

[10] *Péril en la demeure/Death in a French Garden* (1985)
d Michel Deville *p* Emmanuel Schlumberger *pc* Gaumont/TF1/Eléfilm
ph Martial Thury *sc* Deville, Rosalinde Dammame, from René Belleto's novel

Sur la terre comme au ciel, *with* Christophe Malavoy, Nicole Garcia, Richard Bohringer, Anémone, Michel Piccoli.

A murder story, set in leisured, upper-middle-class surroundings, with a penniless student as the central character involved in a complex game. The narrative leaves a lot of work for the audience to do. Technically polished, refined, somewhat heartless, it appeals, like some contemporary French literature, to a mathematical side of the intellect and contrasts with the avid curiosity and openness of *Sunless*.

II HISTORY

[11] *L'Assassinat du Duc de Guise* (1908)
d André Calmettes, Le Bargy *pc* Le Film d'Art *sc* Henri Lavedan *m* Camille Saint-Saens *with* Le Bargy, Albert Lambert, Huguette Duflos.

The best-known production of the Film d'Art, shown to a score specially composed by Saint-Saens, it depicts an episode (1563) in the struggle for power of the Guise family during the minority of King François II. Distantly anticipating popular television historical dramas like that on Mazarin shown in the 1970s, it was one of the first films to give some attention to the development of character and to use experienced actors (Le Bargy of the Comédie Française).

[12] *Napoléon* (1927)
d Abel Gance *pc* Les Films Abel Gance/Société Générale de Films *ph* Jules Kruger *sc* Gance *ad* Alexandre Benois *with* Albert Dieudonné, Gina Manès, Alexandre Koubitzky, Antonin Artaud, Gance.

Gance's excessive, often self-indulgent masterpiece is visually astounding with its use of split-screen effects, etc., and at moments very moving (for example, in the college snowball fight). Its view of French revolutionary and imperial history is epic and Romantic. Norman King's selection of criticism (in *Abel Gance*, 1984) shows that, though the majority of critics praised the film as an artistic achievement, there were doubts about its historical accuracy and its political tendencies. *Candide* (14 Apr 27) compared Bonaparte in one scene to Mussolini, Léon Moussinac, in *L'Humanité* (24 Apr 27) called him 'a Bonaparte for budding fascists', but praised the film's technical brilliance: 'a pernicious work', he concluded in a second article (1 May 27). The accusation of historical inaccuracy centred on Gance's depiction of the Revolution as a bloodbath from which Napoleon had saved the country. There is in France no definitive view of the revolutionary period, such as the one established for most Britons by Burke and Carlyle, and it is not hard to find admiration of Robespierre and intense hatred of Bonaparte, as well as the opposite.

[13]   *La Passion de Jeanne d'Arc/The Passion of Joan of Arc* (1928)
d Carl Theodor Dreyer *pc* Société Générale de Films *ph* Rudolphe Mate
sc Dreyer, Joseph Delteil, from novels by Delteil and records of the trial
ad Hermann Warm, Jean Victor-Hugo, Valentine Hugo *with* Maria Falconetti
Eugène Silvain, Michel Simon, Antonin Artaud, Alexandre Mihalesco.

Dreyer stresses the authenticity of the film with a prefatory sequence showing the documentary record of Joan's trial and concludes with a screen title stating that her memory will live on in the hearts of her countrymen. But this Joan is no nationalist, but a peasant girl standing up for her individual beliefs against the authority of the Church, a Protestant Joan, if you like.

Pierre Audard (*Revue du cinéma*, Feb 1929) said that suffering had never before been shown so nakedly on the screen, 'so close to physical terror'.

[14]   *La Kermesse héroique/Carnival in Flanders* (1935)
d Jacques Feyder *pc* Tobis *ph* Harry Stradling *m* Louis Beydts *sc* Charles Spaak,
Feyder *ad* Lazare Meerson *with* Françoise Rosay, Louis Jouvet, Jean Murat,
Alfred Adam.

The staid bourgeois of a Flemish town flee before the arrival of the Spanish army, leaving their wives to entertain the troops in their own way. A witty comedy, well-written, lavishly produced, it was considered risqué when first shown. Henri Jeanson described it as a 'Nazi' film.

[15]   *La Marseillaise/The Marseillaise* (1938)
d Jean Renoir *ph* Jean Bourgoin, Alain Dovarinou *m* Joseph Kosma,
Sauveplane *sc* Renoir *ad* Léon Barsacq, Georges Wakhévitch *with* Renoir,
Louis Jouvet, Aquistapace, Gaston Modot.

The Popular Front view of the Revolution, in a film financed by public subscription: 'Politics first!', Bernard Barbey commented in *La Revue hebdomadaire* (Feb 1938), and 'in the narrowest and least generous sense'. The bias and left-wing patronage of Renoir's film obliged him to show us Louis XIV as 'indecisive, mediocre, a slave to the tasty dishes that his valets serve him at the most affecting moments in French history' (here, Barbey may have misjudged Renoir's feeling for gourmets), but why show Marie-Antoinette with 'the bored features of Mlle. Lise Delamare'? This is not 'a revolution, or even a revolt; an anecdote, at the most', copying 'the worst American school'.

Other critics appreciated Renoir's sympathetic portrait of the King and, later, his depiction of the Revolution through the reactions of ordinary people (which Barbey condemns as 'anecdotal').

[16] *Remontons les Champs-Elysées/Let's All Go Up the Champs-Elysées* (1938)

d Sacha Guitry *pc* Cinéas *ph* Jean Bachelet *m* Adolphe Borchard *sc* Guitry
ad René Renoux *with* Guitry, Raymond Galle, Germaine Demoz.

A very different view of French history, with Guitry playing six parts, including Louis XV, Napoleon and Napoleon III, as well as the schoolmaster who provides the link for this light-hearted romp down the most famous boulevard in Paris. Its qualities, wit and insouciance are typical of Guitry and sometimes considered 'typically French'. The most interesting aspect of the film now is its picture of French school life before the war.

[17] *Les Visiteurs du soir* (1942)

d Marcel Carné *p* André Paulvé *ph* Roger Hubert *m* Maurice Thiriet, Joseph Kosma *sc* Jacques Prévert, Pierre Laroche *ad* Georges Wakhévitch, Alexandre Trauner *with* Arletty, Marie Déa, Jules Berry, Fernand Ledoux, Alain Cuny.

The devil sends his emissaries in human form to tempt the inhabitants of a fifteenth-century château, but human love defeats his schemes. In the trappings of a purely conventional, legendary Middle Ages, this could be seen as an allegory of resistance. 'Nothing to do with France under the occupation,' Jean-Henri Roy said, categorically, in a review of Carné's later film, *Juliette ou la clé des songes* (in *Les Temps modernes*, Sept 1951), complaining that it was not concerned with any contemporary theme. 'At that time cinema was simply a drug.' If there was an allegory, it was well hidden. *L'Action française* (François Daudet, Jan 1943) was only concerned with its technical qualities, while *La Nouvelle revue française* (Jean Fougère, March 1943) criticized the dialogue ('too literary'), the acting of Arletty and Jules Berry (typecast, because of their previous work, as elegant, disenchanted Parisians) and the tone of the film (Carné is better suited to the realism and 'grey light, the faubourgs with their damp paving-stones').

[18] *Les Enfants du paradis/*US *Children of Paradise* (1945)

d Marcel Carné *pc* Pathé *ph* Roger Hubert *m* Maurice Thiriet, Joseph Kosma *sc* Jacques Prévert, Carné *ad* Léon Barsacq, Alexandre Trauner *with* Arletty, Jean-Louis Barrault, Maria Casarès, Pierre Brasseur, Marcel Herrand, Pierre Renoir.

Everyone's favourite French film? Rivalries in art and love, Parisian low and high life, and murder, against an early-nineteenth-century background beautifully re-created in Trauner's sets. Certainly the most successful of Carné and Prévert's collaborations, *Les Enfants du paradis* (the title refers to the 'gods' in the theatre) owes part of its 'authenticity' to a subtle re-working of literary sources, even though the central characters of the mime Debureau (Barrault), the actor Frédéric Lemaître (Brasseur) and the villainous Lacenaire (Herrand) were historical. Lacenaire bears a strong resemblance to Vautrin in Balzac's *Comédie humaine*, and a number of other features of the film suggest a Romantic literary background that is familiar to everyone from the classroom. All this was patched together in impossible circumstances (Trauner and

Kosma, 'non-persons' under the occupation, worked clandestinely, the actor Robert le Vigan had to flee France because of his collaboration with the Germans, the Italian production company originally involved withdrew and only two parts of the film were shot), to make an enchanting and compelling whole. Before the closure of the Academy Cinema, Oxford Street, London in 1986, they seemed to show it annually and it can afford to be seen over and over again.

[19] *Le Procès de Jeanne d'Arc/The Trial of Joan of Arc* (1962)
   d Robert Bresson *p* Agnès Delahaie *ph* Léonce-Henri Burel *m* Francis Seyrig
   sc Bresson, from records of the trial *ad* Pierre Charbonnier *with* Florence
   Carrez, Jean-Claude Fourneau, Roger Honorat, Marc Jacquier.

'For someone like myself, who is indifferent to [the Christian] myth,' wrote Georges Sadoul in *Les Lettres françaises* (21 March 63), 'the film shows above all ... national resistance in an occupied country.' I doubt if Bresson saw it that way, though Sadoul's remark illustrates how a national 'myth', like Joan's, can sometimes serve Right and Left equally. He continues: 'if anyone had been unwise enough, during the Hitler occupation, to project Dreyer's work, he would have been sent, if not to the stake, at least to the crematorium. Despite this, the Danish director, who believes in God, the immortal soul, vampires, warlocks, miracles and the resurrection of the dead, had an even more mystical argument to his film than Bresson.'

[20] *L'Enfant sauvage* (1970)
   d François Truffaut *p* Marcel Berbert *pc* Les Films du Carrosse/Artistes Associés
   ph Nestor Almendros *m* Vivaldi *sc* Truffaut, from Jean Itard's *Mémoire et
   rapport sur Victor de l'Aveyron* (1806) *ad* Jean Mandaroux *with* Jean-Pierre
   Cargol, Truffaut.

Based on the true story of Dr Jean Itard's attempt to educate Victor, a boy who lived wild in the Aveyron until adolescence, Truffaut's film tackles the themes of education, childhood and 'civilization' in the context of the eighteenth-century Enlightenment (which produced not only the rationalism of Voltaire and Diderot, but also Rousseau's myth of the Noble Savage). Truffaut, himself playing Itard, leaves open the issue of nature *v.* civilization. He asks the question, Christian Zimmer said in *Les Temps modernes* (Apr 1970), 'if all education is a form of dressage/training, what is the use of education?'

[21] *Lancelot du Lac* (1974)
   d Robert Bresson *pc* Mara/Laser/ORTF/Gerico *ph* Pasqualino de Santis
   m Philippe Sarde *sc* Bresson *with* Luc Simon, Laura Duke Condominas, Hubert
   Balsan.

A revised version of the Middle Ages: brutal, tragic and austere, illustrating the

Bressonian theme of divine grace (and its absence). For Jean-Louis Bory (in *Le Nouvel observateur*, 16 Sept 74) it gave 'a more accurate picture of the Middle Ages than all past and future Cecilbedemilleries ... an interior picture: savagery and folly of honour and faith'. And the critic – if not necessarily the film – reflects the influence of the fashionable science of semiotics: '... in harmony with medieval civilization where everything was *sign*, from banners to scarves, from the Graal to the sword-hilt, in the shape of a cross ...'

[22] *Stavisky* (1974)

d Alain Resnais *pc* Cerito/Ariane/Euro-International *ph* Sacha Vierny
m Stephen Sondheim *sc* Jorge Semprun *with* Jean-Paul Belmondo, Anne
Duperey, François Périer, Charles Boyer, Gérard Depardieu.

'Resnais, si! Belmondo, no!' was the title of Jean-Louis Bory's article in *Le Nouvel observateur* (27 May 74), which suggested that the star did not have the right kind of charm for Stavisky, involved in a major scandal of the 1930s. The theatrical elements and the evident pleasure that it takes in period details, made it part of the 1970s fashion for *le rétro* (like granny dresses), despite the political sub-plot involving Trotsky in exile. But this is not how Youssef Ishaghpour and Pierre Samson interpreted it in *Les Temps modernes* (Oct–Dec 1974): 'a film about our own time, about the meaning of inflation and the motive power of the police, in a crisis-ridden society'. They recalled *La Règle du jeu*, 'totally misunderstood at the time: there, too, a story in the style of Beaumarchais ... masked the *danse macabre* of a whole society'.

[23] *Moi, Pierre Rivière .../I, Pierre Rivière ...* (1976)

d René Allio *pc* Arquebuse/Polsim/SEP/Inst. Nat. de l'Audio-visuelle *ph* Nurith
Aviv *sc* Allio, from a text published by Michel Foucault *with* Claude Hébert,
Joseph Leportier, Antoine Bourseiller, Jacques Debarry.

The full title, 'I, Pierre Rivière, having cut the throats of my mother, my sister and my brother ...', tells most of the story. Allio, who made *Les Camisards* (1970), went to the actual site of the crime in Normandy, used peasant actors and meticulously reconstructed the period detail (1835) with the help of Rivière's own confession, the police dossier and other documents. 'He does not judge, he analyses,' Jean-Louis Bory wrote in *Le Nouvel Observateur* (25 Oct 76), to give 'an explanation on several levels', psychological and social, of a crime committed by a solitary, 'savage' man. 'Hence the care he gives to noting a kind of peasant ruthlessness, clarifying, à la Balzac, the mechanisms of money and the harsh material conditions of [peasant] life.' Despite Bory's reference to Balzac, this is at the opposite pole from the literary nineteenth century of *Les Enfants du paradis* and demonstrates the influence and prestige of French historians and sociologists, like Foucault and the group associated with the historical journal *Annales* (Emmanuel Le Roy Ladurie is the best-known), whose work consisted in minute statistical and documentary investigation of the lives of ordinary people, rather than historical generalization or what is usually understood by 'political' history.

[24]   *Perceval le Gallois* (1978)

> *d* Eric Rohmer *pc* Losange/Gaumont/FR 3/RAI/ARD/SSR *ph* Nestor Almendros
> *m* Guy Robert *sc* Rohmer, from the verse novel by Crétien de Troyes
> *with* Fabrice Luchini, André Dussolier, Pascale de Boysson, Marc Eyraud,
> Marie-Christine Barrault.

Another version, again, of the Middle Ages, taken from Chrétien de Troyes's twelfth-century poem on the Graal. Fantasy and enjoyment of the past as a pasture for the imagination coexisted with the sociological work of the *Annales* school.

[25]   *Les Uns et les autres/The Ins and the Outs/Bolero* (1981)

> *d* Claude Lelouch *pc* Films 13/TF1 *ph* Jean Boffety, Jacques Lefrançois
> *m* Francis Lai, Michel Legrand *sc* Lelouch *ad* Jean-Louis Poveda *with* Robert
> Hossein, Nicole Garcia, Geraldine Chaplin, James Caan.

Lelouch's sweeping survey of European and American history through and beyond World War II, shows the enduring temptation of the Hollywood epic school. Superficial, sentimental, loud and colourful, it is closer to Michael Cimino's *Heaven's Gate* (especially in its final scene) than to anything else in French cinema.

[26]   *Danton* (1982)

> *d* Andrzej Wajda *pc* Losange/Production Group X *ph* Igor Luther *m* Jean
> Prodromides *sc* Jean-Claude Carrière, from the play *Afera Dantona* by
> Stanislawa Przybyszewska *ad* Allan Starski *with* Gérard Depardieu, Wojciech
> Pszoniak, Anne Alvaro, Roland Blanche, Patrice Chéreau.

Strictly speaking, perhaps, *Danton* is not a French film, since it was made by a Polish director and, as most critics noted at the time, had as much to do with the struggle of Solidarity in Poland as with the French Revolution. Nonetheless, its contrast between the intellectuality of Robespierre and the earthy passionate nature of Danton, also suggests some of the persistent ideological meanings of the Revolution and the application of its message to contemporary Polish history shows the continuing relevance of those events in France 200 years ago.

[27]   *Mystère Alexina/The Mystery of Alexina* (1985)

> *d* René Feret *ph* Bernard Zitzermann *sc* Jean Gruault, Feret, based on the diary
> edited by Michel Foucault *with* Vuillemin, Valérie Stroh.

The film's punning title (Mister/Mystère) is the only false note in its investigation of the case of a near-hermaphrodite in the 1850s. It questions social attitudes towards sexual identity (Alexina, wrongly classified at birth, is a teacher in a girls' school), but treats the past in a way that does not allow us to be complacent about contemporary society and its attitudes. Intimist history, showing the pervasive influence of Foucault and other socio-anthropologists on the movement of ideas during the past 20 years. It is impossible to imagine such a film being made at any previous time in the history of cinema.

III WAR AND EMPIRE

[28] *Le Bled* (1929)

d Jean Renoir *pc* Société des Films Historiques *ph* Marcel Lucien *sc* Henri Dupuy-Mazuel *with* Arguillière, Manuel Raaby, Enrique Rivero.

Renoir's last silent film was commissioned by the government to commemorate the centenary (1830) of the French conquest of Algeria.

[29] *Verdun, souvenirs d'histoire* (1928)

d Léon Poirier

Poirier's sound version of *Verdun, vision d'histoire* (1928), a reconstruction of the battle of 1916 with a pacifist message, preaching Franco-German rapprochement. There was little documentary material from the fronts of the Great War and by the 1930s, in France as in Britain, cinema was beginning to turn from celebration of military heroism to pacifist themes. Poirier went on to make a number of films set in the French colonies, including *L'Appel du silence* (1935), based on the life of Charles de Foucault.

[30] *Le Grand jeu/Card of Fate* (1934)

d Jacques Feyder *ph* Harry Stradling, Maurice Forster *m* Hanns Eisler *sc* Charles Spaak, Feyder *with* Pierre-Richard Wilm, Marie Bell, Françoise Rosay, Charles Vanel.

A Foreign Legion melodrama, remarkable chiefly because Marie Bell plays two parts, one dubbed with the voice of another actress.

[31] *La Bandera* (1935)

d Julien Duvivier *sc* Charles Spaak, from the novel by Pierre MacOrlan *with* Jean Gabin, Pierre Renoir.

Another legionary drama and Gabin's first major film. *La Revue hebdomadaire* (Sept 1935) praised Gabin ('a great actor') and Renoir ('a fine figure of a Christian soldier, ready for sacrifice') and suggested that children should be taken to see it, not because it is a good idea to show them scenes of war, but because 'they can be taught to learn lessons of generosity, self-denial, courage, all those fine and lovely things necessary to the education of the soul which, in a great people, can be engendered in peace as well as in war.'

[32] *Pépé-le-Moko* (1937)

d Julien Duvivier *pc* Paris Film *ph* Jules Kruger *m* Vincent Scotto *sc* Henri Jeanson, Roger d'Ashelbe, from d'Ashelbe's novel *ad* Jacques Krauss *with* Jean Gabin, Mireille Ballin, Gabriel Gabrio, Lucas Gridoux.

'You don't need a PhD to see a link between the many deaths scriptwriters and the public made Jean Gabin die from the Autumn of 1936 (*Pépé-le-Moko*, ending with his first suicide, was released on Jan 28, 1937) and the disillusionment of the failures and divisions in the [Popular] Front ...' (Jeancolas, *15 ans d'années trente*, 1983). Perhaps not quite how contemporary audiences saw this story of the Algiers casbah, with Gabin as the first in a line of doomed heroes. The colonial setting is present, but merely as a location.

[33] *J'Accuse* (1937)

d Abel Gance *pc* FRD/Star *ph* Roger Hubert *m* Henri Verdun *sc* Gance *with* Victor Francen, Line Noro, Marcel Delaître, Jean Max.

Sound version of Gance's silent film of 1918–19. His melodramatic story of a poet and another man in love with the same woman and reconciled on the battlefield, is a visionary denunciation of war, using experimental camera techniques.

The title is taken from Emile Zola's open letter (1898) defending Dreyfus in the 'affair' which continued to divide left- and right-wing opinion up to World War II. The film inspired an interesting attack by Bernard Barbey in the *Revue hebdomadaire* (Feb 1938), mixing aesthetic and political comment. 'The more art tries to be realistic,' he wrote, 'the more it must know how to adopt artifice and fiction,' expressing 'distress' and 'shock' at Gance's use of live veterans of the Great War as extras. 'It is incredible, at this time of strikes and broken contracts, that a troupe of actors ... and a team of technicians could have been retained long enough to complete the work' (this was written in the aftermath of the Popular Front). More sinister is the comment 'but then, if *J'Accuse* is not a French work, what is its nationality? ... Monsieur Abel Gance's manner, his style, if you like, has no homeland.' The accusation of 'internationalism' at the time, had Fascist overtones. Barbey concludes that the film either 'provokes the spectator to those crude jests to which a Latin public is only too inclined, or else ... creates a neurotic horror of war ... which will only inspire unease, panic and confusion in the minds of our contemporaries.'

[34] *La Grande illusion/Grand Illusion* (1937)

d Jean Renoir *sc* Charles Spaak, Renoir *p* R.A.C. *ph* Christian Matras *m* Joseph

Kosma *with* Jean Gabin, Pierre Fresnay, Erich von Stroheim, Dalio, Gaston Modot.

By a stroke of genius, Renoir set his film on the futility of war, not on the battlefields, but in a POW camp where French and Germans meet as enemies but non-combatants. Among the French prisoners, Gabin, Fresnay and Dalio discover a common national culture that overrides differences of class and ethnic background; while von Stroheim and Fresnay, on the other hand, realize that class crosses national boundaries. From this paradox, the message is that we share a common humanity, the dialectical argument supporting a warm, funny and moving story.

For right-wing critics, it was a problem: an undeniably great French film by a director close to the Communist Party. In their *Histoire du cinéma*, Maurice Bardèche and Robert Brasillach insist that, though 'made by an internationalist', it is a nationalist film. Renoir had fought in the Great War and, 'perhaps before returning to his errors, did not want to betray the truth' of this youthful experience. Bernard Barbey declared that *La Grande illusion* confirmed 'the arrival of a great school of French cinema' (*Revue hebdomadaire*, July 1937), distinguishing between M. Renoir's political ideas, 'apparently identical with those of the organizers of the rather insipid spectacles and celebrations' [of the Popular Front], and his rounded characters: 'the subtlety in the make-up of Maréchal [Gabin], the average Frenchman, de Boeldieu [Fresnay], the aristocrat, Rosenthal [Dalio], the Jew, and Raufenstein [von Stroheim], the Prussian warrior, actually conditions their strength and their humanity; yet they remain typical . . .'

[35] *La Bataille du rail* (1946)
d René Clément *pc* Coop. Gén. du Cinéma Fr. *ph* Henri Alekan *m* Yves Baudrier *sc* Clément, Colette Audry, Jean Daurand *with* Désagneux, André Laurent, Daurand, Jean Clarieux, Leroy.

In a period of six years, France experienced the phoney war, the occupation, the liberation and the postwar purges. The country needed to unite behind a single version of recent history and, in this context, Clément's film is the most authentic record of the Resistance, a fictionalized documentary filmed on actual locations, with a largely non-professional cast.

[36] *Le Silence de la mer* (1947)
d Jean-Pierre Melville *pc* OGC/Melville *ph* Henri Decae *m* Edgar Bischoff *sc* Melville, from the novel by Vercors *with* Howard Vernon, Nicole Stéphane, Jean-Marie Robain.

Vercors's story of passive resistance to the occupier (a cultured German officer, billeted on an old man and his daughter, who eventually force him by their silence to question Nazism and effectively to choose suicide), is full of closely observed details of provincial home life. As a film, Raymond Barkan (*Les Lettres françaises*, 26 Apr 49) found it monotonous and 'the antithesis of cinema' because of the inevitable silence of two leading characters.

[37] *Les Portes de la nuit* (1947)

d Marcel Carné *pc* Pathé *ph* Philippe Agostini *m* Joseph Kosma *sc* Jacques Prévert, Carné *with* Pierre Brasseur, Yves Montand, Nathalie Nattier, Jean Vilar, Serge Reggiani.

Sadoul (*Le Cinéma français*, 1962) speaks of the disharmony between 'outmoded poetic themes and up-to-date reality' after the early scenes and Carné's first postwar film was a commercial disaster. Adapted from a ballet by Prévert, it mixes realism and fantasy and, in retrospect, may translate the atmosphere of the immediate postwar years rather better than its critics have allowed.

[38] *Jeux interdits/Forbidden Games* (1952)

d René Clément *pc* Silver-Film *ph* Robert Juillard *m* Narciso Yepes *sc* François Boyer, Jean Aurenche, Pierre Bost, from the novel by Boyer *with* Brigitte Fossey, Georges Poujouly, Lucien Hubert, Suzanne Courtal.

An antiwar film, at the time, might have been impossible and, like *La Grande illusion*, Clément's film becomes all the more powerful because it does not attack war directly. A peasant boy and a Parisian girl orphaned by the war, create a cemetery for dead animals, caricaturing the behaviour of grown-ups. 'The first "forbidden game" is war,' Clément said. 'A film like no other,' Colette Audry wrote in *Les Temps modernes* (July 1952). 'Next to this profound and serious life of the children, that of the adults (peasants, priest, nun), all well-meaning people, seems elementary, mechanical and often ludicrous. Powerless before the drama of their own lives, ignorant, separated from their own reality by external rituals and a concern for order, they unwittingly devastate the children's lives.'

Catholic opinion was divided. In the *Revue int. du cinéma* (No. 14, 1952), there were mainly favourable reviews by R. M. Arlaud and Stanislas Fumet (who said the film was only disrespectful of 'prejudices which should not be confused with religious convictions'). But Mario Verdone, in the same issue, denounced 'the perverse cleverness of the script' and spoke of 'necrophilia, moral laxity and profanation of sacred symbols'. In *Téléciné* (No. 34, 1952) Paule Sengissen and Claude-Marie Tremois described it as 'the work of intellectuals': 'its message is not pure, but ambiguous and disturbing. The blasphemy . . . in *Jeux interdits* is treated with a complacency that makes the authors part accessories to the evil they denounce. Their reaction is not a fruitful opposition to spiritual and moral decay, but a gloomy, secret delight in the spectacle offered by it.' Undoubtedly, the sensibilities of many French Catholics were wounded by the children's parody of Catholic ritual in the film.

[39] *Ali Baba et les quarante voleurs* (1954)

d Jacques Becker *pc* Cyclope *ph* Robert le Febvre *m* Paul Misraki *sc* Becker, Marc Maurette, Cesare Zavattini *with* Fernandel, Dieter Borsche, Henri Vilbert, Samia Gamal.

A colonial film? In 1954, the war in Indochina ended at Dien Bien Phu and that in

Algeria began, while the French public went to see *Ali Baba*, 'the French cinema's New Year present' (*Le Figaro*), 'the best colour photography' (*Paris-Presse*), 'best direction' (*Le Monde*), Fernandel proving he can 'identify as easily with fairy-tale bedouin as with Don Camillo' (*Dimanche Matin*).

For Catholic and some left-wing opinion, however, the film seemed less innocent. 'Not a film for children,' declared *Télécine* (No. 45, 1955), mentioning violence and belly-dancing, while Raymond Borde (*Les Temps modernes*, Jan 1955) found it 'highly significant that the only evidence the cinema can produce on the Arab World at a time when its consciousness is awaking . . . is a re-working of the *Thousand and One Nights*'. 'Exploitation, hunting down, massacre, then filming jolly tales in which one takes on the clothes of the victim – this is the master's ultimate insult to the slave. Even the Germans behaved better in the worst years of the occupation; but, for us, it is not a matter of one insult more or less towards the "bicots". The joke is a pleasant one and very French. We raid Tunisia, rape native women, burn *douars*, let the witnesses of Oudja die and shoot "sidis", while Fernandel sings "I am Ali, Ali, Ali, Ali, Ba-ba" with that aggressive vulgarity that is uniquely his own.'

[40] *Nuit et brouillard/Night and Fog* (1955)
d Alain Resnais *pc* Argos/Como *ph* Ghislain Cloquet, Sacha Vierny

A short documentary on Auschwitz and one of the first to reveal the full horror of the Nazi concentration camps.

[41] *La Traversée de Paris/Pig Across Paris*/US: *Four Bags Full* (1956)
d Claude Autant-Lara *sc* Jean Aurenche, Pierre Bost *with* Jean Gabin, Bourvil.

'A distorted picture of the war,' Armand-Jean Cauliez called this humorous tale of efforts to transport a black-market pig across occupied Paris (*Télécine*, No. 63, 1957), showing a conservative Catholic distaste for 'a somewhat cynical reaction to an excess of heroism' in other war films. Sadoul, on the other hand, liked it a lot (*Les Lettres françaises*, 1 Nov 56), comparing it with Maupassant's novel *Boule de Suif* as a 'reflexion of the reality of a country at a given time'. The Gabin character was 'sickening', 'suggesting those anarchist artists whose taste for "absolute freedom" eventually led them in 1942 to Weimar (at the gates of Buchenwald) while their pictures were sold, for good prices, to the gentlemen of the black market and aesthetes in grey-green uniforms . . . This intellectual is not imaginary. His like are to be found, now as then, in positions of authority.' The film had a lesson for 1956, then: 'satisfied profiteers, investing in antisemitism (the Arabs are semites, after all) did not disappear with the German occupation, but continue to uphold the established order . . .'

[42] *Un Condamné à mort s'est échappé/A Man Escaped* (1956)
d Robert Bresson *pc* Gaumont/NEF *ph* Léonce-Henri Burel *m* Mozart

sc Bresson, from André Devigny's account of his escape *ad* Pierre Charbonnier
with François Leterrier, Charles Le Clainche.

'As a record of the Resistance, his film was antagonistic, but as true as *La Bataille du rail*,'
Sadoul wrote in *Le Cinéma français* (1962) about Bresson's painfully detailed film, an
interior monologue where the prison becomes a monastery and the escape an
achievement of religious salvation.

[43] *Hiroshima mon amour* (1959)

d Alain Resnais *pc* Argos/Como/Pathé/Daiei *ph* Sacha Vierney, Takahashi
Michio *m* Giovanni Fusco, Georges Delerue *sc* Marguerite Duras
with Emmanuelle Riva, Eiji Okada, Bernard Fressor.

'Great film, great director!' (Georges Sadoul, *Les Lettres françaises*, 18 June 59), though
with reservations about Marguerite Duras's script. A postwar love affair with a
Japanese man evokes memories of a wartime affair with a German: is this a right-wing
film, was one question raised in the round-table discussion on it organized by *Cahiers du
cinéma* (translated in the first volume of selections from *Cahiers* published by Routledge
and Kegan Paul and the British Film Institute in 1985). The general conclusion, in any
case, was that it was a landmark in French cinema.

[44] *Jules et Jim/Jules and Jim* (1961)

d François Truffaut *pc* Films du Carrosse/SEDIF *ph* Raoul Coutard *m* Georges
Delerue *sc* Truffaut, Jean Gruault, from the novel by Henri-Pierre Roché
with Jeanne Moreau, Oskar Werner, Henri Serre.

Truffaut's story of a triangular relationship created a cult ('Jules et Jim' caps, and so on),
because of its enchantment with friendship, youth and physical love. Maybe it also had
to do with the Franco-German rapprochement and the feeling that old animosities had
been buried: the First World War is a mere episode in these three lives, Nazism an
irrelevance from another tragedy. 'The characters ... have no awareness of society,'
Claude Tarare remarked (*Les Temps modernes*, March 1962). 'They live only to please
themselves and for pleasure. Their jobs (writers, musicians, artists) can be done for
amusement like a game ... The only thing which they deign to approach with
seriousness – and more than seriousness – is love. Play and love: it's a child's world.' On
the other hand, he noted that Truffaut's treatment of sex was moving: 'in France
where, if not an excuse for blue jokes, physical love is a taboo subject, this is a *tour de
force*.' Georges Sadoul (*Les Lettres françaises*, 25 Jan 62) felt the film was less about *joie de
vivre* than about 'the disquiet of our century and some of its basic preoccupations'.

[45] *Le Petit soldat/The Little Soldier* (1963)

d Jean-Luc Godard *pc* Georges de Beauregard/SNC/Impéria *ph* Raoul Coutard
sc Godard *with* Michel Subor, Anna Karina, Henri-Jacques Huet, Laszlo Szabo.

Made in 1960, the film was censored until after the end of the Algerian war. This story of a Fascist terrorist is the early, apolitical Godard: Right and Left are identical. This message did not appeal to left-wing critics, though they were in principle sympathetic to the film's problems with the censor. 'Disappointing and outmoded,' concluded Michel Capdenac (*Les Lettres françaises*, 31 Jan 63). 'We see a good deal of torture, but it is the [Algerian] FLN which applies it ... We might applaud a courageous condemnation of torture if the Algerian fighters and those who tried by every means to prolong the war, were not deliberately set on the same level.' Gérard Bonnot, who had seen the film before the censor got to it, described it in *Les Temps modernes* (Nov 1961) as 'quite repulsive, not because of the "realism" of these scenes [of torture], as the stupidity of our censors would have us believe, but, on the contrary, because of their abstract character. The result is that this film which tries to raise the problem of torture in an open manner, seems like an insult to all the victims whose sufferings have not been purely intellectual but very real ...'

[46]   *Paris brûle-t-il?/Is Paris Burning?* (1966)
    d René Clément *pc* Transcontinental/Marianne *ph* Marcel Guignon *m* Maurice Jarre *sc* Gore Vidal, Francis Ford Coppola, from the book by Dominique Lapierre and Larry Collins *with* Jean-Paul Belmondo, Charles Boyer, Claude Dauphin, Bruno Cremer, Alain Delon, Kirk Douglas.

The heroic and spectacular view of the liberation.

[47]   *L'Armée des ombres/The Army in the Shadows* (1969)
    d Jean-Pierre Melville *pc* Corona/Fono *ph* Pierre Lhomme *m* Eric de Marsan *sc* Melville, from the novel by Joseph Kessel *with* Lino Ventura, Paul Meurisse, Simone Signoret.

Melville's account of the activities of a resistance group was 'more brilliant and more exact' than Pierre Kast's *Drôle de jeu* (1968), according to Jeancolas (*Le Cinéma des français*, 1979), 'and doubtless remains the best film on ... the élitist, urban resistance'. Jeancolas also notes the precise depiction of Lyon, as part of a new awareness of the reality of provincial towns.

[48]   *Le Chagrin et la pitié/The Sorrow and the Pity* (1971)
    d Max Ophuls

With the massive documentary *Français, si vous saviez* three years later, this had an enormous impact, challenging accepted myths of the occupation period through the direct testimony of *résistants*, collaborators and ordinary French men and women. Writing in *Les Temps modernes* (May 1971) Christian Zimmer described it as 'history being written and rewritten, alive, continually confronting the present, engaging in a kind of dialogue with it' and giving the image of a France 'cut in half and rising up against itself' (instead of a country united against the occupier), an image that 'bears a strong resemblance to present-day France' in the class realities covered by the terms 'Left' and 'Right'.

[49] *Lacombe Lucien* (1974)
d Louis Malle *pc* Nouvelles Ed. de Films/UPF/Vides/Hallelujah *ph* Tonino delli Colli *sc* Malle, Patrick Modiano *with* Pierre Blaise, Aurore Clément, Thérèse Giehse.

Malle's sympathetic treatment of the young collaborator ('a bastard, but one whose heart is revealed', Jean-Louis Bory, *Le Nouvel Observateur*, 28 Jan 74) divided left-wing opinion. Lucien is a brutal peasant who, when his approaches to the resistance are rejected, joins the Fascist *milice* which offers him a feeling of importance and power. His persecution of a Jewish girl develops into love and their brief idyll, before Lucien is executed, illustrates the ambiguities of the period (revealed on another level by the documentary evidence of *Le Chagrin et la pitié*).

Bory described it as 'the first real, true film on the occupation', praising Malle's attention to the details of life in the Toulouse region: 'this was the daily experience of the time and it was appalling. I know. I was there.' As for Lucien, he sees him as a typical peasant, 'knowing that you have to deceive nature ... It is by chance, not conviction, that he finds himself on the wrong side of the fence', taking 'the revenge of the peasant against the town, the poor against the rich, the humiliated against the proud.'

Christian Zimmer (*Les Temps modernes*, July 1974) saw the film from a different angle. 'The fashion for *le rétro* is not a morbid attraction towards a sinister period of history, but the reflexion and manifestation of a political trend. Gone are the "great designs": the resistance was one, Gaullism another.' Malle's film belongs to the world of de Gaulle's successors, Presidents Pompidou and Giscard, illustrating 'that eminently Giscardian faith in the supremacy of technique ... The only problems are *technical* ones, which is to say, in no way moral ones ... Consequently, good and evil are ideas apparently void of any meaning when set under the pitilessly *realistic* light of circumstances: *Lacombe Lucien* hardly implies anything else: the final scene – that kind of idyllic, paradisiac parenthesis, a remission from history, a utopian arresting of time, in which the young *collabo* and the young Jewess love each other in freedom, under nature ... – is, in brief, an image of the reconciliation preached by the Right.'

[50] *Le Dernier métro/The Last Metro* (1980)
d François Truffaut *pc* Les Films du Carrosse/Andrea/SEDIF/SFP/TF1
ph Nestor Almendros *m* Georges Delerue *sc* Truffaut, Suzanne Schiffman
ad Jean-Pierre Kohut-Svelko *with* Catherine Deneuve, Gérard Depardieu, Jean Poiret, Heinz Bennent, Andrea Ferréol.

Truffaut's film about a theatre company under the occupation marginalizes the events of World War II as *Jules et Jim* [44] dismissed those of World War I. In *Les Temps modernes* (Sept 1981), Françoix Garçon compared it to Fassbinder's *Lili Marlene* and saw it as 'a reverse reply' to Ophuls [48], an attempt 'to ennoble' a shameful page of history. 'The nationalist revival evident in Europe in recent years following the worsening of the economic crisis, partly, at least, explains this fundamental change ... The time has now apparently come for a retreat into an epic vision of past events ... These films are at once the first sign and a warning of this.'

Don Allen (*Finally Truffaut*, Secker and Warburg, 1985) quotes Truffaut's introduction to the published script: 'The Fascist critics regularly denounced "the Jew-ridden plays of Bataille and the effeminate plays of Cocteau" ', and adds that 'the character of Daxiat [Jean-Louis Richard] is based on an episode related by Jean Marais in his autobiography, where he recalls how to beat up the critic of *Je suis partout*, Alain Lambeaux, for his review of Cocteau's *La Machine infernale*.' See my note on [3] above.

[51]   *Coup de torchon/Clean Slate* (1981)

d Bertrand Tavernier *pc* Les Films de la Tour/A2/Little Bear *ph* Pierre William Glenn *m* Philippe Sarde *sc* Jean Aurenche, Tavernier, from the novel by Jim Thompson *with* Philippe Noiret, Isabelle Huppert, Jean-Pierre Marielle, Stéphane Audran, Eddy Mitchell.

The story of a police chief in French West Africa during the 1930s who turns mass murderer is a satire on the anomalies and inherent injustices of colonialism, with elements of black comedy.

[52]   *Fort Saganne* (1984)

d Alain Corneau *pc* Albina/A2/SFPC *ph* Bruno Nuytter *m* Philippe Sarde *sc* Henri de Turenne, Corneau, from the novel by Louis Gardel *with* Gérard Depardieu, Philippe Noiret, Catherine Deneuve, Sophie Marceau.

A left-wing attempt to make a colonialist epic? Corneau's film certainly appears to want it both ways. Saganne is an old-fashioned, swashbuckling hero of the Sahara who comes to realize the limitations of that ethic on the battlefields of the Great War. But the film harks back to the more innocent colonialist dramas of the 1930s, like Léon Poirier's *L'Appel du silence* (1936).

[53]   *Le Temps détruit/Time Destroyed* (1985)

d Pierre Beuchot *pc* Inst. Nat. de l'Audiovisuelle/Ministère de la Culture *ph* Jacques Bouqin, Bernadette Marie *m* Maurice Jaubert.

Beuchot's documentary is constructed around letters written by his father, Roger Beuchot, a signwriter, the composer Maurice Jaubert (whose film scores include *Quai des brumes*, *L'Atalante* and *Zéro de conduite*) and the Communist writer Paul Nizan, all three of whom were killed in the 'phoney war' in 1940. The letters, to women they love, describe conditions at the front, their hopes for the future, their longing to be reunited. The extracts are read over documentary footage from the period and later film of the places where the letters were written. A film with no vast ambitions, but among the most moving and poignant indictments of the idiocy of war.

IV POLITICS AND RELIGION

[54] *Les Nouveaux messieurs* (1929)

d Jacques Feyder *sc* Charles Spaak, Feyder, from the play by Robert de Flers and Francis de Croisset *ad* Lazare Meerson *with* Albert Préjean, Henri Roussel, Gaby Morlay.

Political satire, acceptable on the stage in the play by de Flers and de Croisset, came up against the censor when transferred to the screen. Feyder's film tells the story of a worker who goes into politics, becomes a minister and is involved with a dancer, the mistress of a Royalist *député*. As Sadoul (*Le Cinéma français*, 1962) remarks, there were several Socialist politicians whose careers followed a similar course. But Feyder, surprised by his troubles with the censor, considered that the film was mild in its attack on the parliamentary regime. Even so, it was partly responsible for his removal to Hollywood for the next four years.

[55] *A Propos de Nice* (1930)

d Jean Vigo *ph* Boris Kaufman *dist* Pathé-Nathan.

Almost an amateur documentary, in which Vigo stresses the contrasts between luxury and poverty in the Mediterranean town.

[56] *Le Dernier Milliardaire/The Last Millionaire* (1934)

d René Clair *pc* Pathé-Nathan *ph* Rudolph Maté *m* Maurice Jaubert *sc* Clair *with* Max Dearly, Renée Saint-Cyr, Marthe Mellot, Raymond Cordy.

One of René Clair's failures, at a time when he was undoubtedly the most popular director in France. Its success was not helped by the assassination in Marseilles a few days before it opened of King Alexander of Yugoslavia and a French minister, Louis Barthou: the film, set in the imaginary country of Casinario, is a satire on the economic crisis of the depression. Later commentators tend to find Clair's style of parody ineffectual.

[57] *Topaze* (1936)

d Marcel Pagnol *pc* Les Films Marcel Pagnol *ph* Albert Assouad *m* Vincent Scotto *sc* Pagnol, from his play *with* Arnaudy.

At least four other versions were made of Pagnol's play about a schoolteacher who realizes, after being dismissed for over-honesty, that he can succeed in public life if he abandons all moral principles. Louis Gasnier filmed it in 1933 with Louis Jouvet and in the same year a version was made by Harry d'Abbabbie d'Arrast in the USA. Pagnol tried again in 1951 and Peter Sellers in 1961. The play, and the early films, were indicative of popular disillusionment in the 1930s with business and politics and the naive schoolmaster provides a yardstick against which to measure the sophisticated cynicism of industrialists and administrators.

[58] *La Règle du jeu/The Rule of the Game* (1939)

d Jean Renoir *pc* Nouv. Ed. Fr. *ph* Jean Bachelet *sc* Renoir *with* Marcel Dalio, Nora Gregor, Gaston Modot, Renoir, Roland Tutain.

The Renoir team gathered in 1938 to make this story of a country-house shooting-party which is the most penetrating study of French society of the 1930s. La Chesnaye, the aristocrat, causes tragedy because he has, effectively, no standards to hold his society together.

It was greeted, on first showing, with incomprehension and indifference, then banned by the censor when war broke out, with other films described as 'depressing, morbid, immoral and unsuitable for young people'. Jeancolas (*Quinze ans d'années trente*, 1983) sums up later judgements of the work: Renoir's masterpiece 'and perhaps the finest film in 80 years of French cinema'. Setting it in the context of Renoir's political views in the period, Christian Zimmer wrote (*Les Temps modernes*, June 1965): 'The Popular Front, however things may appear, is already distant. Returning from political commitment, but perhaps thanks to it, the film-maker has "found himself". If his affection for his fellow-men is henceforth without any illusion, if he thinks that mankind can only be helped individually, not saved collectively, for all this, his affection is the stronger and more generous: *La Règle du jeu*, above all, breathes a passion for humanity ...' That this 'morbid, depressing and immoral' film should come to be seen as 'perhaps the finest' in the history of French cinema, says a good deal about changing attitudes during the past half-century.

[59] *La Symphonie pastorale* (1946)

d Jean Delannoy *pc* Gibe *ph* Armand Thirard *m* Georges Auric *sc* Delannoy, from the novel by André Gide *with* Pierre Blanchar, Michèle Morgan.

Gide's scepticism and his preoccupation with the question of individualism and religious authority make him a representative figure of the interwar period, while Delannoy's efficient version of his short novel about a Protestant pastor's love for one of his parishioners is characteristic of the 'quality cinema' of its time and similar in inspiration to his adaptation of Henri Queffélec's *Dieu a besoin des hommes* (1950). For obvious reasons, the political and spiritual outlook of the 1940s was austere.

[60]   *Journal d'un curé de campagne/Diary of a Country Priest*
(1951)
d Robert Bresson *pc* UGC *ph* Léonce-Henri Burel *m* Jean-Jacques Grunewald
sc Bresson, from the novel by Georges Bernanos *with* Claude Laylu, Armand
Guibert, Marie-Monique Arkell.

The austerity of the time perfectly suited Bresson's temperament, as did Bernanos's
preoccupation with evil. Generally, the film met with approval from Catholic sources:
the Centre Catholique des Intellectuels Français held a meeting at the Sorbonne in
1951 where a Carmelite, Father Bruno, recorded that he had seen the film after it was
recommended from the pulpit by a priest who expressed 'no reservations' about it (an
unusual attitude by a Catholic to any film at this time). Father Bruno was jeered when
he told the audience that he had found the film 'morbid' – 'there is no such thing as a
sad saint' (quoted by Robert Drouguet in his study of Bresson, *Premier Plan*, No. 42).

So, among Catholics, Bresson separated the happy saints from those who shared his
sin-laden outlook on the world. It was a question of temperament, not of ideology. *Les
Temps modernes*, not necessarily sympathetic to religious works, published two articles.
In one (Apr 1951), Jean Pouillon used it as the starting-point for an examination of
cinema adaptations of novels and an attack on Bernanos's novel in particular: 'this diary
which would seem simplistic and composed entirely of clichés if it were not that of a
priest' had inspired 'a film as dreary as the book it adapts' (not to speak of the
'mediocrity' of the acting). In March, however, the review had published Jean-Henri
Roy's study of 'Bernanos and the Cinema'; 'no thesis is imposed on us. We are not forced
to choose sainthood ... [the film] makes us feel the fundamental ambiguity of every
vocation ... Never has such fervour been expressed in the cinema and Bresson has
translated it magnificently. But it was entirely contained in a book that surely
represents the most valid example of the contemporary Christian novel.'

[61]   *Le Joli mai* (1962)
d Chris Marker *p* Cathérine Winter *ph* Pierre Lhomme *m* Michel Legrand
sc Marker.

Marker returned from China (*Dimanche à Pékin*, 1955), Russia (*Lettre de Sibérie*, 1957)
and Cuba (*Cuba Si!*, 1961) to make this example of *cinéma-vérité* about one month in
Paris. Sadoul called it 'a great work of art [which] opens a new route for French cinema'
(*Les Lettres françaises*, 9 May 63), rightly pointing out that the camera was 'not a
machine to record indifferently the best and the worst'.

For various reasons, film-makers in the 1940s and 1950s had not been able or
willing to examine the political and spiritual concerns of the period directly (which is
not to say that their films do not, indirectly, give a clue to most of those concerns).
Marker's documentary is a fascinating and convincing portrait of its time. It reacts to
such events as the trial of General Salan and includes testimony from a variety of
people, including that of the worker-priest who describes the reasons for his decision
not to obey the Church's order to leave the movement and return to the priesthood.

Cinéma-vérité is a term particularly applied to the work of Jean Rouch during this
period.

[62] *La Guerre est finie* (1966)

d Alain Resnais *pc* Sofracima/Europa *ph* Sacha Vierny *m* Giovanni Fusco
sc Jorge Semprun *with* Yves Montand, Ingrid Thulin, Geneviève Bujold.

A portrait of a Spanish political activist, Resnais's film showed a new form of realism in the treatment of contemporary political themes.

[63] *Suzanne Simonin, la religieuse de Diderot* (1966)

d Jacques Rivette *pc* Rome-Paris Films/SNC *ph* Alain Levent *m* Jean-Claude Eloy *sc* Jean Gruault, from Diderot's novel (1760) *with* Anna Karina, Liselotte Pulver, Micheline Presle.

Attacked by Catholic organizations even before it was made, this story of eighteenth-century convent life was selected for Cannes, then banned by the Ministry of Information. Even after the *aggiornamento* of the Second Vatican Council, which began to make profound changes in Catholic attitudes, the Church remained particularly sensitive to screen representations of religious subjects. Georges Sadoul (*Les Lettres françaises*, 2 Aug 67) said that the affair had 'unleashed ultra-reactionary forces, against Diderot, against Rivette and against a film which is 'an exemplary and faithful adaptation of a masterpiece of our literature': his defence of the film leads him to a considerable exaggeration of the quality of Diderot's novel.

[64] *Weekend* (1967)

d Jean-Luc Godard *pc* Copernic/Ascot *ph* Raoul Coutard *m* Antoine Duhamel
with Mireille Darc, Jean Yanne, Jean-Pierre Kalfon, Jean-Pierre Léaud.

A bleak Godardian vision of France and Western civilization as a wasteland of industrial and technological debris.

[65] *Z* (1968)

d Costa-Gavras *pc* Reggane/ONCIC *ph* Raoul Coutard *m* Mikis Theodorakis
sc Costa-Gavras, Jorge Semprun, from the book by Vasilis Vassilikos *with* Yves Montand, Irene Papas, Jean-Louis Trintignant, Jacques Perrin.

Méliès's 15-min. film about the Dreyfus affair (1899) was effectively censored until 1950, Feyder ran into difficulties with *Les Nouveaux messieurs* [54] and direct government censorship; and other factors such as libel laws and public indifference have meant that direct representation of parliamentary life and directly political films have been rare in cinema history. But, at the same time, France has long been a land of exile for political activists from abroad (comp. [62]) and, consequently, is involved on more than one level in foreign politics. The Colonels' regime in Greece aroused feelings expressed through demonstrations, petitions and other ways. Costa-Gavras's film popularized a notable sub-genre of political thrillers.

[66] *La Faute de l'abbé Mouret/The Sin of Father Mouret* (1970)
d Georges Franju pc Stephan/Films du Carrosse/Valoria/Amati ph Marcel Fradetal m Jean Wiener sc Jean Ferry, from the novel by Emile Zola with Francis Huster, Gillian Hills, Ugo Tozzi, Margo Lion.

In a political film, the period setting might have dulled the force of the attack; but the Church preaches an unchanging doctrine and, as some of its spokesmen insisted at the time of the Vatican Council less than ten years earlier, more than half believes that it has no need to adjust to the 'modern world'. Consequently, Franju's film about a young priest's discovery of love in an earthly paradise, could be seen as a direct assault on religious values, intensified by the gradual relaxation of censorship.

[67] *Aux urnes, citoyens!* (1971)
d Edouard Bobrowsky.

A documentary on the campaign in Arras for the municipal elections, revealing the mechanism of French parliamentary politics in the Pompidou era. 'The spectacle is horrifying,' writes Christian Zimmer (*Cinéma et politique*, 1974). 'Of course, everything was done to prevent the film being released.'

[68] *Tout va bien* (1972)
d Jean-Luc Godard p Jean-Pierre Rassam ph Armand Marco sc Godard, Jean-Pierre Gorin with Jane Fonda, Yves Montand, Vittorio Caprioli.

Godard's questioning of the forms of communication was as loaded as the satire of a factory-owner or the discussions of the strike committee in perhaps his most overtly political film. It shows his best and worst qualities and, in retrospect, is a telling document about the left-wing conscience at a time of ferment. Jean-Louis Bory (*Le Nouvel observateur*, 8 May 72) found Montand and Fonda extraordinarily truthful 'because, beyond the characters they play ... they rediscover their own personal concerns'. But: 'the provocative analysis of contemporary France is softened into a Gospel According to Saint Jean-Luc. What a relief! At last, we can file away the once-fearful Jojo in a drawer with what is today a quite reassuring label: Brecht.' The film was not a commercial success.

[69] *Coup pour coup/Blow for Blow* (1972)
d Marin Karmitz pc MK2/WDR-Cologne with the workers of Elbeuf.

A drama-documentary about a strike in a textile factory in Elbeuf.

[70] *Je vous salue, Marie/Hail Mary* (1985)
      d Jean-Luc Godard *sc* Godard.

This, on the other hand, really is the Gospel According to Jean-Luc. Joseph is a taxi-driver, Mary works in a petrol station, and the film concentrates on Joseph's very human response to her immaculate conception. The photography is splendid. The Catholic newspaper *La Croix* praised its 'respect for the mysteries of the supernatural and the irrational' and called it 'a great Christian film', but other Catholic voices showed that, in this area at least, they could still be shocked. There were riots in Nantes and elsewhere, demonstrations outside cinemas and calls for the film to be banned. Monseigneur Marcel Lefebvre expressed his disgust and had support from one very influential quarter: Pope John Paul II stated that the film 'distorted and reviled' the spirit of the gospel story and deeply wounded the feelings of believers. Godard replied by acknowledging that the Pope had rights over the original story.

V   THE MIDDLE CLASS

[71] *Un Chapeau de paille d'Italie/The Italian Straw Hat* (1927)
      d René Clair *pc* Albatros *ph* Maurice Despassiaux, Nicholas Roudakoff *sc* Clair,
      from the play by Eugène Labiche and Marc Michel *ad* Lazare Meerson
      with Albert Préjean, Olga Tchekova, Marise Maia.

Updating Labiche's play from the 1850s to the 1890s, Clair satirizes the pretensions of a petty bourgeoisie which is closer to that of his own time, but still divided from it by the war. The satire is without malice, conveyed by visual gags and the careful construction of the narrative.

[72] *L'Argent* (1928)
      d Marcel L'Herbier *pc* Cinégraphic Cinéromans *ph* J. Kruger, J. Letort
      sc L'Herbier, from the novel by Emile Zola *ad* Lazare Meerson *with* Alcover,
      Henri Victor, Alfred Abel, Antonin Artaud, Jules Berry.

L'Herbier's masterpiece, with exteriors filmed at the Bourse, the Opera and Le Bourget emphasizing the updating of Zola's novel and consequently the continuing relevance of its analysis of Capitalism. Noel Burch points out that this interference with a literary 'classic' was the focus of criticism when the film was released (*L'Herbier*, Seghers, 1973). 'Speculative fever has developed prodigiously,' Maurice Sarlat wrote in *Paris-Soir*, 'and the men described by Zola would now look like apprentices, if not fossils.' A number of commentators related it to the collapse of the Gazette du Franc in 1928, which Robert Spa suggested (*Le Figaro*) may have made the events of the film pale by comparison. Jean Fayard (*Candide*) 'would like to have met Armenians, Jews and Levantines' in L'Herbier's bank and stock exchange, 'which could just as well be a large department store' – 'in the cinema, one must not be afraid of stylization'.

[73] *Boudu sauvé des eaux/Boudu Saved from Drowning* (1932)
d Jean Renoir *pc* Michel Simon/Jean Gehret *ph* Marcel Lucien *sc* Renoir, from
the play by René Fauchois *ad* Laurent and Jean Castanier *with* Michel Simon,
Charles Grandval, Marcelle Hainia, Jean Gehret, Jacques Becker.

A respectable gentleman rescues a tramp (Simon) from drowning and takes him to his
home. The tramp responds by continuing to behave as a tramp and seduces the man's
wife and maid, before deciding that he prefers the freedom of the road to the comforts of
a middle-class home. Renoir pokes fun at refined manners and morals, but is not cruel.
The men retain an affection for each other, despite their differences. This is one of
several French films, from *A nous la liberté* [85] to *Vagabonde* [163] in which the
tramp's freedom from social constraints is equated with freedom itself.

[74] *Drôle de drame*/US: *Bizarre, Bizarre* (1937)
d Marcel Carné *pc* Corniglion-Molinier *ph* Eugen Schufftan *m* Maurice Jaubert
sc Jacques Prévert, from the novel by Storer-Clouston *ad* Alexandre Trauner
with Michel Simon, Françoise Rosay, Louis Jouvet, Annie Cariel, Jean-Louis
Barrault.

The middle classes in this Prévert-Carné collaboration are, in fact, the English middle
classes, and eccentric with it; but the farcical goings-on involving a novelist (Simon), a
bishop (Jouvet), a murderer (Barrault) and a character called Mrs Pencil are a 'very
French' (i.e. inaccurate) view of the English side of the Channel.

[75] *Lumière d'été* (1942)
d Jean Grémillon *pc* Discina *ph* Louis Page *m* Roland Manuel *sc* Jacques
Prévert, Pierre Laroche *ad* Max Douy *with* Madeleine Renaud, Paul Bernard,
Pierre Brasseur, Madeleine Robinson.

A love story in which the heroine has to choose between the honest world of the
workmen on a site constructing a dam, and the shallow world of *château* society. She
chooses the former, but it is the scenes of upper-middle-class society that are
memorable: as he showed in such earlier films as *Dainah la métisse* (1931), Grémillon is
admirable when conveying the emptiness of the pleasures of the rich, in contrast to the
working life of the poor. *Dainah*, recently restored by the Cinemathèque, is set in the
engine-rooms and saloons of a luxury liner and contains an extraordinary scene at a
ball suggesting that the passengers are taking part in a dance of death.

[76] *Mon Oncle* (1958)
d Jacques Tati *pc* Specta/Gray/Alter/Centauro *ph* Jean Bourgoin *m* Franck
Barcellini, Alain Romans *sc* Tati, Jacques Lagrange, Jean L'Hôte *ad* Henri
Schmitt *with* Tati, Jean-Pierre Zola, Alain Bécourt, Lucien Frégis, Dominique
Marie.

Tati delights in the eccentricities of the Old Paris and mocks at the pretensions of the new suburbs and the new rich, but the family relationship noted in the title shows that both are aspects of the same class. In the old quarter, we have the traditional lower middle class of tradespeople and employees; in the new suburb, the rising middle class of *cadres supérieurs* who are enjoying the prosperity of the postwar years and exhibiting their culture in their cars, their gadgets, the decoration of their homes, their Franglais and their smart entertainments. 'The ceremonial of the Arpels is, after all, that of the Sun King,' Georges Sadoul wrote in *Les Lettres françaises* (15 May 58), 'and their pitiful fountain the pitiful counterpart of those at Versailles.'

He notes that the film had a mixed reception in Cannes: 'provided one is witty enough, it is possible to make fun of Bernadette and the holy water of Lourdes ... But make fun of the coachwork of the latest Jaguar, the chrome on the DS or the Rolls engine – that really is a sacrilege ... This film is for you, good people, men in the street, who, unlike the others, do not have a Frigidaire for a heart.'

[77] *Thérèse Desqueyroux* (1962)

d Georges Franju *pc* Filmel *ph* Christian Matras *m* Maurice Jarre *sc* Franju, Claude Mauriac, François Mauriac (from his novel) *with* Emmanuèle Riva, Philippe Noiret, Edith Scob, Sami Frey.

Franju brings Mauriac's novel into the present, which some critics found inappropriate: 'in the age of the DS and the 404', Jean Douchet wrote in *Cahiers du cinéma* (Oct 1962), 'the situation could not have developed in this way', and other critics have tended to agree that the provincial bourgeoisie had evolved since 1927, when Mauriac's novel was published.

The film is an encounter between an atheist director (Franju) and a Catholic novelist (Mauriac) – though Mauriac's faith, with its oppressive sense of sin, represents a distinctive current in French Catholicism, if not the only one (see the objection raised to Bresson [60]). The two men met in their strong aversion to the provincial bourgeoisie. The film was 'anti-bourgeois, anti-religious and anti-society', according to Douchet, and Franju considered that he would have had still more trouble with the Office Catholique du Cinéma had it not been for Mauriac: as it was, the Office expressed reservations.

Thérèse, trapped in a loveless marriage, poisons her husband (Philippe Noiret, in one of the first of his roles as an amiable but insensitive middle-class husband). Liberated, she escapes to Paris.

[78] *Un Homme et une femme/A Man and a Woman* (1966)

d Claude Lelouch *pc* Films 13 *ph* Patrice Pouget, Jean Collomb *m* Francis Lai *sc* Lelouch *with* Anouk Aimée, Jean-Louis Trintignant, Pierre Barouh, Valérie Lagrange, Antoine Sire.

The answer to Tati [76], with an equally catchy and not dissimilar theme tune (now, appropriately enough, used in a TV commercial), this represents the lifestyle of a younger version of the Arpels from *Mon Oncle*. He is a racing driver, she is the widow of a stuntman and their previous marriages have given them two lovely children. Free of all other constraints, they agonize over the past.

It won three prizes at Cannes, including the Grand Prix of the Office Catholique International du Cinéma. 'I defy you to find, throughout the length of the film, a single character who is even slightly unlikeable', François Chevassu wrote in *Image et son* (July 1966). 'Lelouch gives us a sugary world beside which *Les Parapluies de Cherbourg* looks like the perverted child of Dante's Inferno ... As for the children, I offer them to grandmas, infertile women, childless couples and naive virgins. They will love them.' The motor car, apparently, takes up around one-third of the total running time and Chevassu points out the 'elegantly rustic' surroundings, 'very *Maison française*' (i.e. *Homes and Gardens*), which the characters inhabit. Nostalgia is a keynote of the film, whether for past loves or for the genuinely rural furniture of the grandparents of this New Class.

[79] *Belle de Jour* (1967)
> *d* Luis Buñuel *pc* Paris Film/Five Film *ph* Sacha Vierny *sc* Buñuel, Jean-Claude Charrière *with* Catherine Deneuve, Jean Sorel, Michel Piccoli, Geneviève Page, Pierre Clémenti.

From *Belle de Jour*, through *Le Charme discret de la bourgeoisie* (1972) to *Cet obscur objet du désir* (1977), Buñuel relentlessly exposed the inadmissible desires behind the façade of conventional society, with a particular hostility to the middle class and the Church. His cinema was also about cinema: 'like each of Buñuel's films, *Belle de Jour* confronts the critic with the problem of the relationship between the mechanism of dreams and that of cinema', Claude Hodin wrote in *Les Temps modernes* (Aug 1967) in a long article on this study of a young woman's sexual fantasies.

[80] *La Femme infidèle*/US: *Unfaithful Wife* (1969)
> *d* Claude Chabrol *pc* Les Films La Boétie/Cinégay *ph* Jean Rabier *m* Pierre Jansen *sc* Chabrol *ad* Guy Littaye *with* Stéphane Audran, Michel Bouquet, Maurice Ronet.

The surface of middle-class life (television, good food, nice children) represses passion, causing a rupture between real feelings and 'civilized' manners. A husband discovers his wife's infidelity and, going to see her lover, ends by killing him. This act of jealousy is also a revelation of love and, as a result of it, she realizes for the first time emotions that have until then been unable to penetrate the façade of their marriage.

[81] *La Truite*/*The Trout* (1982)
> *d* Joseph Losey *pc* Gaumont/Partners/FT1/SFPC *ph* Henri Alekan *m* Richard Hartley *sc* Monique Lange, Losey, from the novel by Roger Vailland *with* Isabelle Huppert, Jean-Pierre Cassel, Jeanne Moreau, Daniel Olbrychski.

'A social comedy with bitter and sometimes tragic overtones', was Losey's tentative description of this adaptation of Vailland's novel about the impersonality of big business. In fact, it illustrates how far, since the early 1960s, certain middle-class milieux had become the 'natural' setting for the study of sexual relationships.

[82] *Pauline à la plage/Pauline at the Beach* (1983)

d Eric Rohmer *pc* Losange *ph* Nestor Almendros *m* Jean-Louis Valero
sc Rohmer *with* Amanda Langlet, Arielle Dombasle, Pascal Greggory, Féodor Atkine, Simon de la Brosse.

Rohmer followed his series of Moral Tales with one of Comedies and Proverbs, of which this is the third. Marion and her 15-year-old cousin, on holiday, become entangled with Pierre, Henri and Sylvain. The class to which the central characters belong is, once more, treated as 'natural'. In the cultured Parisian middle class, their proper environment, these people would pass merely as 'people', with no salient social background at all, as their counterparts do in so many other films of the time. Here, in a 'foreign' setting (a Breton resort) where Henri becomes fleetingly involved with a working-class girl who sells peanuts on the beach, we have some yardstick by which to situate them: but the film constitutes an episode, distinct from 'real' life (it starts and ends with Marion and Pauline's arrival and departure by car).

One indication of changing standards: the Office Catholique Français du Cinéma which, 20 years earlier, would have almost certainly condemned such a film for immorality, merely recommended it as suitable for adolescents: 'Rohmer emphasizes the contrast between the amorous discourse and reality.'

[83] *Notre histoire/Separate Rooms* (1984)

d Bertrand Blier *pc* Sara/Adel/A2 *ph* Jean Penzer *m* Laurent Rossi *sc* Blier
with Alain Delon, Nathalie Baye, Michel Galabru, Geneviève Fontanel.

A frenetic tale which 'lays bare the social and sexual hypocrisies of French middle-class society', in the words of Derek Elley's programme note when it was shown at the London Film Festival. In fact, it is more remarkable for its use of the devices of narrative fiction (stories within stories), though the climax in the bedroom could be construed as a satire on bourgeois standards.

VI   WORKING CLASS AND INDUSTRY

[84] *La Roue* (1923)

d Abel Gance *pc* Les Films Abel Gance *ph* Léonce-Henri Burel *sc* Gance
with Séverin-Mars, Ivy Close, Gabriel de Gravone, Pierre Magnier.

The version of Gance's film eventually released cut out much of the social comment in the original. His railway-driver hero is elevated to the stature of a figure from classical myth, but the real hero is the railway engine. Gance's early critics praised his visual poetry and René Clair, in an article several times reprinted, wished that he would abandon fiction altogether and stick to 'pure film'.

[85]　*A nous la liberté* (1931)

> *d* René Clair *pc* Tobis *ph* Georges Perinal *sc* Clair *ad* Lazare Meerson *with* Henri Marchand, Raymond Cordy, Rolla France.

Emile and Louis start as comrades in jail, but in the world outside Louis's success separates them and Emile finds himself as the production-line worker, Louis as the boss. In the end, reduced to the same level as tramps, they rediscover happiness and comradeship.

Clair's satire on industrial life (the factory is explicitly compared to the prison) inspired Chaplin's *Modern Times*. Its use of song and other vaudeville elements softens the satire, but Claude Aveline (*La Revue hebdomadaire*, 6 Feb 32) was pleased that Clair had not chosen the form of a political tract. ' "Let's have freedom" ', he wrote, 'is not only the cry of the escaping prisoner . . . or of the worker whose submission to discipline and to work on a production "chain" – the word is significant – is almost indistinguishable from prison; it is also the secret wish of the boss whom wealth, acquired too quickly, has thrown into a life that stifles him.' Interestingly, Aveline makes a point about the inadaptability of the *nouveau riche*, when most spectators would understand Clair to mean that wealth and class in themselves are as alienating as poverty or prison.

[86]　*L'Atalante* (1934)

> *d* Jean Vigo *pc* Gaumont *ph* Boris Kaufman, Louis Berger *m* Maurice Jaubert
> *sc* Vigo, from a story by Jean Guinée *with* Dita Parlo, Jean Dasté, Michel Simon.

Vigo's film about a couple on a working barge, travelling through the industrial landscape of France during the depression, is a classic of 'poetic realism': that is to say, it transforms everyday reality.

In *L'Humanité* (7 June 34), Emile Cerquast expressed indignation at the fact that Gaumont, having acquired the rights to Vigo's 'very fine film', had tried to popularize it by adding a theme song and re-titling it *Le Chaland qui passe* ('The Passing Barge'). Even 'poetic realism' could be too close to reality for popular consumption.

[87]　*La Belle équipe* (1936)

> *d* Julien Duvivier *pc* Ciné Arts *ph* Jules Kruger, Marc Fessard *m* Maurice Yvain
> *sc* Charles Spaak, Duvivier *with* Jean Gabin, Charles Vanel, Viviane Romance, Raymond Aimes, Robert Lynen.

A 'Popular Front' message? Five workmen win some money on the lottery and decide to invest it in a co-operative venture, a riverside cabaret. Spaak and Duvivier preferred the unhappy ending of the first version, but the producers persuaded them to adopt a happier one, apparently after a poll taken when the film was previewed. In either case, the 'co-operative' idea is weak and Duvivier's original ending would have brought the film closer in spirit to the pessimistic melodramas in which Gabin usually starred at the time, than to the optimism of *Le Crime de Monsieur Lange*.

Georges Sadoul (*Commune*, Nov 1936) said that, in any case, 'five cannot create a little world of happiness. Happiness is an affair concerning the whole world, millions of men'; but, despite this limitation of the film, 'Duvivier does not disguise his indignation at the fate of the unemployed'.

[88]   *Le Crime de Monsieur Lange/The Crime of Mr. Lange* (1936)
      d Jean Renoir pc Obéron ph Jean Bachelet m Jean Wiener sc Jacques Prévert
      with René Lefèvre, Jules Berry, Florelle, Nadia Subirskaia.

'Irony and feeling are indistinguishably mixed', Bernard Barbey wrote in *La Revue hebdomadaire* (Feb 1936) of Renoir's film which tells the story of a small printing works whose manager absconds, leaving his workers faced with unemployment. Instead they decide to run the enterprise as a co-operative and do so with the help of Lange, a writer of pulp fiction. When the manager threatens to return and destroy the co-operative, Lange kills him. It was premiered three months before the elections that brought the Popular Front to power.

Both Renoir's film and that of Prévert and the Groupe Octobre, it encapsulates the spirit of the Front and Renoir's political leanings at the time. The political importance of cinema and the debate on its significance can be judged by Renoir's assertion two years later that *Quai des brumes* [2] was a 'fascist' film because it showed morally tainted and dishonest characters, making you feel that a dictator was necessary to restore order.

For a writer like Barbey, not sympathetic to the Front, the film was 'an important stage in cinema technique' and marked 'a great moment in the uncertain and painful history of French cinema'. He felt, however, that to be counted a masterpiece it needed 'some of that pity which one finds in the works of Tolstoy' or in German films like *The Blue Angel*.

[89]   *La Bête humaine/Human Beast/Judas was a Woman* (1938)
      d Jean Renoir pc Paris ph Curt Courant m Joseph Kosma sc Renoir, from the
      novel by Emile Zola with Jean Gabin, Simone Simon, Fernand Ledoux, Carette.

Another film banned by the censor at the start of World War II as 'depressing, morbid and immoral'. Renoir updates the story from the nineteenth century to 1938, but retains the theme of fatality: Zola's railwayman is a sex murderer because of a tainted heredity. Most of all, the film is interesting because of the picture it gives of life on the railways, as Sadoul remarked (*Regards*, 5 Jan 39): 'Renoir may even have surpassed Zola ... Zola, as Abel Gance was later to do in *La Roue*, allowed himself to be too often carried away by the "lyricism" of the railways ... From the first images we are transported into the noise of the locomotive on its way to Le Havre; then we enter the staff dormitories and changing-rooms at the express terminus, the station-master's apartment . . . We also see the obsessive and tragic shunting yards where night conceals the clandestine love of Jacques and his mistress; we go with them to the railway-workers' ball . . .'

[90] *Le Jour se lève* (1939)

  d Marcel Carné *pc* Vog/Sigma *ph* Curt Courant *m* Maurice Jaubert *sc* Jacques Viot *with* Jean Gabin, Arletty, Jacqueline Laurent, Jules Berry.

Honesty against corruption. What is remarkable about Gabin's working-class hero is that he is credible both as an individual and as a representative of the 'ordinary man', which at the time meant a workman with a bicycle, not a racing-driver. Carné takes us inside the machine-shop where Gabin works, shows us where he lives, his entertainment and his dreams. At the end, when he is surrounded by the police, the crowd tries to defend him.

[91] *Remorques*/US: *Stormy Waters* (1940)

  d Jean Grémillon *pc* SEDIF *ph* Armand Thirard *m* Roland Manuel *sc* Jacques Prévert, André Cayatte, from the novel by Roger Vercel *with* Jean Gabin, Michèle Morgan, Madeleine Renaud, Fernand Ledoux.

An eternal triangle, with Gabin between Morgan and Renaud. It is interesting chiefly because of the scenes on the waterfront and at sea: though the effects are appalling (the model of the tug-boat looks like a bathtime toy), the film shows the life of sailors which was Grémillon's passion.

As a director, Grémillon was unlucky. His films of the 1930s are flawed, but demonstrate his talent. Work on *Remorques* was interrupted by the outbreak of war.

[92] *Aubervilliers* (1945)

  d Eli Lothar.

Lothar's shocking documentary on the slums of a Parisian suburb.

[93] *Le Sang des bêtes* (1949)

  d Georges Franju *pc* Forces et Voix de la France *ph* Marcel Fradetal *m* Joseph Kosma.

Franju's documentary, on the Paris abattoirs, is singularly unpleasant to watch: it describes systematically the method for killing different kinds of animal for meat. It suggests, too, the burden that society imposes on those who do necessary, but disagreeable jobs.

[94] *Le Point du jour* (1949)

d Louis Daquin *ph* André Bac *sc* Vladimir Pozner *with* Desailly, René Lefèvre, Loleh Bellon.

'With the films of Renoir,' Sadoul wrote in *Les Lettres françaises*, 12 May 49, '*Le Point du jour* is one of the few French films to have gone beyond the facile travesties of populism to show the reality of popular life.' He compared Daquin's film, set in a mining community in northern France, to Ford's *How Green Was My Valley*: 'Ford, in his paternalistic and sermonizing adaptation of Richard Llewellyn's novel, imagined his miners living in smart apartments and the mine itself was chiefly an excuse for him to show the subtle interplay of lifts.'

[95] *Le Salaire de la peur/The Wages of Fear* (1953)

d Henri-Georges Clouzot *pc* CICC/Filmsonor/Vera/Fono Roma *sc* Clouzot, Jérôme Géronini, from the novel by Georges Arnaud *with* Yves Montand, Charles Vanel, Véra Clouzot, Folco Lulli.

A brilliant suspense film with a sardonic ending, set in an imaginary South American country from which the four central characters try to earn their escape by driving lorries packed with nitroglycerine up a bumpy mountain road. Industry? Working-class? Yes, if only because of Montand. Most popular singers in Britain or the USA, whatever their background, projected an image of suave gentility. Montand, as singer and actor, was resolutely working-class.

B. Dort analysed the film at length in *Les Temps modernes* (June 1953), praising it for its use of cinematographic effects to achieve suspense, and its depiction of character: these are not 'the abstract heroes of Westerns', though in the second part Clouzot sacrifices character to action. He notes, too, the implied homosexuality in the bond between the men. 'He never defines them as homosexuals, but merely shows them, at times, acting as such.' The ending is 'debatable in terms of simple credibility, but an astounding metaphor, carrying us from the realm of necessity to that of myth'.

However, the film attracted a hostility that seems surprising today, notably from the Catholic press. The Centrale Catholique du Cinéma rated it 4A ('For adults, with reservations'). In *Télé-Ciné* (Nos. 40–41, 1954), Gilbert Salachas quoted Pierre Kast's description of it as 'a great atheist film': 'we share that opinion'. It gives, he said, 'a deliberately negative and unhealthy moral picture' and exhibits 'a conscious determination to exclude any spiritual dimension'. The cult of the *unhappy end* had become systematic and no more justifiable than the opposite and Clouzot's work was 'the expression of a *mal du siècle* far more harrowing in its aggressive, nihilistic despair than the tears of the Romantic generation'.

[96] *Gervaise* (1956)

d René Clément *pc* Agnès Delahaie/Silver/CICC *ph* Robert Juillard *m* Georges Auric *sc* Jean Aurenche, Pierre Bost, from Emile Zola's novel *L'Assommoir* (1877) *with* Maria Schell, François Périer, Suzy Delair, Mathilde Cassadessus.

'That rare thing: a successful adaptation of a great novel,' Jean Pouillon wrote in *Les Temps modernes* (Apr 1957). Should it have been updated? 'In choosing to recreate, very precisely, a period and an atmosphere, Clément has undoubtedly achieved a *tour de force*, but at the expense of dating the plot, distancing it from the spectator and making what was polemical in the novel, aesthetic in the film.' On the other hand, 're-read the book and ask yourself if the current conformism of French cinema (and not only cinema) could have tolerated such a violent and profoundly pessimistic indictment! "Reconstructing" was surely the only way not to soften Zola's message. And if you think that is a pity, it is not Clément who should be blamed.'

Even a historical film about the working-class, especially one that depicts its life so convincingly, could not be consigned merely to the status of 'literature' and 'history'. In *Télé-Ciné* (No. 60, 1956), Claude-Marie Tremois described Clément as 'a moralist who adopts an authoritative language to express appalling realities which will remain an insult to humanity until all trace of them has disappeared'.

[97] *Le Bonheur* (1965)

> *d* Agnès Varda *pc* Parc *ph* Jean Rabier, Claude Beausoleil *sc* Varda *with* Jean-Claude Drouot, Claire Drouot, Sandrine Drouot, Marie-France Boyer.

This story of an eternal triangle is set in a working-class family but uses the working-class as a 'neutral' background. 'The tone . . . is uniformly idyllic' and 'nothing could be further from social realism than the make-believe world it constructs' (Roy Armes, *French Cinema*, Secker and Warburg, 1985).

[98] *La Dentellière/The Lacemaker* (1977)

> *d* Claude Goretta *pc* Action/FR 3/Citel/Janus *ph* Jean Boffety *m* Pierre Jansen *sc* Pascal Lainé, Goretta, from Lainé's novel *with* Isabelle Huppert, Yves Beneyton, Florence Giorgetti.

One of the few films to suggest that class divisions might still persist in French society, it tells the story of a love affair between a middle-class student and a working-class girl which eventually drives her to insanity. Her exclusion from his intellectual world is well-observed.

VII PROVINCIAL AND RURAL LIFE

[99] *Marius* (1931)

> *d* Alexander Korda *pc* Marcel Pagnol/Paramount *ph* Ted Pahle *sc* Pagnol *with* Raimu, Orane Demazis, Pierre Fresnay, Alida Rouffe, Charpin.

The first part of the Pagnol Marseilles trilogy. It was followed by *Fanny* (1934), directed by Marc Allégret, and *César* (1936), directed by Pagnol, with the same actors in the leading roles. Together, the three films established an image of Provençal life: the bitter-sweet story of the love affair between Marius and Fanny and the older generation of 'characters' in César's waterfront bar recreated on film by the actors who had played them on stage. In 1937, *La Cinématographie française* (12 March 37) published its first poll showing *César* as the most popular film of the year and the trilogy enjoyed considerable success abroad. Dilys Powell (*Sunday Times*, 18 Feb 51), quoting a colleague who regretted, after seeing *César*, that there were no more of them, wrote: 'I find myself forgetting the editing and the camera angles and all the other narrative devices of the cinema, and thinking only that here is an entrancing tale, at once funny and touching, about people.' That, perhaps, is the answer to the argument about Pagnol's films being simply 'filmed theatre'.

Claude Berri's adaptations of *Jean de Florette* and *Manon des Sources* (1986) show the continuing popularity of Pagnol's stories of Provençal life.

[100] *Angèle* (1934)

d Marcel Pagnol *pc* Les Films M. Pagnol *sc* Pagnol, from Jean Giono's novel *Un de Baumugnes with* Orane Demazis, Fernandel.

Like *Jofroi* (1934), another Giono adaptation, this was filmed on location in Provence from Pagnol's Marseilles studios – a phenomenon at a time when the French cinema industry was otherwise totally centred on Paris-Joinville. *L'Humanité* (7 Nov 34) criticized the film for having 'too much dialogue': 'there is also in *Angèle* a bias towards aestheticism not to be found in Giono'.

[101] *Toni* (1935)

d Jean Renoir *pc* Les Films Marcel Pagnol.

Set among immigrant workers in southern France, *Toni* is often seen now as a precursor of Italian neo-realism. 'The subject of the film is taken from an incident which actually happened in part of southern France ... This region is inhabited mainly by immigrants of Italian origin, half-workers, half-peasants. Among these uprooted people, passions run high and the men who served as my models in *Toni* seemed to me to carry with them that heavy atmosphere which indicates the fatal destiny of the heroes of tragedy, or indeed of popular song' (Jean Renoir, in *Comoedia*, 8 Feb 35).

[102] *Pension Mimosas* (1935)

d Jacques Feyder *pc* Tobis *ph* Roger Hubert *sc* Feyder *with* Françoise Rosay, Paul Bernard, Alerme, Lise Delamare, Arletty.

In *L'Action française* (25 Jan 35), François Vinneuil compared the theme (the undeclared love of a woman for her godson) with Greek tragedy and with Racine's

Phèdre, pointing to Feyder's boldness in tackling such a subject with 'the still scanty resources of the cinema', but feeling that it lacked the 'sombre poetry' of characters from Feyder's *Le Grand jeu* (1934), who would hardly be found 'in the limiting environment of a small, middle-class hotel, among its humble or weak-minded guests'. Bernard Barbey (*La Revue hebdomadaire*, March 1935), noting that the film had been criticized for neglecting the landscape of the Côte d'Azur, wrote: 'I cannot share these reservations ... it is indeed a fact of life in a *pension*, even in the sunniest part of the Riviera, that its guests, and still more its proprietors, barely see beyond the entrance hall, the veranda and the palm trees in the garden. Their horizon is limited to the terrace of the casino.'

Recalling the problems Feyder had experienced with *Les Nouveaux messieurs* [54], Emile Cerquast described it as 'morally clean' (*L'Humanité*, 25 Jan 35), demonstrating that 'directors who have remained "independent" are obliged to limit their imagination and to weigh carefully every part of a script'. He considered the film excessively sentimental in parts, 'a simple concession to the supposed taste of the audience'.

[103] *Regain* (1937)

d Marcel Pagnol *pc* Les Films M. Pagnol *sc* Pagnol, from the novel by Jean Giono *with* Orane Demazis, Gabriel Gabrio, Fernandel.

An abandoned Provençal village is brought back to life by Panturle (Gabrio) and Arsule (Demazis) who was formerly the mistress (almost the slave) of an itinerant knife-grinder. Jeancolas (*Quinze ans d'années trente*, Stock, 1983) describes it as 'naive cinema, like naive painting' and 'medieval', with scarcely any reference to contemporary society or events; 'in its picture of women, Pagnol's cinema is not medieval, but neolithic. Woman is not an object, but merchandise. In *Angèle*, Jean Servais and the father negotiate her fate in her absence. In *Regain*, Panturle reimburses Gedemus the amount which represents Arsule's upkeep. Arsule is an animal.'

Jeancolas also discusses the question of the relationship of the film to the doctrines of Vichy's wartime Révolution Nationale: *Regain* 'would be, three years in advance, the ideology of the Révolution Nationale were it not so clearly distinguished from the "priest-ridden" dimension' of Vichy. I discuss this question above [pages 40–41]. Giono's anarchism seems to me quite distinct from the ideology of Vichy, and the non-Catholic dimension a significant one. But some aspects of Giono did appeal to Vichy. The documentaries *Manosque, pays de Jean Giono* and Maurice Labro's *Le Pain* appeared during the occupation and were praised in *L'Action française* by Ed. Michel in lyrical terms: the first celebrated 'the joy of the earth, the song of the water and the wind', the second was 'a fine hymn to the basic foodstuff of Frenchmen and the virtues of the race'. But to make Pagnol and Giono responsible for Vichy's promulgation of peasant and family life, is an attempt to establish their guilt by association.

[104] *La Femme du boulanger* (1938)

d Marcel Pagnol *pc* Les Films M. Pagnol *sc* Pagnol, from Giono's novel *Jean le Bleu*, *with* Raimu, Ginette Leclerc.

When the village baker's wife runs off, he refuses to work and the villagers are pressed into helping him to secure her return. 'A very broad farce,' according to Georges Sadoul (*Regards*, 22 Sept 38), 'in the good old tradition of Molière and peasant humour', but at the same time tragic in its depiction of the betrayed husband: 'an admirably French work'. There is a curé, caricatured perhaps rather too much by 'facile and conventional anti-clericalism' but 'we defy all Herr Goebbels' directors to make a film as completely German, all those employed by Sig. Mussolini to create a work as utterly Italian, as this *Femme du boulanger* is French, for all it was produced in a France still in the hands of the Judeo-Marxists, the half-castes and the Slavonic hordes of the Popular Front.'

[105] *Goupi-Mains-Rouges*/US: *It Happened at the Inn* (1943)

d Jacques Becker *pc* Minerva *ph* Jean Bourgoin, Pierre Montazel *m* Jean Alfaro *sc* Becker, Pierre Véry from his novel *with* Fernand Ledoux, Blanchette Brunoy, Robert Le Vigan.

A peasant family, hostile to outsiders, with the conventional traits of rapacity and greed, settles its own scores. This is no idealized view of country life. Becker's next film, *Falbalas*, was set in the very different world of *haute couture* and made just as the war ended.

[106] *Le Corbeau*/US: *The Raven* (1943)

d Henri-Georges Clouzot *pc* Continental *ph* N. Hayer *sc* Louis Chavance, Clouzot *with* Pierre Fresnay, Ginette Leclerc, Pierre Larquey, Roger Blin.

Inspired by a case of poison pen letters in Tulle, this would have passed as a conventional thriller had it been made 20 years later. In the event, it caused a scandal and was banned after the war.

The criticisms were moral and ideological. The Office Familial de Documentation Artistique rated it grade 6. Grade 5 was not recommended even for adult audiences, so grade 6 was indescribably bad. François Vinneuil, who had expressed his own aesthetic reservations about it in *Je suis partout* (9 Oct 43: 'we are becoming more demanding of Clouzot's brilliant gifts'), wondered in the same paper (15 March 44) just what the Office *did* consider suitable for French audiences. The Centrale Catholique du Cinéma's ratings did not go beyond grade 5 ('proscribed'), so that is what the film got. 'What people find unpardonable in Henri-Georges Clouzot,' Roger Régent wrote in *Les Nouveaux temps* (Oct 1944), 'is his talent.'

Ideologically, the film did not appeal to the Right (despite Vinneuil): 'It is clear that, throughout the length and breadth of his script, M. Louis Chavance has been seized by the desire to scandalize,' wrote *L'Action française* (3 Oct 43). '*Le Corbeau* has deliberately infringed the most elementary principles of the most common morality.' Still less to the Left: in the clandestine *Lettres françaises* (15 Apr 44), G. Adam and P. Blanchar compared it unfavourably to Grémillon's *Le Ciel est à vous* (1944): 'The Germans can rub their hands: after many mistakes in judging the worth of their French valets, they have finally dug up two who, under cover of a spotless and sometimes even attractive piece of merchandise, will be superb standard-bearers for the enemy's cleverly-concealed ideology ... In contrast to the morally crippled, abnormal and corrupt characters who, in *Le Corbeau*, dishonour one of our provincial towns, *Le Ciel est à vous* offers characters full of French vigour, genuine courage and moral health in whom we rediscover a national truth which will not and cannot die.' Hurray! Unfortunately, the (non-clandestine) Fascist press was also claiming *Le Ciel est à vous* for its own (which just shows how careful you have to be in assigning an ideological tendency to works of fiction).

[107] *Premier de cordée* (1944)

   d Louis Daquin *sc* from the novel by Roger Frison-Roche.

Like Grémillon, the work of a left-wing director who had no intention of upholding the ideology of the Révolution Nationale, this story of man's battle against the mountains was also later accused of 'Pétainism' in its preference for the countryside over the town, etc. 'I was, after all, in charge of the clandestine trade union organization,' Daquin wrote in his own defence (*Cinématographe*, May 1978), while accepting that there are 'elements of Pétainist ideology in *Premier de cordée*: whatever one is, one is always subject to the influence of the dominant ideology.'

[108] *Farrebique* (1946)

   d Georges Rouquier *pc* L'Ecran Français et Les Films *ph* André Dantan
   sc Rouquier.

See next entry.

[109] *Biquefarre* (1982)

   d Rouquier *pc* Midas/Mallia *ph* André Villard *m* Yves Gilbert *sc* Rouquier
   with the inhabitants of Goutrens (Aveyron)

Rouquier's two documentary dramas about Goutrens must be considered together, though they show contrasting worlds, because they make up the most convincing portrayal of peasant life in French (perhaps in European) cinema. The first is a record of the 'unchanging' face of village life and of farming people whose customs and relationship to the soil had hardly changed since the Middle Ages. The second, centring on the sale of a property, does indeed show some 'unchanging' aspects of the outlook of the same characters, but emphasizes above all the profound alterations that have occurred in their circumstances: mechanization of farming, pollution, even the effects of the Common Agricultural Policy. It is a painful and sad film, but at the same time an extraordinarily penetrating examination of the thoughts and feelings of country people.

Of the first film, Georges Sadoul wrote (*Les Lettres françaises*, 21 March 47): 'it is above all a hymn to the "eternal" peasant and to nature, immutable since the beginning of time ... We see, only or almost only, a "family cell", cut off from the rest of mankind and France'; but, 'despite obvious omissions, the peasants of *Farrebique* do not belong to all time: they are farmers and landowners in the Aveyron in 1946. This is why the film is a great work of art, for the eternal can only be reached through the present.'

[110] *Les Vacances de Monsieur Hulot/Mr Hulot's Holiday* (1953)

d Jacques Tati *pc* Cady/Discina/Eclair Journal *ph* Jacques Mercanton, Jean Mousselle *m* Alain Romans *sc* Tati, Henri Marquet *with* Tati, Nathalie Pascaud, Louis Perrault, Michèle Rolla.

A delightful comedy of manners which tells a good deal about the atmosphere of a holiday resort on the Normandy coast (near to Paris, and so popular just after the war). Needless to say, there are a couple of English tourists.

[111] *Le Beau Serge* (1958)

d Claude Chabrol *pc* AJUM/CGCF *ph* Henri Decae *sc* Chabrol *with* Gérard Blain, Jean-Claude Brialy, Bernadette Lafont, Michèle Meritz.

In an open letter to Chabrol, Bernard Dort (*Les Temps modernes*, Apr 1959) compared this with the director's second feature, *Les Cousins* (1959), contrasting the 'reality' of the village of Sardent in the first to the artificiality of the Parisian bourgeoisie in the second. 'We see Sardent through your eyes, through those of your hero ... The square in front of the church, the children's games, the inhabitants walking past, the *bistrot*, the hotel room, the bad morning coffee, the hop ... This village, both open and shut, impenetrable, warm and cold, intimate and foreign, is more than just true: we all know it, we have all seen and lived it.' Through the central character we discover Sardent and Serge, 'his wasted life, his drunkenness, his irritability'.

Serge is the provincial who didn't get away, François the one who did. But, starting from this apparently clear-cut distinction, Chabrol makes us question the ideas of success and failure, and operates a 'Hitchcockian' transfer of guilt.

[112] *Les Parapluies de Cherbourg/The Umbrellas of Cherbourg* (1964)

d Jacques Demy *pc* Madeleine/Beta (Munich) *m* Michel Legrand *sc* Demy *with* Catherine Deneuve, Nino Castelnuovo, Marc Michel, Anne Vernon, Ellen Farner.

The plot is similar to that of *Marius*: a girl finds herself pregnant after her boyfriend has gone away and enters a marriage of convenience to someone else. In this case, the boyfriend is called up for military service in Algeria and the film does give a powerful feeling of the times and the everyday life of the city where it is set – incredibly, in view of the fact that all the dialogue is sung. Georges Sadoul recognized this realistic element in a package so obviously artificial: 'If I was a lawyer or an obstetrician, I could tell you fifty stories like this one' (*Les Lettres françaises*, 20 Feb 64). 'I saw people weeping near me at some scenes in the film and I was myself profoundly moved by it.'

[113] *Mouchette* (1967)

d Robert Bresson *pc* Parc/Argos *ph* Ghislain Cloquet *sc* Bresson, from the novel by Georges Bernanos *with* Nadine Nortier, Jean-Claude Guilbert, Marie Cardinal.

Bresson's heroine, humiliated and despised, lives in a tragic world, cut off from love and communication with others. Rural life is depicted as cruel and unpleasant, its timeless dimension (like that of Bernanos' story) being indicated by the deliberate juxtaposition of old and new, neither of which is shown as in any way attractive. Bernanos' sense of sin and of the meanness of human existence, finds a perfect expression in Bresson.

[114] *Le Boucher* (1970)

d Claude Chabrol *pc* Les Films La Boétie/Euro International *ph* Jean Rabier *sc* Chabrol *with* Stéphane Audran, Jean-Pierre Cassel, Jean-Claude Drouot.

The village schoolteacher (Audran) falls in love with the butcher, who turns out to be killing more than dumb animals. In *Les Temps modernes* (Apr 1970), Christian Zimmer wrote of 'the loving way in which he has photographed the little village of Trémolat, teaching us in our turn to love its main street, its school, its church, its square and its war memorial ...' and said that the film achieved a perfect balance between 'spectacle' and 'meaning'.

[115] *La Veuve Couderc* (1971)

d Pierre Granier-Deferre *pc* Lira *ph* Walter Wottitz *m* Philippe Sarde *sc* Granier-Deferre, Pascal Jardin, from the novel by Georges Simenon *with* Simone Signoret, Alain Delon, Jean Tissier.

In the 1920s, a country widow shelters a man wanted by the police and falls in love with him. Not, perhaps, on anyone's list of the greatest French films, it is enchantingly photographed in the Burgundy countryside and the details of rural life (except for Signoret's accent) carefully reproduced.

[116] *Poulet au vinaigre/'Cop au vin'* (1985)

d Claude Chabrol *pc* MK2 *ph* Jean Rabier *m* Mathieu Chabrol *sc* Chabrol, Dominique Roulet from his novel *Une Mort en trop,* with Jean Poiret, Stéphane Audran, Lucas Belvaux, Michel Bouquet, Caroline Cellier.

Chabrol's favourite territory: the darker side of the provincial bourgeoisie, with in this case a very vicious police inspector who seems to believe that anything is justified, provided it arrives at the truth.

VIII PARIS

[117] Fantômas (1913–14)
d Louis Feuillade *pc* Gaumont *sc* Feuillade.

Followed by the series of *Judex* and *Les Vampires*, and filmed in the studio and on location in Paris and its suburbs, these helped to reinforce a particular image of the city, derived ultimately from Eugène Sue's novels *Les Mystères de Paris* (1842–43) which were also filmed before World War I. This mythical Parisian underworld thus persists from the popular literature of the 19th century to *Subway* [126], and no doubt beyond.

[118] Sous les toits de Paris (1930)
d René Clair *pc* Tobis *m* Armand Bernard, Raoul Moretti, R. Nazelles *ph* Georges Périnal, Georges Paulet *sc* Clair *ad* Lazare Meerson *with* Albert Préjean, Pola Illéry, Gaston Modot, Edmond Gréville.

The first great success of French sound cinema depicts a less sinister underworld Paris than that of *Fantômas*, but still suggests the mixture of classes and professions through the device of the apartment house: cheap lodgings upstairs, more luxurious ones on the lower floors. 'Alas, it looks as if everyone must get there eventually', Pierre Bost wrote in *La Revue hebdomadaire* (May 1930), admitting that Clair's film was the best French contribution to the 'talkies'. 'A fairly average script, not very successfully situated in *bals-musette*, among somewhat outdated characters (the bandit, the shop-girl, the honest street-vendor) once more demonstrates M. René Clair's skill and intelligence.' The comedy was better, though, in the silent scenes and the *genre* could only lead to less brilliant achievements.

[119] La Chienne (1931)
d Jean Renoir *pc* Braunberger/Richebé *ph* Theodore Sparkuhl, Roger Hubert *sc* Renoir, from the novel by Georges de la Fouchardière *with* Michel Simon, Janie Marèze, Georges Flamand.

Set in Montmartre, Renoir's early venture into sound was disappointing, but includes some stock characters of French cinema in the period, notably the prostitute played by Janie Marèze.

[120] Hôtel du Nord (1938)
d Marcel Carné *pc* Sedif *ph* Armand Thirard *m* Maurice Jaubert *sc* Jacques Prévert, Henri Jeanson, Jean Aurenche, from the novel by Eugène Dabit

ad Alexandre Trauner *with* Arletty, Annabella, Louis Jouvet, Jules Berry, Jean-Pierre Aumont.

The district of the Canal Saint-Martin provides the setting for the story of two couples which has the doom-laden atmosphere of all the Prévert-Carné films of this time. It is remarkable chiefly for the performance of Louis Jouvet, a leading figure in French theatre who was also a great cinema actor.

[121] *Bob le Flambeur/Bob the Gambler* (1955)

d Jean-Pierre Melville *pc* OGC/Jenner/Play Art/La Cyme *ph* Henri Decae
m Eddie Barclay, Jean Boyer *sc* Melville *with* Isabelle Corey, Roger Duchesne, Daniel Cauchy, Guy Decomble, André Garret.

Melville's experience of the underworld around Pigalle (as a *résistant* in the war) served him in good stead. The plot has an ironical twist: a plan to rob the casino at Deauville goes wrong. The film was overshadowed when first released by the successes of *Touchez-pas au grisbi* and *Du rififi chez les hommes*, but Jean-Yves Gonte said that it caught the 'poetic truth' of Montmartre (*Cahiers du Cinéma*, Oct 1956).

[122] *French Cancan* (1955)

d Jean Renoir *pc* Franco-London/Jolly *ph* Michel Kelber *m* Georges van Parys
sc Renoir *with* Jean Gabin, Françoise Arnoul, Maria Félix, Jean-Roger Caussimon.

The history of the Moulin Rouge: a celebration of tourist Paris, perhaps, but filmed with reference to impressionist and post-impressionist paintings, to give a picture of the city's more obvious charm. 'René Clair on an off day,' was the verdict of *Les Temps modernes* (Aug 1955).

[123] *Porte des Lilas/Gate of Lilacs* (1957)

d René Clair *pc* Sonor/Cinetel/Seca/Rizzoli *ph* Robert Le Febvre *m* Georges
Brassens *sc* Clair, Jean Aural, from René Fallet's novel *La Grande ceinture*
ad Léon Barsacq *with* Pierre Brasseur, Brassens, Henri Vidal, Dany Carrel.

'One of the best French films of 1957.' *L'Humanité* proclaimed, in its cinema review of a year that was 'not only that of Brigitte Bardot' (1 Jan 58). 'René Clair takes us back to the films of his youth with his usual affection for the inhabitants of the slums. His romantic crooks are slightly ridiculous: but friendship, the *valse-musette*, the corner *bistrot* and thwarted love are the stars.'

It also marked the only screen appearance of Brassens, a unique figure in French popular music.

[124] *Deux ou trois choses que je sais d'elle/Two or Three Things I Know About Her* (1967)

d Jean-Luc Godard *pc* Annouchka/Argos/Les Films du Carrosse/Parc *ph* Raoul Coutard *sc* Godard, from an investigation by Cathérine Vimonet *with* Marina Vlady, Anny Duperey, Roger Montsoret, Jean Narboni.

Godard's study of the satellite housing estates which were growing up around Paris at this time ('homes for the incurable'), suggesting that bored housewives, left alone during the day, resorted to prostitution. This is combined with Godard's habitual reflexions on communication and other matters.

[125] *Playtime* (1967)

d Jacques Tati *pc* Specta *ph* Jean Bourgoin *m* Franck Barcellini, Alain Romans *sc* Tati, Jacques Lagrange *with* Tati, Jean-Pierre Zola.

Tati's most savage attack on the New Paris, centring on a group of tourists who visit this 'anywhere' of glass and concrete, rather than the real city which was still somewhere to be found.

[126] *Subway* (1985)

d Luc Besson *pc* Loup/TFS/Gaumont/TF1 *ph* Carlo Varini *m* Eric Serra *sc* Besson, Pierre Jolivet *ad* Alexandre Trauner *with* Christophe Lambert, Isabelle Adjani, Michel Galabru, Jean-Hughes Anglade, Richard Bohringer.

Subway opens with a splendid car chase that actually finishes in the *métro* where Christophe Lambert escapes from his pursuers to become a latter-day Fantômas brandishing a light-stick and surrounded by a collection of *marginaux* who are supposed to inhabit the passageways behind the subway stations. No wonder Adjani prefers the company of these freaks to the ones in the polite dining-rooms of her husband's friends. It was one of France's most successful film exports of the year.

IX   CRIME AND THE LAW

[127] *L'Alibi* (1937)

d Pierre Chenal *pc* BN *ph* Ted Pahle, Jacques Mercanton *m* Georges Auric *sc* Marcel Achard *with* Jany Holt, Margo Lion, Louis Jouvet, Erich von Stroheim, Albert Préjean, Roger Blin.

'Melodrama and a complete absence of taste', was Georges Sadoul's description of *L'Alibi* in *Le Cinéma français* (Flammarion, 1962), but Chenal is still one of the most varied and neglected directors of the period. He produced documentaries (*Les Petits métiers de Paris*, 1932, on Parisian street life), dramas (*La Rue sans nom*, 1934, an example of 'poetic realism') and thrillers. This confronts a murderer (von Stroheim) with an early type of the unscrupulous and cynical detective (Jouvet). Its chief weakness lies in Achard's script.

[128] *Le Dernier tournant* (1939)

> *d* Pierre Chenal *pc* Gladiator *ph* Claude Renoir, Christian Matras *sc* Henri Torrès, from James M. Cain's novel *The Postman Always Rings Twice ad* Georges Wakhévitch, Maurice Colasson *with* Corinne Luchaire, Florence Marly, Fernand Gravey, Robert Le Vigan, Michel Simon.

One of the many adaptations of Cain's thriller in which the murderer gets away with his crime, only to be convicted of the killing of his accomplice (Luchaire) for which he was not responsible. The seedy American roadhouse is successfully transformed into a seedy French roadhouse, and the American depression atmosphere to France. In neither case is one surprised that the characters will stick at nothing to escape, even if it is fate, rather than justice, that punishes them in the end.

[129] *Justice est faite* (1950)

> *d* André Cayatte *pc* Silver *ph* Jean Bourgoin *m* Raymond Legrand *sc* Charles Spaak, Cayatte *with* Valentine Tessier, Claude Nollier, Jacques Castelor, Michel Auclair.

One of Cayatte's four social dramas: the others are *Nous sommes tous des assassins* (1952), *Avant le déluge* (1953) and *Le Dossier Noir* (1955) which dealt with euthanasia, the death penalty and other topics. On the first two of these films, *Les Temps modernes* (July 1952) carried articles by Jean Cau and Bernard Dort. 'If a family was not forced to live in one room, a tired and overwrought father would not brain his child because it was crying,' Cau wrote. 'And if the Assistance Publique was not a jail for children, the children would not later become adult jailbirds.' Dort replied by questioning Cau's criteria for judging *Nous sommes tous des assassins*, describing it as 'a sensation-seeking film', propagandist and simplistic in construction, and preferring *Justice est faite*.

An interesting reaction in *Télé-Ciné* (No. 35, 1953), in an article by J.-P. Noel on *Nous sommes tous des assassins* – a reminder that Catholic opinion was (and is) divided on the abolition of the death penalty: 'Does not "understanding" the criminal mean absolving him, at least partially? Is this not an implicit encouragement to all other possible murderous acts? . . . Major objections can be raised to Cayatte's underlying thesis.'

On the death penalty, see Lelouch's *La Vie, l'amour, la mort* [146]. The treatment of juvenile offenders was dealt with in the documentary fiction *Chiens perdus sans colliers* (1955), Jean Delannoy's adaptation of Gilbert Cesbron's novel, starring Jean Gabin.

[130] *Casque d'Or* (1952)

> *d* Jacques Becker *pc* Speva/Paris *ph* Robert Le Febvre *m* Georges van Parys

sc Backer, Jacquez Companeez *ad* Jean d'Eaubonne *with* Serge Reggiani, Simone Signoret, Claude Dauphin, Raymond Bussières.

A period piece, set at the turn of the century, this could probably have as well gone under Paris or History; but the period setting is largely incidental, though carefully recreated, like the Parisian sets. 'This Paris 1900 does not come out of a fashion book,' Colette Audry wrote in *Les Temps modernes* (July 1952), adding that Becker 'has a gift for satire which he should exploit'. Georges Sadoul (*Les Lettres françaises*, 18 Apr 52), said that the plot was taken from a celebrated court case of the time. An ordinary working man falls in love with the mistress of a criminal and is eventually guillotined after committing a justifiable murder and being betrayed by the woman's lover.

Sadoul compared Reggiani's role with those played by Gabin in the 1930s: 'Serge Reggiani does not labour under the weight of a destiny that comes direct from old German films and Greek tragedy. He is, to speak the language of 1900, "a victim of society".' As for Becker, 'he has rediscovered the realistic poetry of Paris and its suburbs, the secret of which seemed to have disappeared with Feuillade.'

[131] *Touchez-pas au grisbi/Grisbi* (1954)

d Jacques Becker *pc* Del Duca/Silver/Antarès *ph* Pierre Montazel *m* Jean Wiener *sc* Becker, Maurice Griffe, Albert Simonin, from Simonin's novel *ad* Jean d'Eaubonne *with* Jean Gabin, René Dary, Paul Frankeur, Lino Ventura, Jeanne Moreau, Victor Franken.

Gabin's 'middle period': friendship takes the place of love, world-weariness has at last overcome hope and the ambition is not to escape, but to get enough money to settle down. Colette Audry analysed Gabin's part at length in *Les Temps modernes* (Nov 1954): 'the story of a gangster, a womanizer, cynical, intrepid, who can only finally be defeated by his own heart which is too loyal to his feeble and clumsy friend'. The ageing Gabin becomes the opposite of the stereotype, imagining rest 'because the life he leads seems *ridiculous to him at his age* . . . We have reached the moment when the genre still persists and keeps its style, but empty of substance. This is illustrated by the hero's relationships with women. It is nothing new to discover that gangster films are misogynistic, but women were still expected to produce a certain effect on "men". Max has moved beyond that. Perhaps the conversation of little dancing-girls does bore him, that one understands; that he does not, like his friend Riton, risk being taken for a ride, is his bounden duty as a gangster; but that he should prefer to sleep alone, is quite new.'

In *Télé-Ciné*, Gilbert Salachas admitted that, *à la limite*, the film might teach fraternity and humility, but in the main it was 'far from edifying'.

[132] *Les Diaboliques/Diabolique* (1955)

d Henri-Georges Clouzot *pc* Filmsonor *ph* Armand Thirard *m* Georges van Parys *sc* Clouzot, Jérôme Géronimi, from the novel *Celle qui n'était plus* by Boileau and Narcejac *with* Simone Signoret, Véra Clouzot, Paul Meurisse, Charles Vanel, Pierre Larquey.

A shocker: the story of a plot by two women to murder the husband of one of them, with a totally improbable twist in the tail (very similar to the 1985 Boileau-Narcejac adaptation *Les Louves/Letters to an Unknown Lover*, made by the British director Peter Duffell). The shameless audience manipulation was not what attracted critical attention at the time. Gilbert Salachas in *Télé-Ciné* (No. 46, 1955): 'The world described . . . is the most sordid, the most base, the most negative in modern mankind. Everything there is unhealthy, tainted, vile or twisted.' Clouzot 'does not seem to be repulsed by the emptiness and the sickening monstrosity of his little world. He appears to enjoy it and to glut himself with horrors . . . If *Les Diaboliques* is a joke, it is not a very agreeable one' and 'one can only be amazed . . . at the almost collective aberration of journalists and critics who are usually better informed and who have managed to promote such a desperately empty work.'

[133] *Du Rififi chez les hommes/Rififi* (1955)

d Jules Dassin *pc* Henri Bérard *ph* Philippe Agostini *m* Georges Auric *sc* Dassin, René Wheeler, Auguste le Breton, from le Breton's novel *ad* Alexandre Trauner *with* Jean Servais, Carl Möhner, Robert Manuel.

A suspense thriller with all the ingredients of the French version of the genre: friendship, irony and Parisian locations, and a celebrated scene of a jewel robbery filmed in total silence which remains one of the most gripping moments in the cinema.

[134] *Ascenseur pour l'échafaud/Lift to the Scaffold* (1958)

d Louis Malle *pc* Nouvelles Editions de Films *ph* Henri Decae *m* Miles Davis *sc* Malle, Roger Nimier, from the novel by Noel Calef *with* Maurice Ronet, Jeanne Moreau, Georges Poujouly, Yori Bertin, Lino Ventura.

The conventional ingredients of suspense and irony combine in Malle's first film. Moreau plots with her lover Ronet to kill her husband, but it all goes wrong when he gets stuck in a lift (the suspense) and his car is stolen by a young tearaway who uses Ronet's gun to commit another murder. Ronet escapes from the lift, only to be arrested for the crime he did not commit. Georges Sadoul wondered why a young director (Malle was 25) should have to tackle such a ridiculous theme, imposed on him because producers found such subjects 'commercial', though the public was sick of them (*Les Lettres françaises*, 30 Jan 58).

Other critics looked more closely at Malle's treatment of this conventional plot and found the characters and style of the film deeply significant. 'His characters belong precisely to our time, to 1957,' Armand Monjo wrote in *L'Humanité* (1 Feb 58). '. . . they evoke, in a few gestures or a few lines, the important problems of our age: the ultra-rich arms dealer who has interests in Saharan oil ("How many thousand million francs did you make out of the war in Indo-China? And now, how much from Algeria?", asks his "right-hand man" [Ronet] before killing him); the former parachutist [Ronet] who coldly and meticulously plans the murder of his mistress' husband . . .'

In *Les Temps modernes* (May 1958), Raymond Borde went further along the same path to conclude that 'in every sense of the word, *Ascenseur pour l'échafaud* is a Fascist film.' Right-wing critics, 'understandably, have hailed Louis Malle as a new Vadim ... Like Vadim, he is the victim of certain myths ... One can see that he is obsessed by the exterior marks of wealth ... the motorway motel where you drink champagne with former SS officers, now Common Market businessmen ... These monied Teutons take pride of place in the mythology of Louis Malle and Roger Vadim. They have lived through the Hitler "adventure".' But 'the human model which Louis Malle offers for mass admiration is still more suspect and repulsive [Ronet] ... He kills the arms dealer. This noble murder recommends him to the sympathy of the audience ... He is admired: "That bloke, he's covered with medals and wounds ... He's got incredible style." ' Finally, there is 'a young tearaway in a leather jacket ... a future parachutist' – 'a fashionable little tough guy, a 35-year-old ex-officer and a neo-Nazi capitalist, make up the three reference points of Louis Malle's inner dream'.

[135] *En cas de malheur/Love is My Profession* (1958)

d Claude Autant-Lara *pc* Iéna *ph* Jacques Natteau *m* René Cloerec *sc* Jean Aurenche, Pierre Bost, from the novel by Georges Simenon *ad* Max Douy *with* Jean Gabin, Brigitte Bardot, Edwige Feuillère, Franco Interlenghi.

One of the three films chosen to represent France in Venice, it brought together old and new figures in French cinema, in conventional characters: Gabin as a lawyer, Feuillère as his wife and Bardot as a young prostitute. It was less a herald of the New Wave, however, than the meeting of the commercial cinema and the 'cinema of quality'.

[136] *La Tête contre les murs/The Keepers* (1958)

d Georges Franju *pc* Attica/Sirius/Elpenor *ph* Eugen Shuftan *m* Maurice Jarre *sc* Jean-Pierre Mocky, from the novel by Hervé Bazin *ad* Louis Le Barbenchon *with* Mocky, Pierre Brasseur, Paul Meurisse, Anouk Aimée, Charles Aznavour.

The central character is a young delinquent whose father, a middle-class lawyer, has him put away after an apparently 'inexplicable' crime. Filmed inside an actual asylum, it questions both the treatment of mental illness and society's definition of it.

[137] *Pickpocket* (1959)

d Robert Bresson *pc* Agnès Delahaie *ph* Léonce-Henri Burel *sc* Bresson *with* Martin Lassalle, Marika Green, Pierre Leymarie, Pierre Etaix.

The inspiration came from Dostoievsky's *Crime and Punishment*, but the style and atmosphere are entirely Bresson's. Sadoul (*Le Cinéma français*, Flammarion, 1962) said that the director had advanced still further into Jansenist asceticism, depriving the film of any dramatic artifice, but noted that however 'mystical' his approach, 'he knows how to recreate, intensely, certain contemporary realities'.

[138]   *A bout de souffle/Breathless* (1960)

d Jean-Luc Godard *pc* Georges de Beauregard/SNC/Impéria *ph* Raoul Coutard
m Martial Solal *sc* Godard, from an idea by François Truffaut *with* Jean-Paul
Belmondo, Jean Seberg, Claude Mansard, Daniel Boulanger.

Godard's first feature uses the conventions of the Hollywood 'B' movie and makes them
entirely his own. This new version of the New Wave did not appeal to Georges Sadoul
(*Les Lettres françaises*, 31 March 60); the Left had just started to come to terms with the
old one. 'I prefer the sincerity of *Le Beau Serge* or *Les 400 coups* to this astonishing
success, in which neither the heroes nor the plot appeal to me.'

He goes on to quote Godard's assertion that, since it was 'conformist' to hate the
police, his hero was unconventional when he said 'I like cops'. 'This anti-conformism is
worse than the worst conformism . . . Godard declared in these pages: "I have made the
anarchist film I dreamed of." Fine. But one may judge that his rebellion is far from being
a left-wing one.'

In *Les Temps modernes* (Apr–May – 1960), Gérard Bonnet saw the film more in terms
of the influence of Hollywood on society and 'the priority given to effect, this taste for
style pushed if necessary to the point of murder.' 'Conventional opinion has long
wondered whether cinema can express the whole of human reality. Jean-Luc Godard's
film offers an unexpected solution to this aesthetic problem . . . It predicts that there will
soon be no other human reality than that which the cinema can express. It
demonstrates this with convincing talent. But should we rejoice?'

[139]   *Le Trou/The Hole* (1960)

d Jacques Becker *pc* Play Art/Filmsonor/Titanus *ph* Ghislain Cloquet *sc* Becker,
José Giovanni, Jean Aurel, from Giovanni's novel *ad* Rino Mondellini
with Michel Constantin, Jean Keraudy, Philippe Leroy.

Becker returns to his favourite themes of loyalty and friendship in this story of a prison
escape, with no background music and non-professional actors. Raymond Borde (*Les
Temps modernes*, Apr–May 1960) called it 'an astonishing "drama of objects"' and
praised its 'micro-sociological' descriptions, using the opportunity for a dig at the New
Wave: 'the film shows a mastery beside which the little audacities of the New Wave are
feeble stammerings'.

[140]   *Le Cave se rebiffe*/US: *The Counterfeiters of Paris* (1961)

d Gilles Grangier *sc* Michel Audiard, Albert Simonin *with* Jean Gabin.

One of many gangster movies of the period, none of which could equal *Touchez pas au
grisbi* [130] or *Du rififi chez les hommes* [131], though many of them seemed to use Gabin
whose personality dictated the real meaning of the film. 'A million French people have
already seen *Le Cave se rebiffe*,' Claude Tarare wrote (*Les Temps modernes*, Dec 1961),
quoting the distributors' publicity for the film. 'One might more truly say: a million
French people have *already seen themselves* in *Le Cave se rebiffe* . . . as they are and as they
imagine themselves to be.' The crooks talk slang, but think as *bourgeois* and live like

bourgeois: 'A documentary on our contemporaries ... average Frenchmen, reading *L'Aurore* and *Le Parisien libéré.*' And Tarare's description of Gabin's 'godfather' role might have suggested some interesting comparisons to his readers: 'The Father has retired from active life, but in his field, he was a master. He *is* a master, so much so that former colleagues come and ... beg him to go back to work. Coquettish, the Father takes a little persuasion; then he accepts, nostalgic for a job well done and irritated at seeing his successors blundering about in the work he loves. Combining authority, calmness, seriousness, prudence, efficiency and humour, the Father sees the job through successfully, defeats and tricks his associates who intended to trick him, then goes back to his distant rural retreat ...'

Three years earlier, de Gaulle had been persuaded (with the support of the Army, which expected him to maintain the French presence in Algeria) to leave his country home in Colombey-les-Deux-Eglises and take over the presidency. Finding that French rule in Algeria was doomed, he granted the country independence, to the dismay of some elements of the Army who rebelled on the barricades of 1960 and later formed the Organisation Armée Secrète for a terrorist campaign which reached its height in 1962. De Gaulle did not return to his country retreat until 1969.

[141] *Le Doulos*/US: *Doulos – The Finger Man* (1963)

d Jean-Pierre Melville *pc* Rome-Paris/Champion *ph* Nicolas Hayer *sc* Melville, from the novel by Pierre Lesou *with* Jean-Pierre Belmondo, Serge Reggiani, Jean Desailly, Fabienne Dali, Michel Piccoli, Monique Hennessy.

'Le doulos' means 'the informer'; so, too, does 'la balance' (see [150]) – and in both films the informer is a woman, though the male lead is suspected. Melville's complex plot is really a morality about appearance and reality, love and betrayal, though Patrick Bureau, in *Les Lettres françaises* (14 Feb 63) saw it as a 'disturbing apology of the informer's trade'. Jean Rochereau (*La Croix*, 16 Feb 63) interpreted it as showing the 'universal implications and tragic dimension' of the police informer. *Le Monde* (Jean de Baroncelli, 14 Feb 63) described the film as 'great cinema', though it found the police mythology questionable.

[142] *Bande à part*/*The Outsiders*/US: *Band of Outsiders* (1964)

d Jean-Luc Godard *pc* Annouchka/Orsay *ph* Raoul Coutard *m* Michel Legrand *sc* Godard, from the novel *Fool's Gold* by D. and B. Hitchens *with* Anna Karina, Sami Frey, Claude Brasseur, Louisa Colpeyn.

The publisher Gallimard's celebrated detective fiction list, the *série noire*, specialized in translations of American thrillers and give its name to a particular sub-genre of the crime novel. French film-makers were attracted to the cynical outlook and sleazy atmosphere of these works, which could easily be translated to a French setting. *Bande à part*, set in the Paris suburbs, is a tribute, with the usual Godardian interjection of reflexions on a variety of apparently unconnected topics.

[143] *Pierrot le Fou* (1965)

d Jean-Luc Godard *pc* Rome-Paris Films/Dino de Laurentis *ph* Raoul Coutard *m* Antoine Duhamel *sc* Godard, from a novel by Lionel White *with* Jean-Paul Belmondo, Anna Karina, Dirk Sanders, Raymond Devos.

Once more, Godard transforms his basic material to make a completely individual work. Belmondo and Karina meet, fall in love, commit murder and rampage across France, enjoying one of those brief idylls that recur in the genre. Godard is 'consistent in his inconsistency,' Jeancolas remarks (*Le Cinéma des français*, Stock, 1979). '. . . like a street urchin who does not respect the rules of the game, he expresses the unease of an increasing number of young people in a country ruled by a very old man according to very old principles.'

Pierrot's adventures are 'not absurd'. Georges Sadoul wrote (*Les Lettres françaises*, 11 Nov 65), calling this the 'best French film of the year'.

[144] *Le Deuxième souffle/Second Breath* (1966)

d Jean-Pierre Melville *pc* Montaigne *ph* Marcel Combes *m* Bernard Gérard *sc* Melville, José Giovanni from his novel *with* Lino Ventura, Paul Meurisse, Raymond Pellegrin, Christine Fabrega, Michel Constantin.

To combat the terrorists of the OAS, De Gaulle's secret service established its own force of '*barbouzes*', a 'parallel police' working under deep cover and using the same methods as their enemies. The existence of these, and the *brigades territoriales*, formed later to combat organized crime by similar means, caused a great deal of disquiet which crime films began to show through the interrogation methods of brutal inspectors and an implied identification of police and criminals. The inspector in Melville's film, a torturer and a coward, is the double of the criminal he pursues; only an accident puts them on different sides. 'An intuitive policeman ... and an honourable crook,' was Jean Rochereau's conclusion in *La Croix* (5 Nov 66). Marcel Martin in *Les Lettres françaises* (10 Nov 66) wrote that this was 'a work of very high class'.

[145] *Le Samourai/The Samourai* (1967)

d Jean-Pierre Melville *pc* Filmel/CICC/FIDA *ph* Henri Decae *m* François de Roubaix *sc* Melville *with* Alain Delon, Nathalie Delon, François Périer, Cathy Rosier.

Delon establishing his type as an amoral hired assassin. Melville's concern is with the solitary outsider. 'A masterpiece, precise, painful and ironical,' Samuel Lachize said in *L'Humanité* (28 Oct 67).

Melville's concentration on the technical details of the contract killer's work, Christian Zimmer wrote in *Les Temps modernes* (Dec 1967), 'has something of a religious ceremony and, at the same time, the fastidious routine of a minor civil servant.' Comparing the film to Bo Widerberg's *Elvira Madigan* ('Classical Melville and Romantic Widerberg'), he said that Melville believed exclusively in a Bergsonian notion of time: i.e. time as relative and subjective, not as simple duration. He noted too, in a survey of three recent Melville films, *Le Doulos* [141], *Le Deuxième souffle* [144] and *Le Samourai*, similarities in the contrast between policemen and criminals: 'those who talk, compose phrases, sayings, literature, are the policemen; the crooks do not express themselves either in words or in facial expressions, but in their appearance, their behaviour and their gestures.' And, in Melville's choice of theatre actors to play the policemen, in a theatrical style, and cinema actors for the criminals (Desailly/Belmondo, Meurisse/Ventura, Périer/Delon), he suggested a permanent struggle between 'naturalness and lies' in society.

[146] *La Vie, l'amour, la mort/Life, Love, Death* (1968)

d Claude Lelouch *pc* Ariane/Films 13/Artistes Associés *ph* Jean Collomb *m* Francis Lai *sc* Lelouch *with* Amidou, Caroline Cellier, Janine Magnan.

A polemic against the death penalty (not finally abolished until 1981, though hardly ever applied in the 1970s). The central character is an Arab who kills a prostitute after a sexual humiliation. The inhuman ritual leading to the guillotine is described in minute and gruesome detail. 'There is a new dimension in Lelouch's work, the mature and secret virtue of compassion,' Danièle Heymann wrote in *L'Express* (19 Jan 69).

There were doubts, however, about the evident weighting of the case: the criminal is shown as 'so likeable, outside his lethal crises, that the spectator is in danger of being convinced by a sentimental rather than a rational reaction', Marcel Martin objected in *Les Lettres françaises* (Jan 1971). 'We seem to have returned to the (prewar) Gabin myth', with Gabin as the model working man denied happiness because of the wickedness of others or the blindness of fate. '*La Vie, l'amour, la mort* is a perfect consumer durable ... The problem it raises, being stated in terms of psychology and morality, can only be resolved in terms of feeling and pathos. This is why the case is biased.'

[147] *Le Cercle rouge/The Red Circle* (1970)

d Jean-Pierre Melville *pc* Corona/Selenia *ph* Henri Decae *m* Eric de Marsan *sc* Melville *with* Alain Delon, Bourvil, Yves Montand, François Périer, Gian-Maria Volonte.

The Melville themes taken a step further, to create an enclosed, entirely mythological world. Delon, again, is the criminal: he was to star in Melville's last film, *Un Flic*, made in the following year.

[148] *Diva* (1981)

d Jean-Jacques Beineix *pc* Galaxie/Greenwich/A2 *ph* Philippe Rousselot *m* Vladimir Cosma *sc* Beineix, Jean van Hamme, from the novel by Delacorta *ad* Hilton McConnico *with* Frédéric Andrei, Roland Bertin, Richard Bohringer, Wilhelmina Wiggins Fernandez.

Despite the operatic theme and treatment and the confused and confusing plot, *Diva* resolves itself into a fairly conventional shoot-out. It became something of a cult movie.

[149] *La Balance* (1982)
> *d* Bob Swaim *pc* Ariane/A2 *ph* Bernard Zitzermann *m* Roland Bocquet, Boris Bergman *sc* Swaim *with* Nathalie Baye, Philippe Léotard, Richard Berry, Maurice Ronet.

'Superficial characterization and gratuitous violence', based on the worst American TV series, according to Roy Armes (*French Cinema*, Secker and Warburg, 1985). This is to ignore the film's close attention to its location (Belleville, with a mixed population, mainly from North Africa), and the particular significance for a French audience of the assertion that certain units of the police, in this case the *brigades territoriales*, are, if anything, worse than those they try to bring to justice (compare *Le Doulos* [141]). Even the character of the warm-hearted and loyal prostitute, though a cliché, is a cliché from French cinema going back to the 1930s.

[150] *Vivement dimanche/Finally Sunday*/US: *Confidentially Yours* (1983)
> *d* François Truffaut *pc* Les Films du Carrosse/A2/Soprofilms *ph* Nestor Almendros *m* Georges Delerue *sc* Truffaut, Suzanne Schiffman, Jean Aurel, from the novel *The Long Saturday Night* by Charles Williams *with* Fanny Ardent, Jean-Louis Trintignant, Jean-Pierre Kalfon, Caroline Sihol.

Truffaut's last film was disappointing in some ways, but at the same time a summary of one aspect of his work and a further expression of his admiration for Hitchcock: the plot concerns an estate agent's relationship with his secretary who has to be convinced of his innocence when he is accused of killing his wife (suggesting a number of Hitchcock plots, from *The Thirty-Nine Steps* onwards, as well as the Hitchcock themes of guilt and suspicion). The Riviera and night club locations are conventional, but part of the same celebration of Hollywood *film noir* and comedy. The Office Catholique Français du Cinéma, recommending it for adolescent audiences, described it as 'quality entertainment which does not take itself too seriously.'

X   WOMEN AND THE FAMILY

[151] *La Vérité sur Bébé Donge* (1952)
> *d* Henri Decoin *pc* UGC *ph* Léonce-Henri Burel *m* Jean-Jacques Grunewald *sc* M. Auberge, from the novel by Georges Simenon *with* Danielle Darrieux, Jean Gabin, Daniel Lecourtois.

A wife murders her husband, disillusioned with the stifling environment of her bourgeois marriage. 'There is a dimension of love which seems excluded from this view,' *Télé-Ciné* (Nos. 32–33, 1953) wrote. 'It is that of suffering, of gratuity . . . Another "truth" also emerges from the film . . . the need for realistic and spiritual preparation for marriage.'

[152] *Papa, Maman, la bonne et moi* (1954)
d Jean-Paul Le Chanois.

A successful comedy (Le Chanois did a sequel in the following year), but, as Raymond Borde noted (*Les Temps modernes*, Jan 1955), the director 'gives his films a social content and at times a political one'. He praised the opening scene showing the typical inhabitants of an apartment house and the portrait of the (typical?) middle-class family, 'the father, science teacher at Saint-Beuve, a sadico-anal type who keeps his money in a tin, the mother, who does translations of detective novels in her spare time . . .'

[153] *Et Dieu créa la femme/And God Created Woman* (1956)
d Roger Vadim *p* Raoul Levy *with* Brigitte Bardot, Curt Jurgens.

Not at first successful in France, Vadim's film did enormously well in the United States and established Bardot's image. France was entering a brief period of 'star fever' which culminated around Bardot's marriage to Jacques Charrier and the birth of their child. The intense interest of the press in such events was bewailed by some cinema-lovers and the films were condemned by Catholics and conservatives who found them immoral. However, in a round-table discussion organized by *Cahiers du cinéma* (May 1957), Jacques Doniol-Valcroze described Vadim's film as 'a very good essay' on his ideas about love and sexual relationships. *Cahiers* liked Vadim most of all because he did not set out to make films of social comment (they condemned Jean-Paul Le Chanois and André Cayatte for doing precisely that). Vadim's films, they felt, expressed deeper truths about contemporary society.

[154] *Le Miroir à deux faces* (1959)
d André Cayatte *pc* Gaumont/Franco-London/Union/CEI *ph* Christian Matras *sc* Cayatte, Gérard Oury *with* Michèle Morgan, Bourvil, Oury, Ivan Desny.

'The young wife has accepted it all: the kids, the money put aside, penny by penny, the bawling-out by her mother-in-law and the passive idiot of a husband. She is the prisoner of these hideous worms. Thousands of women are in her position.' (Raymond Borde, *Les Temps modernes*, Jan 1959). '. . . an important film . . . full of genuine glimpses of the petty bourgeoisie of Le Vésinet or Montreuil . . . Some women spectators will, perhaps, on returning home, have the courage to rebel.'

[155] *Cléo de 5 à 7/Cleo from 5 to 7* (1961)

d Agnès Varda *pc* Rome-Paris *ph* Jean Rabier *m* Michel Legrand *sc* Varda
with Corinne Marchand, Antoine Bourseiller, Dorothée Blank, Michel
Legrand.

Cléo waits, around the Luxembourg Gardens and the Parc Montsouris, for the result of a medical test. She meets a young soldier on leave from military service. Her private anxieties about cancer, his about being killed in Algeria, suggest more public concerns. Georges Sadoul (*Les Lettres françaises*, 12 Apr 62) called it 'a real film, modern and profoundly of our time', telling the story of 'two victims of two cancers, one of them (which one neither dared nor was able to name) being called "Algerian war"'.

[156] *Une Femme mariée/The Married Woman* (1964)

d Jean-Luc Godard *pc* Annouchka/Orsay *ph* Raoul Coutard *sc* Godard
with Macha Méril, Philippe Leroy, Bernard Noel, Roger Leenhardt, Rita
Maiden.

Originally '*la* femme mariée', but the censor refused this on the grounds that it might be taken to mean that the film depicted married women in general, rather than just one of the species. The Godard mixture of parody, quotation, documentary, pseudo-documentary and fiction is, as with all his films, impossible to summarize in a few words.

[157] *La Peau douce/Silken Skin/*US: *The Soft Skin* (1964)

d François Truffaut *pc* Les Films du Carrosse/SEDIF *ph* Raoul Coutard
m Georges Delerue *sc* Truffaut, Jean-Louis Richard *with* Françoise Dorléac,
Jean Desailly, Nelly Benedetti, Daniel Ceccaldi.

The break-up of a marriage, a theme that Truffaut was later to treat as part of his cycle of films about Antoine Doinel in *Domicile conjugal*. In this case, the man is a middle-aged academic who falls in love with an air hostess: his feelings and the needs and feelings of the two women are sympathetically analysed, without moralizing.

[158] *La Fiancée du pirate/*US: *A Very Curious Girl* (1969)

d Nelly Kaplan *pc* Cythère *ph* Jean Badard *m* Georges Moustaki *sc* Kaplan,
Claude Makovsky *ad* Michel Landi *with* Bernadette Lafont, Georges Genet.

Like the central character in Varda's *Sans toit ni loi* [163], the 'pirate's fiancée' chooses to live alone, implying that to be free a woman must always be an outsider in a male-dominated society. Happily prostituting herself, she becomes the exploiter, not the victim of men, whom she despises as she despises their conformist wives. When finally they combine against her, she turns the tables on them all and marches off triumphant. A very funny, anarchistic and anti-clerical film, including a bitter satire on rural life.

[159] *L'Enfance nue/Naked Childhood*/us: *Me* (1969)

d Maurice Pialat *pc* Parc/Les Films du Carrosse/Renn/Para-france *pc* Claude Beausoleil *sc* Pialat *with* Michel Tarrazon, Marie-Louise Thierry, René Thierry, Marie Marc.

Pialat's first feature, by a director who also worked in television, was the story of an unwanted child (see [161]).

[160] *La Cage aux folles* (1978)

d Edouard Molinaro *pc* Artistes Associés/Da Ma Produzione *ph* Armando Nannuzzi *m* Ennio Morricone *sc* Francis Veber, Molinaro, Marcello Danon, Jean Poiret, from Poiret's play *with* Ugo Tognazzi, Michel Serrault, Claire Maurier, Remi Laurent, Michel Galabru.

The family? Certainly. A homosexual couple who run a night club on the Riviera have to resort to subterfuge when the son of one of them falls in love with the daughter of a respectable politician and the boy's mother, a successful businesswoman, refuses to join in the deception. The homosexual couple are caricature gays, but the film did reverse some other preconceptions as well as finding a wide audience for a comedy entirely sympathetic to a homosexual relationship. It led to the inevitable sequels and it is interesting to note that the Office Catholique, which would undoubtedly have condemned them had they been made earlier, classified *La Cage aux folles II* as grade 4, 'suitable for adult audiences' and regretted that a dull film had been made of a story 'that might, as well as laughter, have provoked reflection on homosexuality, old age and the way we are seen by others'.

[161] *Le Destin de Juliette/Juliette's Fate/Juliette's Destiny* (1982)

d Aline Issermann *pc* Laura/A2/PR Communication *ph* Dominique le Rigoleur *m* Bernard Lubat *sc* Issermann, Michel Dufresne *with* Laure Duthilleul, Richard Bohringer, Véronique Silver, Pierre Forget, Didier Agostini.

Juliette is forced into marriage with Marcel, a railway worker, so that her family can keep their SNCF tied cottage. He is frustrated in this loveless match and takes to drink. The Office Catholique du Cinéma, recommending it for adolescent audiences, said that it showed the persistence of patterns from one generation to another in the lives of the working-class and peasantry, and the complex relationships of 'a couple made up of two solitudes … A powerful film, without complacency, in which tenderness overrides melodrama.'

[162] *A nos amours/To Our Loves* (1983)

d Maurice Pialat *pc* Les Films du Livradois/Gaumont/FR 3 *ph* Jacques Loiseleux *sc* Pialat, Arlette Langmann *with* Sandrine Bonnaire, Pialat, Evelyne Ker, Dominique Besnehard.

Pialat examines the nuclear family, centring in turn on the sexual awakening of an adolescent girl, her parents' marriage, her downtrodden mother, her mixed-up and over-protective brother, her boyfriends and her relationship with her father. Where other films on family life have tended to show it in terms of a single conflict (husband and wife, child and parents), he reveals a complex bundle of relationships, each problematic, each impinging on the others.

The Office Catholique du Cinéma recommended it for adolescents with reservations ('some ideas may offend') and called it 'a hard film' which did not set itself up as a model of behaviour. 'It leads to reflection on love and relationships, seeing them as something other than ... conformity with accepted notions, mere appearances and the deceptive "sexual revolution".'

[163] *Sans toit ni loi/Vagabonde* (1985)
  d Agnès Varda *pc* A2/Ministère de la Culture/Ciné-Tamaris *ph* Patrick Blossier *m* Joanna Bruzdowicz *sc* Varda *with* Sandrine Bonnaire, Macha Méril, Stéphane Freiss, Marthe Jarnais, Yahiaoui Assouna.

In the style of a documentary-drama, Varda traces the last days in the life of a girl found dead in a vineyard in southern France, uncovering a fiercely independent character, envied by most of those who came in contact with her for her determination to remain free of all social obligations. Filmed on location, using mainly non-professional actors, the film shows, too, the local people, immigrant workers and drop-outs (*les marginaux*) who inhabit the area and has a definite documentary interest (e.g. in recording the Franglais used by the young people with whom Mona associates). The story of her bid for freedom is at times moving, ultimately depressing, because it implies that such total independence is unattainable.

XI CHILDHOOD AND YOUTH

[164] *Visages d'enfants/Faces of Children* (1923)
  d Jacques Feyder *pc* Zoubaloff-Perchet *ph* Léonce-Henri Burel, Paul Parguel *sc* Feyder *with* Jean Forest, Victor Vance, Arlette Peyran.

A boy coming to terms with the arrival of a step-mother. Feyder achieved extraordinary performances from his child actors and Burel's photography explores the scenery of the Valais, in Switzerland, where the film is set.

[165] *Zéro de conduite* (1933)
  d Jean Vigo *pc* Gaumont/Franco/Aubert *ph* Boris Kaufman *m* Maurice Jaubert *sc* Vigo *with* Jean Dasté, Louis Lefebvre, Gilbert Pruchon, Delphin.

'We feel almost obliged to defend this moralizing, demagogic and tedious film,' Raymond Borde wrote in *Les Temps modernes* (Apr 1959), 'when it is attacked from the Right. Imbeciles have protested, respectable fathers have deplored the bad example it gives to young people and the Mayor of Nice ... has taken out a banning order against *Les Tricheurs*. Marcel Carné's timid provocations ... have been enough to scandalize unrepentant Pétainists ... We are likely to end by defending what we hate: false daring which hides conformism, and a delight in punishment ... Marcel Carné describes the youth of Saint-Germain-des-Prés in 1958. They go to the café, dance, ride their scooters ... The girls sleep around ... Now, there's something you don't often see. Will *Les Tricheurs* strike a new note in French cinema? No such luck! The girls are punished.' Clo, the rich girl, is pregnant; when asked if she is going to keep the baby, she says 'yes ... I'm a Christian', much to the relief of the bourgeois audience; Mic, her friend, commits suicide at the wheel of her Jaguar: 'you have to pay for pleasure.' 'These clichés flatter the audience with a vague scent of Poujadism' (the 1950s saw the rise and fall of Pierre Poujade's reactionary party of small businessmen). 'These young people are nothing, not Communist, or Fascist, or very busy, or very loose-living, or artistic, or rebellious, or religious, or atheistic.' Carné may have done a lot of research for his film, but 'it is not enough to take a few phrases from the slang of a period' to describe its young people.

[171] *Les Coeurs verts*/US: *Naked Hearts* (1966)
>*d* Edouard Luntz *pc* Raoul Ploquin/Sodor *ph* Jean Badel *m* Serge Gainsbourg, Henri Renaud *sc* Luntz *with* Gérard Zimmerman, Erick Penet, Marise Maire, Françoise Bonneau.

Zim (Zimmerman) and Jean-Pierre (Penet) hang around cafés, pick up girls and indulge in petty crime. The contrasting fate of the two boys suggests the narrow line between social integration and delinquency.

[172] *Le Souffle au coeur*/*Murmur of the Heart* (1971)
>*d* Louis Malle *pc* Nouvelles Ed. de Films/Marianne/Vides/Franz Seitz *ph* Ricardo Aronovitch *sc* Malle *with* Léa Massari, Benoît Ferreux, Daniel Gélin, Michel Lonsdale, Henri Poirier.

Set in 1954, the year in which the Algerian war broke out and also the year of Autant-Lara's screen adaptation of *Le Blé en herbe* [168], Colette's novel of an adolescence far removed from social or political concerns. The wider issues of the time hover on the fringes of Malle's film, seen from the viewpoint of its adolescent central character, but its focus is elsewhere. The mother-son incest is treated delicately, but the director would hardly have expected it not to shock. It did.

[173] *L'Argent de poche*/*Small Change* (1976)
>*d* François Truffaut *pc* Les Films du Carrosse/Artistes Associés *ph* Pierre-

William Glenn *m* Maurice Jaubert *sc* Truffaut, Suzanne Schiffman *ad* Jean-Pierre Kohut-Svelko *with* Geory Desmouceaux, Philippe Goldman, Claudio Deluca, Pascale Bruchon.

An affectionate picture of the lives of children, filmed in Triers with what critics have considered an excess of charm and sentimentality. Maurice Pialat's *Passe ton bac d'abord* (1979), also in a provincial town, showing children at a later stage in their school careers, probably gives a more accurate picture of young people at the time. But Truffaut's film, because it is virtually restricted to pre-adolescent children as a group, betrays a particular idea of the child's emotions and mentality, as yet 'uncontaminated' by the adult view of the world.

XII FANTASIES

[174] *Le Grand Méliès* (1952)

d Georges Franju *pc* Armor *ph* Jacques Mercanton *m* Georges van Parys *sc* Franju *with* Madame Marie-Georges Meliès, André Méliès.

Franju's tribute to Méliès shows how the work of this cinema pioneer had been forgotten by the 1950s, and it remains probably the most convenient place to see footage from the Méliès films. The possibility of using the camera to perform conjuring tricks (special effects, in later jargon) was realized from the start and Méliès used it in such films as *Le déshabillage impossible* (1900) where characters find themselves in the frustrating situation of trying to undress while instantly being reclothed, usually in garments belonging to others. Méliès also filmed an imaginary journey to the moon (1902) and numerous other scientific reconstructions or illusions. Also before World War I, the comedies of Boireau and Rigadin used different effects, including one in which time is speeded up.

[175] *Paris qui dort/The Crazy Ray* (1923)

d René Clair *pc* Diamant *ph* Maurice Defassiaux, Paul Guichard *with* Henri Rollan, Marcel Vallée, Albert Préjean, Madeleine Rodrigue, Charles Martinelli.

René Clair's first film owes a good deal to Méliès: it is the story of a mad scientist who paralyses Paris with a ray gun.

[176] *La Fin du monde/The End of the World* (1930)

d Abel Gance *pc* L'Ecran d'Art *ph* Jules Kruger, Roger Hubert *sc* Gance, from a story by Camille Flammarion *effects* Nicolas Roudakoff *sd* Lazare Meerson *with* Victor Francen, Colette Darfeuil, Gance, Samson Fainsilber, Jean d'Yd.

The first spectacular French talkie, and a commercial disaster. It was dismissed by Philippe Soupault (*L'Europe nouvelle*, 7 Feb 31) as ridiculous, scientifically improbable and an example of the direction cinema should not take. Soupault compared it, unfavourably, with Clair's *Paris qui dort* [175]. Despite these two films, and the experiments of Méliès, French cinema never took to science fiction as a genre, perhaps partly because of Gance's failure.

[177] *Les Yeux sans visage*/*Eyes Without a Face*/(dubbed) *The Horror Chamber of Dr Faustus* (1959)

d Georges Franju *pc* Champs-Elysées-Lux *ph* Eugen Shuftan *m* Maurice Jarre *sc* Jean Redon from his novel *effects* Assola, Georges Klein *ad* Auguste Capelier *with* Pierre Brasseur, Alida Valli, Edith Scob, François Guérin.

A famous Franju horror: plastic surgeon tries to rebuild his daughter's face after a car accident, using faces from girls he has had kidnapped for the purpose. He fails and is savagely torn apart by the dogs he uses for experiments. When it was first shown at the Edinburgh Film Festival, members of the audience fainted.

As well as the conventional horror elements, it tackles the question of misuse of science (of universal interest in the atomic age) and nature (going back to Franju's exposure of our inhumanity to animals in *Le Sang des bêtes* [93]). Both suggest a narrowness of vision that the film illuminates: this scientist is prepared happily to sacrifice not only animals, but also other human beings for the sake of his own daughter. Perhaps, as Raymond Durgnat says in his book on Franju (University of California Press, 1968) an attack on the right-wing, Pétainist glorification of the family?

[178] *Le Monocle noir* (1961)

d Georges Lautner *pc* Orex *ph* Maurice Fellous *m* Jean Yatlove *sc* Jacques Robert, Pierre Laroche *with* Paul Meurisse, Pierre Blanchar, Albert Rémy.

The first in a series of popular thrillers, with a tongue-in-cheek element that brings them closer to the later James Bond movies than to the conventions of the thriller.

[179] *Alphaville* (1965)

d Jean-Luc Godard *pc* Chaumiane/Filmstudio *ph* Raoul Coutard *m* Paul Misraki *sc* Godard *with* Eddie Constantine, Anna Karina, Akim Tamiroff, Howard Vernon, Michel Delahaye.

'Alphaville or Betafilm?', Arlette Elkaim asked in *Les Temps modernes* (June 1965). 'Intellectual hysteria', 'simplicity or banality (in the dialogue)' and 'pseudo-philosophical verbiage', she went on. Most people were far more worried by the present realities inside President Johnson's very human head than by this 'inhuman technocracy': 'True, large housing estates are depressing and in the *métro*, after work, people look dull or moronic. But computers are not to blame.'

In the following month, *Les Temps modernes* returned to the attack with an article by Pierre Samson. The film's 'wholesale culture' was a means to distract our attention from Lemmy Caution's real role, as a cop. 'However, this manifestly reactionary film has succeeded in mystifying left-wing critics in *L'Humanité* and *Le Nouvel Observateur* ... Godard is the product of a society that has chosen Gaullism ...', his 'petty-bourgeois individualism' offering us love as the answer to anxieties about the unknown and the future.

Constantine plays a typical tough guy role in Godard's very untypical SF thriller. Dislike of Godard among the critics of *Les Temps modernes* reached its height around this time, and the fact that the review was prepared to devote two articles to this one film is evidence of how seriously his influence was taken by the 'unofficial' Left. As the two writers quoted above argue, they saw him serving the régime by distracting attention from the real problems of the time and disguising a 'reactionary' message behind a torrent of (pseudo-)philosophy. Ironically, Godard himself converted to the Left after 1968, adopting many of the attitudes of his earlier critics.

[180] *Coplan sauve sa peau/Coplan Saves His Skin* (1968)
  d Yves Boisset *pc* Comptoir Français du Film *ph* Pierre Lhomme, Alain Derobe
  sc Boisset, Claude Veillot, from Paul Kenny's novel *Coplan paie le cercueil*
  with Claudio Brook, Margaret Lee, Jean Servais, Jean Topart, Bernard Blier.

Le Monocle, Le Gorille, Le Tigre, O.S.S. 117 and Coplan were among the French answers to the James Bond type of spy thriller. These series may have concealed many political assumptions about the Cold War or the superiority of Whites. They were made entirely for commercial reasons, however, and owed any hidden political message partly to their Hollywood models.

[181] *Fahrenheit 451* (1966)
  d François Truffaut *pc* Anglo Enterprise/Vineyard *ph* Nicholas Roeg, Alex
  Thompson *m* Bernard Herrmann *sc* Truffaut, from the novel by Ray Bradbury
  ad Syd Cain *with* Oskar Werner, Julie Christie, Cyril Cusack, Anton Diffring,
  Bee Duffell.

Made in English, Truffaut's film is about a society in which books are banned and destroyed (451° is the combustion temperature of paper), and about the value of language and the liberating power of literature – remember Antoine's love of Balzac in *Les quatre cents coups*. Perhaps because of the language difficulties, it was not Truffaut's most successful work.

[182] *Barbarella* (1967)
  d Roger Vadim *pc* Marianne/Dino de Laurentis *ph* Claude Renoir *m* Michel

Magne *sc* Vadim, Jean-Claude Forest, Claude Brûlé, Vittorio Bonicelli, Robert Scipion from Forest's cartoons strip *with* Jane Fonda, John Philip Law, Anita Pallenberg, Ugo Tognazzi, David Hemmings, Claude Dauphin.

The cast also includes Milo O'Shea as Duran Duran, a character who gave his name to a 1980s British pop group, indicating that Vadim's film continued to enjoy a cult following. Far from serious SF, it is also a tribute to the comic strip (see *Jeu de massacre* [7]). Fonda travels round the galaxy, making love with everyone and everything, including a pleasure machine which succumbs in the face of unfair competition.

[183] *Le Gendarme et les extra-terrestres/The Policeman and the Extraterrestrials* (1978)
d Jean Girault *sc* Jacques Vilfrid *with* Louis de Funès, Michel Galabru, Jean-Pierre Rambal.

The Louis de Funès comic policeman starred in a highly popular series which has a good deal to say about everyday life and attitudes, little about police work. The officious, stupid, self-important and, above all, accident-prone policeman satisfies a need to make fun of authority figures without questioning the system. In an earlier film in the series, *Le Gendarme de Saint-Tropez*, de Funès' comic adventures centred on his prudish attempts to ban nude bathing on the Riviera beach. This sample of the type draws on the conventions of another (alien?) genre; perhaps the inspiration of the producers was beginning to flag.

Index of film titles

Numerals in square brackets denote an entry number in the reference material starting on page 91. Numerals in **bold** denote the number of a **photograph**

A

A bout de souffle [138], 61, 76
Age d'or, L', 35
Alerte en Méditerrannée, 37
Ali Baba et les 40 voleurs [39], 43
Alibi, L' [127]
Alphaville [179]
Alsace, 33
A Man and a Woman, see *Un homme et une femme*
Amour l'après-midi, L', 81
And God Created Woman, see *Et Dieu créa la femme*
Angèle [100], 50
Année dernière à Marienbad, L' [4]
A nos amours [162], 46, 85, 80
A nous deux, Madame la Vie, 30
A nous la liberté [85], 34, 37, 68, 69, 70, 83, **14, 25**
A nous les p'tites anglaises, 83
Appel du silence, L', 35–36, 67
A Private Function, 46
A propos de Nice [55], 73
Argent, L' [72], 34, 59, 67, 68
Argent de poche, L' [173], 80
Armée des ombres, L' [47]
Army in the Shadows, see *Armée des ombres, L'*
Arroseur arrosé, L', 15
Ascenseur pour l'échafaud [134], 10, 43, 60, 72–73, 76, **27**
Assassinat du Duc de Guise, L' [11], 16
Atalante, L' [86]
Aubervilliers [92], 73
Au-delà des grilles, 48
Aux urnes, citoyens! [67], 66
Avec le sourire, 69
A Very Curious Girl, see *Fiancée du pirate, La*
A Window in London, 59

B

Baccara, 30, 32, 34
Baker's Wife, The, see *Femme du boulanger, La*
Balance, La [149], 46, 61, 73, 82
Ballet mécanique, Le, 18
Ballon rouge, Le, 80
Bande à part [142], 61, 76, **36**
Bandera, La [31], 35
Barbarella [182]
Bataille du rail, La [35], 39, 43
Beau Serge, Le [111], 44, 47, 49, 53
Belle de jour [79], 6
Belle équipe, La [87] 37–38, 48, 58, 69, 83, **15**
Bête humaine, La [89], 59, 67, 70, 74, **17**
Biquefarre [109], 46, 49, 52–53

Bizarre, Bizarre, see *Drôle de drame*
Bled, Le, 35
Blé en herbe, Le [168], 32, 52, 79, **44, 45**
Bob le Flambeur [121]
Bof!, 71, 82
Bolero, see *Uns et les autres, Les*
Bonheur, Le [97]
Boucher, Le [114], 56
Boudu sauvé des eaux [73], 68
Breathless, see *A bout de souffle*
Butcher, The, see *Boucher, Le*

C

Cage aux folles, La [160], 84
Card of Fate, see *Grand jeu, Le*
Carnival in Flanders, see *Kermesse héroïque, La*
Caroline chérie, 65
Carry on Sergeant, 35
Caserne en folie, La, 35
Casque d'Or [130], 49, 59, 73, **11, 32**
Cave se rebiffe, Le [140], 44
Celui qui doit mourir, 67
Cercle rouge, Le [147]
Chagrin et la pitié, Le [48]
Champion du régiment, Le, 35
Chantecoq, 33
Chariots of Fire, 46
Charron, Le, 52
Chasseur de Chez Maxim's, Le, 30
Cheaters, The, see *Tricheurs, Les*
Chienne, La [119]
Chinoise, La [6], 76, **28**
Choc en retour, 37
Clean Slate, see *Coup de torchon*
Cléo de 5 à 7 [155]
Coeur de française, 33
Coeur et l'argent, Le, 16
Coeurs verts, Les [171], 81
Compères, Les, 84, 88
Confidentially Yours, see *Vivement dimanche*
Cop au vin, see *Poulet au vinaigre*
Coplan sauve sa peau [180]
Coq du régiment, Le, 35
Corbeau, Le [106], 56, 67
Counterfeiters of Paris, The, see *Cave se rebiffe, Le*
Coup de torchon [51], 36
Coup pour coup [69]
Crazy Ray, The, see *Paris qui dort*
Crime de Monsieur Lange, Le [88], 34, 48, 56, 58, 69, 16
Croisade, La, 34
Croisade de l'air, 52
Croix de bois, Les, 35

D

Dame aux camélias, La, 16
Danton [26], 64, 89
Daybreak, see *Jour se lève, Le*

157

General index